Contents

Foreword by Sir Dermot Turing   6
Foreword by Professor Richard Aldrich   8
Acknowledgements   9
Introduction   11

1   Lesmahagow   20
2   The Red Generation   30
3   A Foreign Country   41
4   The Third Secretary   50
5   An Unsatisfactory Probationer   60
6   LISZT   70
7   KURORT: Bletchley Park and Ultra Intelligence   83
8   A Semi-Monastic Life   92
9   On His Majesty's Secret Service   103
10 The Venona Project   115
11 The 'Ealing' Spy   125
12 New Careers   138
13 Confession   149
14 The Hunt for the Fifth Man   162
15 Agent for the Duration   171

Afterword   180
Appendices – Interviews with John Cairncross   187
Notes   204
Bibliography   237
Index   252

Foreword by Sir Dermot Turing

John Cairncross's own book about his life is called *The Enigma Spy*. The title is something of an embellishment, since Cairncross spent only a year at Bletchley Park, and what he did there in the way of spying for the Soviet Union was of doubtful value. It is remarkable that Cairncross's efforts were the high-water-mark of Soviet penetration into the agency which would, in due time, become the front line of the Cold War; in one sense, it is a tribute to the Government Code & Cypher School, the official name of the code-breaking organisation at Bletchley, and its somewhat unorthodox methods of recruitment, that the Soviets did no better.

The sensational title of Cairncross's book gives something away about who he was, and how he perceived himself. He was a complex figure, who seems to have striven for most of his life to make a name for himself, and to achieve recognition and acceptance. His own story about spying for Russia in World War II is couched in defensive terms : it was acceptable, because Russia was an ally and everyone was trying to defeat Germany, and the Russian victory at the Battle of the Kursk Salient (which Cairncross attributes in part to the decrypts he stole from Bletchley) was an important milestone on the road to Allied victory. Was Cairncross writing to achieve notoriety, to justify himself, to explain away the fact that he had not been exfiltrated by the KGB, or was it an exercise in self-deception?

This new study of Cairncross by Chris Smith re-examines the story of John Cairncross, as a misfit, as a hapless spy, as someone perpetually outside the cliquey British intelligence establishment. We discover that there is a lot more to Cairncross's life than the selective autobiography was willing to

BEDFORDSHIRE LIBRARIES

3B

29/May/12 AS
13/July/21 give

BOOKS SHOULD BE RETURNED
BY LAST DATE STAMPED ABOVE

The Last Cambridge Spy

The Last Cambridge Spy

JOHN CAIRNCROSS, BLETCHLEY CODEBREAKER AND SOVIET DOUBLE AGENT

CHRIS SMITH

Dedicated to the memory of my late aunt, Marty Kilby

First published 2019

The History Press
The Mill, Brimscombe Port
Stroud, Gloucestershire, GL5 2QG
www.thehistorypress.co.uk

British Library Cataloguing in Publication Data.
A catalogue record for this book is available from the British Library.

ISBN 978 0 7509 8147 7

Typesetting and origination by The History Press
Printed and bound in Great Britain by TJ International Ltd

give away. Notwithstanding his unsuitability for tradecraft, Cairncross had a searing intelligence, a superlative gift for language, and a multi-faceted career. Cairncross should never have been a spy : his unqualified successes were in the academic world, and it is the tragedy of Cairncross's life-story that his spying background ultimately ruined the best chance he had for academic success and the reputation for which he hungered. Although he was 'the last Cambridge spy', he was never part of the 'Cambridge spy ring' – forever on the outside, and in the final analysis deemed too unimportant by the Establishment to be worth prosecuting. Cairncross's own book looks like a last attempt to regain entry to the charmed circle.

The Last Cambridge Spy is not just a fascinating, well-paced book about an interesting individual, but it also invites us to re-appraise the very idea of the 'Cambridge spy ring'. We have been conditioned to think about the Soviet infiltration of British intelligence in terms which show up the failings of old-boy networks, recruitment on the basis of social background rather than skills, and inability to confront prejudices even in the face of overwhelming evidence. That narrative is beginning to look tired: here we can see a more subtle Establishment at work, making a carefully-calculated decision about the value of prosecuting Cairncross through the courts; and the very idea of a homogeneous group of 'Cambridge spies' begins to seem less of a reality than a headline for twentieth-century journalists. Perhaps it is appropriate to ask afresh how significant the penetration of MI6 by the Soviet Union actually was. *The Last Cambridge Spy* is a timely and lively account of an interesting figure, whose confused relationships with Moscow and Whitehall might just help us get closer to an understanding of that question.

Sir Dermot Turing
2019

Foreword by Professor Richard Aldrich

Chris Smith offers us a remarkable account of John Cairncross, one of the most significant spies of the twentieth century. Less of a household name than flamboyant figures like Guy Burgess and Kim Philby, he was none-theless effective. He secured thousands of secret documents from the most sensitive areas of British government, including its intelligence agencies and passed them to the Soviet Union between 1937 and 1952. He siphoned off material from Bletchley Park's cryptanalytic efforts in the run-up to the Battle of Kursk, the greatest tank battle of the Second World War. This was a period when the Russians were at their greatest peril and arguably his espionage had a significant impact on the course of the twentieth century's most important conflict. The KGB showed its gratitude by awarding him not only medals but money to buy a car and even a wedding present.

This book sheds light on an elusive figure. Cairncross was above all a shy and awkward intellectual. He left home in 1929 to study at the University of Glasgow, the Sorbonne and finally the University of Cambridge from which he graduated with a First Class degree in 1936. An absent-minded professor type – he was prone to mistakes, lapses of memory and was poor at espionage tradecraft. He finally felt the net closing on him soon after the defection of Guy Burgess and Donald Maclean in 1951, but artfully traded a formal confession to MI5 to avoid prosecution a decade later. Hoping to make a name for himself as a translator of Racine and Corneille and also as an expert on Moliere, he was instead exposed in 1979 and spent the latter years of his life in flight from journalists and eager book writers. But Chris Smith has captured him at last and tells his story – it is a riveting read.

Professor Richard Aldrich

2019

Acknowledgements

Over the course of writing this book I have incurred a considerable number of debts. Much of the research upon which this book is based was conducted in Scotland and the Society of Antiquaries of Scotland were generous enough to provide a grant to subsidise that research. I have also been lucky enough to receive a great deal of advice and help from friends and colleagues. In particular, I would like to thank Richard Aldrich and Chris Moran, who read the manuscript and made key suggestions for improvement. Similarly, I'd also like to thank Benet Vincent, Jim Clarke and Kris Lovell, who also read chapters of the book, spotting errors and highlighting terrible prose in equal measure. My thanks also go to The History Press, and to my commissioning editor Mark Beynon in particular, who have supported this project since its infancy, endured my delays and offered nothing but unwavering support.

The original seeds for this book were planted during my Doctoral research, conducted at Aberystwyth University, under the supervision of Siân Nicholas and Iwan Rhys Morus. Without their formative influence, careful instruction and tireless patience, neither this book, nor my previous effort, *The Hidden History of Bletchley Park* (2015), could have been written. I have greatly profited from discussion with friends, colleagues and experts who helped me form my ideas. Particular mention must go to Björn Weiler, Peter Lambert, Brett Sanders, John Grima, Jacques Gallagher, Sonja Astley, Darren Reid, Juliette Pattinson, Amy Blakeway, Emily Guerry, Phil Slavin, Philip Boobbyer, Kate Terkanian, Kate Murphy, Rosie Wayne and Angela John. Of particular note is Rosie Toy, a former student whose First Class dissertation has informed my perception of MI5. The staff and patrons of The Cricketers Arms, Leamington Spa, have also been excellent sounding boards for my ideas, so my thanks go to them and, in particular, Ben Houghton O'Connor, who bore the brunt of this – so I apologise for having been the proverbial and literal pub bore.

I am also grateful to the archivists and librarians who held my hand through much of the research process. These include staff at the National Archives, Kew; the British Library, London; the National Library of Wales, Aberystwyth; the National Library of Scotland, Edinburgh; Lesmahagow Library; South Lanarkshire Council Archives, East Kilbride; Glasgow City Library; the Centre for Buckinghamshire Studies, Aylesbury; the University of Glasgow Archives; the University of Cambridge Library; the University of Bristol Library and the Bletchley Park Trust Archive, Bletchley. Of special note are the staff of the Burns Library, Boston College, Massachusetts, who were kind enough to send me copies of correspondence between John Cairncross and Graham Greene, free of any charge, and have allowed me to quote from this material liberally. I would also like to thank two of my former students Rosie Wayne and Rosie Toy.

I owe a huge debt of thanks to Gayle Gowe, who allowed me to access and quote from John Cairncross' papers, gave up her time to talk to me about John, and offered encouragement regarding my proposed book. I would also like to thank Frances Cairncross, who has kindly allowed me to quote from the papers of her father, Sir Alexander Kirkland Cairncross.

My mother, Susan Smith, in addition to offering moral support and love, also read sections of the book and assisted me greatly by researching the genealogy of the Cairncross family. Finally, my love and thanks to my partner, Kellie, and our cat, Heath, who have been forced to live with the ghosts of the Ring of Five for many years.

Introduction

In 'One of us', a 1986 episode of the BBC's classic political sitcom, *Yes, Prime Minister*, Sir Humphrey Appleby (Nigel Hawthorne), is put on the spot by his former boss, Sir Arnold Robinson (John Nettleton). Suspicion has fallen on Humphrey: despite his long, distinguished career, has he been a Soviet intelligence agent operating at the heart of the Civil Service all along? In answer to the allegation, Sir Humphrey indignantly responds 'But I couldn't have been, I wasn't at Cambridge! I'm not one of them, I'm a married man, I'm one of us!'[1] The Soviet Union, the show joked, knew more about what was going on in the British government than the hapless Prime Minister, Jim Hacker (Paul Eddington). Soviet spies had infiltrated the heart of Whitehall and had gone unnoticed throughout long distinguished careers in the Civil Service. They got away with their treasonous subterfuge because they were chaps who travelled in the right circles and who had the right school and university ties. They were above suspicion. They were English gentlemen.

Though the subject of comedy by the 1980s, the naivety and class prejudice of the British Civil Service, so mercilessly lampooned in *Yes, Prime Minister* was very real and very serious. Crude assumptions and prejudices regarding class among Britain's civil servants facilitated the worst intelligence failure in modern British history, and the Soviet Union ruthlessly exploited this blind spot. Throughout the 1930s, Soviet 'illegals' – resident agents operating in Britain – carefully selected, recruited and nurtured emerging talent at Britain's ancient universities of Cambridge and, to a lesser extent, Oxford. After their graduation these recruits forged high-flying careers in the civil and intelligence services, all the while leaking key information to their Soviet handlers. Their elite education and backgrounds ensured that they were trusted implicitly and without question. Over the course of the Cold War, as these agents were eventually discovered, a steady stream of embarrassing revelations emerged in the press.

Of the agents that Moscow recruited in this fashion, five emerged who stood out from the rest. The quality and quantity of the material they supplied was unparalleled; they were, in the words of the former KGB (Komitet Gosudarstvennoy Bezopasnosti or Committee for State Security) officer Yuri Modin, 'the most valuable spies.'[2] These men, Guy Burgess, Donald Maclean, Anthony Blunt, Kim Philby and John Cairncross have widely been labelled the 'Cambridge Five'. Both fact and conjecture regarding their activities have filled countless books and newspaper column inches.

The questions regarding Soviet infiltration of the British state first created a media storm in 1951 when the Foreign Office officials Burgess and Maclean sensationally disappeared, only to emerge later living in the Soviet Union. Throughout the remainder of the Cold War and beyond, there has been a constant flow of information regarding those Soviet agents who operated in Britain and the sheer enormity (both in terms of quantity and importance) of the material they passed to Moscow. For many years, from the 1950s onwards, much of this amounted to speculation regarding the identity of these spies and the damage their betrayals wrought. At first, there were the two 'missing diplomats', Burgess and Maclean. However, in 1961 the Soviet defector Anatoliy Golitsyn asserted that the two were part of a 'Ring of Five'.

In 1963, a 'third man' was revealed when Kim Philby, following in the footsteps of Burgess and Maclean, absconded to the Soviet Union. The public had to wait until 1979 to learn the identity of a 'fourth man', Anthony Blunt, who was publicly unmasked by the journalist Andrew Boyle.[3] This was then confirmed on 21 November 1979 by the Prime Minister, Margaret Thatcher, in the House of Commons.[4] From that point on, the hunt was on for the 'fifth man'. This book is about that fifth man – John Cairncross.

It should be remembered that decades later the identity of the fifth man remains controversial. Over the years, authors, journalists, historians and fellow travellers have presented a variety of 'true' fifth men. For instance, the Australian writer Roland Perry made the case that it was Victor Rothschild.[5] However, today the overwhelming consensus among historians and the weight of evidence – based on what has emerged from Soviet archives and former KGB officers – suggests John Cairncross was that fifth man. For his own part, Cairncross, though admitting that he was a spy, downplayed the extent of his activities; he always rejected the label 'the fifth man' and indeed the notion that there was a 'Ring of Five' at all. In this book I will present the highly compelling evidence arranged by others suggesting that Cairncross' espionage activities were far more considerable than he was willing to admit. However, I will also present Cairncross' arguments and leave it to readers to draw their own conclusions.

★

Today John Cairncross is perhaps most well known as a minor character in the biopic film about the mathematician and cryptanalyst Alan Turing, *The Imitation Game* (2014).[6] The central action of the film takes place in Britain's secret Second World War code-breaking centre, Bletchley Park, and the main characters are all mathematicians. Cairncross' role in the film is as one of Turing's cryptanalyst colleagues, working in secret for Moscow. This is true inasmuch as Cairncross was posted to Bletchley Park and did use his position to pass highly secret intelligence, among the most closely guarded secret information of the war in fact, to the Soviet Union. Such was the significance of the material generated at Bletchley Park, the official historian of British wartime intelligence, Sir Harry Hinsley, estimated that it reduced the length of the war by no less than two years.[7] However, Cairncross was no cryptanalyst; indeed, it is near certain that he never met Turing or any of the other main characters depicted in the film. Cairncross, who worked shifts as a translator in a system that operated like a production line, occupied a very different environment to key figures such as Turing.

Nevertheless, Cairncross was indeed there. Contrary to some of the somewhat whimsical claims that the wartime inhabitants of Bletchley Park were the 'geese who laid the golden egg and never cackled', Stalin's intelligence officials had enjoyed first-hand access to Britain's most secret intelligence nerve-centre.[8] Before that he had served in the Foreign Office, the Treasury and had been the personal private secretary to Lord Hankey, a member of the Cabinet. Afterwards he would serve in MI6, the Treasury and the Ministry of Supply.

The Blunt affair of 1979, which revealed that a Knight of the Realm, the Keeper of the Queen's Pictures and former MI5 man, Anthony Blunt, was a traitor, shocked the nation. In its wake, thanks to revelations provided by John Colville, Cairncross was soon also publicly revealed as a spy in the pages of the *Sunday Times* by Barrie Penrose and David Leitch.[9] Over the course of the early 1980s, Cairncross continued to feature in the press and also appeared in Chapman Pincher's 1981 and 1984 works, *Their Trade is Treachery* and *Too Secret Too Long*.[10] Similarly, he also appeared in Penrose and Simon Freeman's 1986 biography of Anthony Blunt *Conspiracy of Silence*, was named in Peter Wright's 1987 memoir *Spycatcher*, and in Robert Cecil's 1988 biography of Donald Maclean.[11]

In all of these books, Cairncross was depicted as a relatively minor figure. However, in 1990 the historian Christopher Andrew, in conjunction with the Soviet defector Oleg Gordievsky, made headlines. They alleged that Cairncross had been the first Atomic spy.[12] They further claimed, based on Gordievsky's information, that they could show definitively that Cairncross was indeed the fifth man of the Cambridge spy ring. Cairncross, they alleged, had leaked many thousands of pages of highly sensitive material to Moscow throughout a lengthy relationship with Soviet intelligence lasting from 1937 to 1952. This was soon followed, in 1993, by revelations from the former KGB officer, Oleg Tsarev, who named Cairncross as the 'sixth man' (awarding Michael Straight the title of 'fifth man'), in reference to the order in which the spies were recruited.[13] Adding further fuel to the fire, the memoirs of Cairncross' former handler, Yuri Modin, presented Cairncross as one of the most important spies the Soviet Union had ever possessed.[14]

It was in this atmosphere that Cairncross decided to write his own memoirs, which were published in 1997 by his widow, Gayle, two years after his death in 1995. The central argument at the heart of *The Enigma Spy* was that the author had been motivated by patriotism. Cairncross' purpose, he claimed, was to serve Britain by aiding Moscow. The logic of this outwardly contradictory position was that if the Soviet Union fell during the Second World War, then Britain would undoubtedly be next. Churchill and his inner-circle were remiss in not sharing the wealth of Bletchley-generated information at their disposal with their Russian allies, so Cairncross had taken matters into his own hands.

Cairncross also claimed that the Cambridge Five, such as it was, did not really exist and that he worked alone. Certainly he had known the other key players. He worked with Maclean in the Foreign Office and Philby in MI6, he had been in the same Cambridge college (Trinity) with Blunt and knew Burgess socially, but he claimed to be ignorant of their activities. He categorically denied being part of an intelligence cell with them. Further, he said that the charge that he had been an atomic spy was risible. He had been, he claimed, a very small fish in a very large pond. However, despite his efforts, the accusations continued to flood in as more information from both former Soviet intelligence officers and even the Soviet archives became available.[15] Nevertheless, despite the interest and accusations that plagued his later years, no biography, beyond his own account, has yet been dedicated to him. Moreover, though he has sometimes featured fairly prominently in other books narrating the activities of the Ring of Five, Cairncross has typically been awarded only a few pages worth of attention. I aim in this book to remedy this situation.

★

This book cannot, however, possibly be seen as the final word on John Cairncross. Far from it. I have attempted to reconstruct his life from the sparse official files produced by the British state, but also the rather more wholesome letters and diaries that were produced by Cairncross, his friends, his colleagues, and his family. Yet though there have been partial releases, such as the KGB files to pre-selected authors such as Nigel West and John Costello, free and open access to the Soviet Union's intelligence archives is at the time of writing unavailable. In short, historians cannot check the original records for themselves.

Writing about spies and the dark, dangerous and secret world which they occupied is fraught with obstacles. The key challenge to an intelligence historian typically is acquiring documentary evidence. Exploring the case of John Cairncross has proven to be no exception. Given the extensive penetration of the British state by Soviet intelligence, the scale of the records collected about agents by the British (and American) intelligence services after they were revealed is likely to be vast. This has certainly been confirmed in the case of recent releases of files regarding Burgess and Maclean to the National Archives, Kew, which comprise many thousands of documents. However, there are far fewer materials available relating to Cairncross. Indeed, to date, only four files have been released for public inspection that deal with Cairncross in any serious detail: a Foreign Office personnel file partially detailing the information they collected on him after his initial interrogation in 1952; an MI5 file on the Burgess and Maclean affair that includes reports on those interrogations; a Cabinet Office file; and a Home Office file, heavily redacted, I obtained via a freedom of information request.[16] Clearly, there are many relevant files still to be released to the National Archives, Kew, by the intelligence services.

Given the relatively meagre official source material available, it is clear that a 'standard' intelligence history, based on careful sifting of state documents, is not easily achievable. Meanwhile, what evidence there is of John Cairncross' specific activities has already been reported elsewhere. Since the late 1990s, a wealth of material emanating from both former Soviet intelligence officers and Soviet and British archives has become available and outlined in a variety of excellent books, many of which have provided good accounts of Cairncross' espionage activities.[17] Naturally, this biography narrates (and draws upon) much of the same story as already outlined in these works. However, it is not the intention that this biography reinvent the Cairncross wheel. Instead, the central objective is to provide an exploration of John Cairncross' character, to tell the wider story of his life and to place him within the broader context of twentieth century British society and its history.

Understanding why spies offered their assistance by divulging their country's secrets to an enemy power is inevitably a key consideration for intelligence historians. In order to understand the *why*, as opposed to only the *what* and *how*, it is necessary to turn to social, cultural and economic history. Unsurprisingly, therefore, issues such as social class and attitudes towards sexuality have been the subject of commentary by authors examining the successful Soviet infiltration of British institutions. However, the exploration of such factors has tended to be fairly limited. With this in mind, in this book, I have endeavoured to invert that arrangement – this is a biography not just of Cairncross, but of Britain's secret world and it aims to explain Cairncross' place within it. It also considers his personal and professional life beyond espionage, his relationships with family and friends – not least the celebrated author, Graham Greene.

To date, a number of linked hypotheses have been postulated to explain the actions of the Cambridge Five. Among the first was crude homophobia as satirised by *Yes, Prime Minister* (Sir Humphrey couldn't be a spy because, as he explained, 'I'm a married man'). When, in 1955, the British government finally admitted in a White Paper that Burgess and Maclean had fled to Moscow, it invoked the spectre of homosexuality – Burgess being unapologetically gay at a time when it was still illegal in Britain – but refused to comment on the matter. Naturally, elements of the press jumped on the issue of sexual 'deviancy'. For instance, the scurrilous *Sunday Pictorial* asserted '[t]his sordid secret of homosexuality – which is one of the keys to the whole scandal of the missing diplomats – is ignored by the Government White Paper.'[18] Further impetus was added to this theory when, in 1979, it was revealed that Blunt, also gay, was the fourth man. Andrew Boyle, in the book that paved the way for Blunt's exposure, was keen to emphasise sexuality, in witheringly negative terms, at one point even conflating homosexuality with Communism.[19]

This hypothesis, despite its considerable longevity in the imaginations of certain parts of the press and public, holds no water at all. Burgess and Blunt were indeed homosexuals, and although happily married, there has been speculation that Maclean was bisexual.[20] However, Cairncross, to borrow the historian Christopher Andrew's words, was 'like Philby a committed heterosexual'.[21] In fact, on a number of occasions Cairncross demonstrated some discomfort in the presence of homosexuals. For instance, he once described a party he attended with Burgess as 'markedly and unpleasantly homosexual'.[22] Nevertheless, as late as 1995, in an obituary of Cairncross, the journalist Bernard Levin took to the pages of *The Times*, writing, 'Then there was Sir Anthony Blunt, who cared for nothing but art and a ripe bum-boy, and who had been an early believer in the wonders of the Soviet Union.'[23] While, of course, Levin did not explicitly link Blunt's sexuality (or his love of art) with his role as a Soviet agent, the purpose of his crass homophobic remark was clear.

Of course, associating hostile espionage and Communism with homosexuality in the 1950s (and beyond) reflected the attitudes of the period. However, it muddied the waters. Rather than demanding a serious investigation into how the Soviet Union had infiltrated the nation's instruments of government and security, publications such as the *Sunday Pictorial* instead encouraged fruitless sexual profiling. A significantly more nuanced and persuasive argument regarding sexuality has been proposed by both Rhodri Jeffreys-Jones and Christopher Andrew. Each of the Cambridge Five, in their own way, found the sexual mores of their class to be ostracising, be it womanising or homosexuality. The promise of a more enlightened future under Communism, coupled with class rebellion, made a compelling cocktail.[24]

A second hypothesis is that these men were drawn to ideological Communism. Certainly, in the case of Maclean, his biographer Robert Cecil noted that once in Moscow, he was happy to have left pretence behind him and embrace the Soviet ideology openly.[25] Cairncross, on the other hand, even after his wide public exposure as a spy, denied anything other than a brief and youthful flirtation with Communism while at Cambridge. However, it is difficult to accept that conclusion after examining his life. After all, he did spy for the Soviet Union. One of his later MI5 inquisitors, Peter Wright, claimed that even long after his espionage career was over, his Communist sympathies remained undiminished.[26] However, this still leaves the question of why Cairncross found Communism attractive in the first place. Despite his careful efforts to underplay this issue in his autobiography, Cairncross grew up in the coalmining community of Lesmahagow in South Lanarkshire, which was beset by considerable social and economic hardship and upheaval. It is, therefore, imperative to at least consider the impact of episodes such as the post-First World War recession, the 1926 General Strike, and the Great Depression on his development.

The third hypothesis often cited is that the rise of fascism in Europe had a profound influence on the mindset and political outlooks of Britain's Soviet spies. In particular, they were concerned by the rise of Nazism in Germany and the threat it posed to peace, security, minority groups, both in Germany and the world more generally. The Cambridge Five seem to have viewed western democracies as lacking both the moral fibre and the ideological commitment to defeating such a menace; salvation could only lie with the Soviet Union. Certainly, although Kim Philby was already a Communist, it was only after a period aiding stricken refugees from Nazi Germany, while in Vienna in 1934, that he turned decisively towards the Soviet Union.[27] As we will see, Cairncross as a young man also saw Nazism first hand and this would prove a significant moment in his political development. It was this, in combination with his early awareness of the injustices of poverty and hardship, which would steer him towards the Soviet Union.

Perhaps more important though was the fact that Cairncross never fit in with the aristocratic and upper middle-class world that he would join. He was a difficult man, keen to argue and lacked the social and economic graces to succeed in an environment where born privilege ruled. He was propelled to reveal his country's secrets, not only because of a contrarian personality, but because he felt rejected by the high society he had worked so hard to enter – a fact that he greatly resented.

★

A brief note on terms: throughout this book the Soviet intelligence apparatus that conducted foreign intelligence is described as the NKVD (Narodnyy Komissariat Vnutrennikh Del or the People's Commissariat for Internal Affairs) and, after 1954 as the KGB. Strictly speaking, this is incorrect. The organisation went under numerous guises, names and bureaucratic restructuring before finally becoming the KGB in 1954. Yet, for the sake of simplicity, prior to 1954 the organisation will be referred to as the NKVD and after as the KGB.[28]

1

Lesmahagow

The Cairncross family was an old and prosperous one, which had produced a number of senior clergymen. In 1390, a Simon de Cairncross was noted in the Exchequer rolls and in 1439, under the great seal of Balmashannar, the family was granted lands in Inverness, Forfar, Perth and Aberdeen.[1] A century later, Robert Cairncross was appointed Bishop of Ross in 1539 and served as Chaplain to James V.[2] In 1585, Nicol Cairncross, president of the Edinburgh Dean of Guild, built a home comprising three towers at Colmslie Hill on their land near Melrose; this was an estate of no small worth and by 1643 was valued at £1,630.[3]

Alexander Cairncross (1637–1701), the son of a dyer in the Canongate at Edinburgh and the heir to the Colmslie estate, like Robert before him became an important clergyman. An educated man, Alexander gained a Doctorate, at the University of Edinburgh. As he was a favourite of the Duke of Queensbury, it was eventually arranged that a small bishopric be provided for him in 1684. However, before the end of the year he was promoted further to become the Archbishop of Glasgow and with it Chancellor of Glasgow University, positions he enjoyed from 1684 until 1687.[4] However, he fell out of favour with the Lord Chancellor (the Earl of Perth) and lost his position. In 1693 he obtained a position as a bishop in Ireland, which he retained until his death.[5]

By the eighteenth century, John's branch of the family had lost its status and Alexander Cairncross (b. 1777), John's great-grandfather, worked as a gardener at Douglas Castle in South Lanarkshire, not far from Lesmahagow. This was the estate of Charles Douglas-Home – the 12th Earl of Home and the grandfather of the future Prime Minister Alec Douglas-Home.

Alexander's tenth child, Andrew, was a businessman, and rose to be the chief buyer at a major Glasgow warehouse with a handsome salary of £600 per annum. In 1864 he left the firm to marry Margaret, the daughter of Thomas McCartney, a Lesmahagow draper, who owned a shop on the village high street.

Thomas was a man of some wealth, but his daughter and her children saw little of it upon his death. At the age of 83, Thomas remarried and left his property to his new wife. Within six months he had died and his widow promptly left the village, taking the inheritance with her. Instead, Andrew, Margaret and their eldest son sustained and developed the drapery and eventually converted the family business into an ironmongery. Margaret and Andrew's son, following family tradition named Alexander, would go on to marry Elizabeth Wishart, an elementary school teacher.

Alexander and Elizabeth had eight children; the final child, John, was born on 25 July 1913. This large family, comprised of two parents, four boys and another four girls, was certainly not affluent. Her marriage and the birth of her children ensured that Elizabeth's career in the classroom had come to an end long before John was born, leaving Alexander, a partner in the family business, as the sole earner.

★

Lesmahagow is situated in the heart of the Scottish lowlands, some 20 miles south-east of Glasgow as the crow flies. The village had been the site of a medieval priory founded in 1144, which was burned to the ground by Edward III's brother, John of Eltham, Earl of Cornwall, in 1336. It was soon rebuilt, only to be destroyed yet again in the early 1560s by the iconoclasts.[6] Primarily, the community was centred on agriculture, and would remain so for many centuries. By 1801 the parish was comprised of some 3,070 people, around two-thirds of whom made their living from the land.[7] There was, however, a major economic resource beneath the soil – coal.

The first individuals likely to have exploited coal in the area were the medieval monks of the priory; mining continued in the years thereafter, presumably on a relatively small scale. By the eighteenth century, the local Stockbriggs estate was drawing a sizeable income from the ground.[8] However, agriculture continued to be the chief source of income and employment in the parish. Such was its status that, in 1805, the Lesmahagow Farmers Society was founded.[9] The early nineteenth century was a point of transition away from arable farming and increasingly towards animal husbandry. By the mid-nineteenth century, the sale of dairy produce had become the chief source of rents for the farmers and an annual cattle show attracted large numbers of spectators.[10]

This situation would not, however, last much longer. Interest in exploiting resources beneath the ground was growing. When gas lighting was introduced in Glasgow, local sources for coal gas became increasingly significant. In 1832 some 8,000 tons of coal were mined; by 1857 that would rise to 60,000 tons.[11] This increase followed wider trends throughout the lowlands of Scotland, described by Christopher Harvie as an 'unlovely "third Scotland" [that] sprawled from South Ayrshire to Fife ... neither much liked nor at all well known'.[12] This region rapidly dominated the Scottish coal industry and, in turn, other industries reliant on coal-fire smelting. By 1870 some 158 blast furnaces were in operation in Scotland, ninety-two of which were located in Lanarkshire, and by 1890 some 63 per cent of those living in west central Scotland were employed in the mining industry.[13]

The natural impact on Lesmahagow was that the population of the parish began to rise as individuals flooded in looking for work. Where the population of the parish stood at a little over 3,000 at the beginning of the nineteenth century, by 1861 it had risen to 9,266.[14] The increase in the population led to social and economic side effects, such as rising rates of pauperism, from an average of forty-two paupers in the parish at the end of the eighteenth century to nearly 200 by 1862.[15] The increasingly urbanised industrial population also brought with it a certain disapproval from wealthy observers, such as J.B. Greenshields. 'It does not, however, appear very evident,' he wrote in 1863, 'that either the conduct or morals of the people have been improved by the increased facilities of education; the vices of drunkenness and pilfering ... have certainly not decreased, while discontent has made rapid strides.'[16]

All the while the mining industry would continue to grow, reaching its peak levels of production by the outset of the First World War.[17] In short, Lesmahagow, like many other communities in the immediate region of south Lanarkshire, had become increasingly in thrall to the coal mining industry. The industry not only changed the nature of employment within the community and parish, but transformed its very shape and population. What had been a small agricultural community had become a small urban town, complete with outlying mining villages, centred primarily on that single industry.

★

It was into this small mining and agricultural community that John Cairncross was born in 1913. As we have seen, his was a large family and it is clear that the Cairncrosses were certainly not wealthy. Cairncross himself remembered that there were financial burdens, but they endured. He wrote that the family's 'needs were simple – food and basic clothing – but even there economy was practiced.'[18]

It has been on this basis, the community from which Cairncross was born and raised and the relatively low socio-economic status of his parents, that he has been assumed to have been a working-class Scot. Such a claim is indisputably untrue; Cairncross was very clearly lower middle class. Not only did he identify his own status as lower middle class, but so too did his other family members. His brothers, Andrew and Alec, both described their father as a 'merchant' on the University of Glasgow matriculation forms.[19] Alexander senior, when surveyed for the valuation and assessment roll for the 1926–27 financial year, was similarly listed as a merchant as well as the proprietor (as opposed to tenant) of his property. Its yearly potential rental value was judged to be £30 8s.[20] To provide some context for that sum, a Lesmahagow miner, Guy Bolton, a filler in a nearby pit, recalled the joy of briefly earning double pay in 1926: 'If you earned twelve shillins a day you wouldnae tell naebody. That was a big wage.'[21] This was indeed a lot of money. A few years earlier, in 1920, the average weekly wage packet for coal miners was 16s 9d – approximately £45 a year according to the Miner's Federation of Great Britain.[22] Thus, while Alexander Cairncross was certainly not a wealthy man, he was part of the lower middle-class professionals, a self-employed shop owner as opposed to a member of the working classes, and from his business he clearly was able to draw a reasonable income. Indeed, despite the expenses incurred in raising a large family in a period of economic hardship, Alexander could still afford to ease the household burdens on his wife by hiring a live-in maid.[23]

John Cairncross placed significant store by his lower middle-class origins. He went as far as to complain that he had been wrongly pigeonholed as a working-class 'rebel against social injustice. In fact, my parents were sturdy middle class, and though we were not high up the ladder, my father was proud of his relative eminence.' His father was also a 'staunch Conservative', in contrast to the Labour-voting miners. Cairncross was also keen to note that though the Clyde valley has a reputation for working-class militancy, Lesmahagow saw little of it. Moreover, he was insulated from the lives and travails of the working-class miners in the town, which he described in less than a page of his autobiography. Highlighting this point he wrote, 'we remained apart from the grime of the coalpits.'[24]

His elder brother, the economist Sir Alec Cairncross, however, took a very different view in his own autobiography. For him the miners and the industrial struggles of the period played a formative role in his early life. As he explained, 'Glasgow and the region around it had begun to feel the effects of the Depression, of the long miners' strike of 1926 ... for an economist ... it was an ideal environment in which to grow up.'[25] He further described, as a child, watching the miners returning from the pits, black with coal dust.[26] He also grew up with the children of the miners; they went to the same village school and Boys' Brigade. His early life 'involved contact ... with a wide variety of occupations and very different social backgrounds.' On the subject of class, he wrote 'to a boy who lived in the village community ... the reality was never class [difference] as such but manners and interests. ... there were those who drank heavily and led disorderly lives. Then there were those of less aggressive habits who enjoyed a game and had interesting hobbies or unfamiliar skills.'[27]

★

The years in which the two youngest Cairncross boys, Alec and John, were in school, first in Lesmahagow and then at Hamilton Academy, were tumultuous ones. The community in which they lived had undergone a radical evolution on the back of the coal industry in the previous century. By the inter-war period that community was, as Sir Alec suggested, again in the midst of rapid change.

This was a period of marked industrial decline, and the reasons for that decline were many and multifaceted. In the immediate aftermath of the First World War, Britain enjoyed a brief economic boom as wartime controls on markets and labour were lifted. This, however, was followed in 1920 by collapse. Demand for British products abroad sharply declined as a global recession set in and people and nations began to tighten their belts. This resulted in sharp falls in exports (30.1 per cent), industrial production (18.6 per cent), real income (3.2 per cent) and employment (14.4 per cent).[28] The coal industry was closely tied to other traditional industries, such as iron and steel production, industries that were suffering as the export market collapsed and the home market was inundated with cheap steel from abroad.[29]

For the workers of Glasgow, the brief boom enjoyed by the rest of the country prior to recession in 1921 never materialised. The two major industries in the city were shipbuilding and engineering; as military and civil demand for both fell in the advent of peace, joblessness in the city rose. Unemployment in these two key industries rose from 0.15 per cent and 0.5 percent cent during the war to 4.9 per cent and 8 per cent by February 1919.[30] The sharp decline in these local industries was soon followed by major problems in other industries, such as iron and steel. This perfect storm in turn led to further catastrophe in west central Scotland's coal mining industry.

In the year that John Cairncross was born, 1913, there were a little under 80,000 people employed by the coal industry in west central Scotland. That figure would remain at around the same level in 1919, representing the peak of employment in the Scottish coal industry. Over the following decade those numbers would come tumbling down. By 1929, the year before Cairncross departed to the nearby city of Glasgow for university, the tally stood at approximately 50,000. By 1932, during the heights of the Great Depression, the figure fell to below 39,000.[31] Though all other mining communities in Scotland suffered, none did so like the communities in the small towns and villages of Lanarkshire.

Miners also had to contend with the steady increase in the number of machines down the mines. These were coal-cutters, hulking devices armed with saws and disks that ate into the seam. The purpose of those machines was specifically to replace the hewers. These skilled men were relegated to the even more arduous, yet menial, job of removing the undercut coal from the seam, breaking it up, and loading it for transport back to the surface. The shifts also grew longer, due to machine malfunctions and the need to complete the length of a wall before the next shift began.[32]

Such rapid changes to the industry and, after the First World War, declining employment and poor conditions, resulted in increased industrial action. The mining industry in west central Scotland was no stranger to strikes in the ten years prior to the First World War, with an average of fifteen per year. Yet, the number of recorded strikes in the decade after the war was twice that figure. Moreover, these strikes were also considerably more intense, involving many more workers.[33]

The social and economic impact both of the recession and of industrial action on Lanarkshire towns was severe. Out of work or striking miners and their families were regularly forced to call upon the generosity of the parish and local council. During the 1920s, new applications for poor relief poured in. In the final two weeks of September 1921 alone, during the post-war recession and a year of widespread industrial dispute, there were more than 131 recorded applications for poor relief. As the wider economy began to improve the number of applications reduced over time to an average of twenty to twenty-five applications a month. This lasted until the end of the decade, when the Great Depression hit, after which numbers reached an average of forty-six a month during the first quarter of 1930.[34]

The impoverished also had to turn to the parish for other forms of assistance. Each year, throughout the 1920s and '30s, the parish clothing committee bought and collected items of clothing and fabric. These were distributed to men and women who had been so impoverished that they were incapable of clothing themselves or their children. To give an example of just one individual, Alec Susley received 3.5yd of yarn, two suits, two shirts, two combs and three pairs of boots in 1930. He also had to clothe his little girl and so received a dress, a chemise, a pair of knickers and a petticoat. Such items were not always of the highest quality. In 1930 the Second District Council received complaints regarding the poor quality of dresses being issued to girls. The articles were soon inspected by the councillors.

After careful consideration, the district council unanimously agreed that the type of dresses supplied was made of unsuitable material, especially for exposed rural areas, and they recommended to the public assistance committee that a heavier dress material should be issued as well as knickers and petticoats for girls.[35]

Despite being of sometimes questionable quality, in that year alone, the parish would distribute: more than 400 yards of fabric; more than seventy suits; more than 100 shirts; nearly 100 chemises; and more than 200 pairs of boots and shoes.[36] As a relatively successful member of the community and proprietor of a local shop, Alexander Cairncross did his bit in aiding his neighbours. In 1923 he and his business partner were recorded and thanked for having sold clothing to the parish for poor relief.[37]

Yet even with these forms of assistance and intervention on both the district and parish level, food poverty was a major problem and some resorted to crime. In 1921, Guy Bolton, then aged just 14 years old, had recently begun working in the coal mines at the nearby village of Coalburn, when a wave of industrial action saw him on strike for thirteen weeks. He was forced into acts of petty theft of food to support himself. He too endured clothing poverty. As he explained, he was:

> out stealin' hens' eggs, stealin' tatties [potatoes] and turnips. In fact, that's a' ye got tae eat after the first couple o' weeks. But your mother went in debt in the Store and she got the basics, jist the rough basics. ... maybe ye got a pair o' troosers frae [from] the minister tae weer cut doon. ... You got a pair o' boots, tacky boots, aboot the month o' October. And when thae boots war run down – and that wasnae to long – that was the summer started. It wis your bare feet then till October again, no matter the weather. That was the position then: a' the bairns [children] went wi their bare feet.[38]

The most significant industrial action of the 1920s was, of course, the General Strike of May 1926. As Sir Alec Cairncross noted, the General Strike had a profound impact on the lives and living standards of the Lesmahagow miners. Just as the industrial action of 1921 sent miners in search of poor relief from the parish, so too did the General Strike – only on a vast scale. There was a huge spike in the number of applications that month to a staggering 415.[39] Once again, Guy Bolton described the crushing poverty that ensued, 'Ye had tae go oot and look for your food, because there was nothing, nothing.' Unlike in 1921, however, rather than acts of petty theft, he and his brothers and friends resorted to poaching. This soon landed him in trouble with the authorities and he was fortunate that the older boys deliberately took the entire blame to spare the younger among them. The older boys each received three-month prison sentences.[40]

★

Against this backdrop of growing poverty and hardship, the inter-war period saw working-class political activism and militancy. Though a politically Liberal city by the turn of the century, Glasgow was at the heart of the growing Labour movement, the Labour Party and the Independent Labour Party, the latter of which was founded in 1882. The ILP's early newspapers of the Labour movement, with titles such as *Labour Leader* and the *Miner*, were published in Glasgow.[41] Its leader, who is now perhaps more closely associated with the Labour Party, Keir Hardie, was a native son of the Clydesdale area. This was also the era of Red Clydeside, a period of intense political radicalism and revolutionary sentiment. Cairncross' Clydeside was, then, a place of rebelliousness.

Unsurprisingly, the Lesmahagow of Cairncross' childhood was also a politically active town, though he himself claimed that this activity was relatively low level and rarely crossed his radar. The only political activity he was to describe was a march during the 1926 General Strike, when mine workers proceeded to the town hall in protest that poor relief payments had been suspended.[42] Aside from the usual activities at election times, this was not the full extent of political activity in the area. Lesmahagow contained an active branch of the National Unemployed Workers' Movement (NUWM), an organisation founded by the Communist Party of Great Britain (CPGB) in 1921, to highlight the plight of the unemployed.

During the Great Depression, activists such as Bolton were able to call NUWM meetings that would attract hundreds of participants and later, in the mid-1930s, organise hunger marches.[43] By his reckoning, the Lesmahagow branch of the NUWM had a thriving membership of no fewer than 300 by the Depression years of the early 1930s. By and large, these men (and they were nearly all men), though not necessarily all card-carrying members of the CPGB, were at least sympathetic to its aims. 'I couldnae tell ye how many o' the N.U.W.M. Members were in the Communist Party,' he recalled, but 'There was a goodly number. But I can say that they were to a man behind the Party leadership. … We had a good solid core and that was the main thing.'[44] Bolton, who himself had joined the CPGB years earlier in 1924 at the age of just 17, had a long history of political activism that had, on occasion, cost him his job.

The poverty of mid-central Scotland did not go unnoticed by Cairncross' siblings. Andrew recalled in 1964, an 'early boyhood pastime' involved watching the miners, covered in coal dust, returning to their homes. 'They would speed down the hill and through the streets, all of them on bicycles, you know. They looked like a black, moving line.' He was also closely familiar with the rural element of Lesmahagow's population, spending his school holidays tending sheep.[45] However, Andrew, who was born in 1901 and had departed to university in the early 1920s, would likely have been more removed from the impact of the inter-war years on his home town than his brothers and sisters.

For Sir Alec, the General Strike and the Great Depression, had a profound impact. Not only was he clearly aware of the impact of industrial disputes, particularly the 1926 General Strike, it shaped his entire future. These events 'reduc[ed] many of the miners' families to extreme poverty. These economic and social strains formed the background to my years at university.'[46] It was no coincidence that he would go on to forge a career as an economist, since that was the discipline asking the central questions relating to the future of the community in which he had been raised:

How could alternative employment be found for the miners and what could be done in the meantime to provide them with a livelihood? The social consequences of high unemployment in poverty, ill health and low morale were all too apparent. The tensions of the General Strike in 1926 and the deepening of the depression a few years later brought home to me the urgency of seemingly intractable problems and the importance of economics as a discipline for resolving them.[47]

It is impossible to know how much, if at all, the economic hardship he witnessed as a child influenced John Cairncross' view of the world, his politics as an adult or his sense of place in a class-riven society. Nor can we establish with certainty whether the rebelliousness of the Clydesdale region had much, if any, effect on him. However, it is difficult to reconcile his own account of his childhood with that provided by his brothers. In John's case, his childhood might have been somewhat Spartan, but nevertheless a middle-class cocoon that insulated and isolated him from the harsh realities faced by the majority of his neighbours. Yet, according to Sir Alec's autobiography, his observations of poverty and industrial dispute proved formative and they loom large in his account of everyday realities of Lesmahagow. Such crushing poverty was ubiquitous, as Guy Bolton observed, 'if I knew the population of Lesmahagow at that time I could tell you hoo many were unemployed. ... There wis nae industry – nothing.'[48]

2

The Red Generation

In 1934 at Trinity College, Cambridge, resided a young don named Anthony Blunt. Blunt had arrived at Cambridge in October 1926 to read Mathematics. He was soon joined by the other young Communist radicals with whom he would become forever associated: Kim Philby embarked on his Cambridge studies at Trinity in October 1929; Guy Burgess arrived at Trinity in October 1930; Donald Maclean started at Trinity Hall in 1931.[1]

A few months before Cairncross arrived at Cambridge in 1934, another young man and important figure in this story entered Britain from continental Europe. Arnold Deutsch was a brilliant academic who was awarded a PhD in 1928 from the University of Vienna, a mere five years after first beginning his undergraduate studies. He was 24 years old. His interests were wide-ranging, including chemistry – the subject of his doctoral research – but also psychology. By that time he was already a committed Communist and he soon began work for the secret International Liaison Department of the Communist International (Comintern) – a Moscow-backed, directed and funded apparatus for spreading world revolution. In 1932 he was moved to the foreign intelligence department of the NKVD to work as an 'illegal'; that is, a spy operating abroad without formal diplomatic status. After a posting in France, Deutsch was soon transferred to London in early 1934, where he swiftly set about recruiting twenty agents and making contact with twenty-nine – including the Cambridge Five.[2]

★

Throughout the 1920s and '30s, MI5 turned its sights on suspected Communist subversives. In particular, the Communist Party of Great Britain and various journalists, trades union members and other shady characters suspected of links to Moscow. This included the figures in the Soviet trading organisation, Russian Oil Products, but also the Russian, Cambridge-based scientist and Nobel laureate, Pyotr Kapitsa. Kapitsa worked at the famous Cavendish Laboratory of the University of Cambridge, and was suspected of being involved in scientific espionage. Yet this was, in all likelihood, a red herring and MI5's attention on the highly respectable, highly middle-class university was limited.[3] This was a mistake.

In the late 1920s, there was little in the way of radical left-wing political activity at the University of Cambridge. There were, of course, some exceptions to this – Maurice Dobb, for instance, was an economist who had visited Moscow in 1925 and soon became a well-known exponent of Communism.[4] Dobb's close associate, Roy Pascal, the noted philologist, was also a convert. There were also figures among the Cambridge scientists, such as John Desmond Bernal and J.B.S. Haldane, who were attracted to Communism because of the Soviet Union's apparent scientific and industrial progress.[5] Yet even so, Communism had made little headway in Cambridge during the 1920s.

However, by the end of the decade and in the early 1930s things had begun to change in Cambridge. For a start, Ludwig Wittgenstein, the Austrian-born philosopher, returned to Cambridge. Wittgenstein had a long and chequered history at Cambridge dating back to before the First World War. Though certainly not a Marxist in the formal sense, he was an important radical thinker within the faculty. Wittgenstein had left Cambridge in 1914 to fight for the Austro–Hungarian Army. He would return to University of Cambridge in 1929, where he was awarded a Doctorate and appointed lecturer and fellow of Trinity College. According to one of his students, Maurice Cornforth, Wittgenstein's return 'immediately caused an upheaval in the circles of students (and lecturers) who were studying philosophy.' Moreover, he soon gained a following of left-leaning students who, including Cornforth, who would 'sit at Wittgenstein's feet, drinking in his new ideas'.[6] Cornforth, in turn, would become a leading figure in energising support for Communism amongst the student body.[7]

The greatest change, however, was brought about by the Great Depression, which began with the Wall Street crash of 1929 and rapidly escalated into a global economic crisis of desperate proportions. In Britain, unemployment, which had stood at 10.4 per cent in 1929, was more than double that rate at 22.1 per cent by 1931.[8] Extreme crisis in the country soon resulted in the rise of radical politics in Cambridge. Having returned a Marxist from a year of study in Germany, the student David Haden-Guest joined the Communist Party and formed a Communist student group in 1931, which within a year swelled to a modest twenty-five members.[9] The Communist group was co-founded by another, very able, very radical student – James Klugmann.

Klugmann arrived at Trinity College from Gresham's School, with his school-friend Donald Maclean, in 1931. Like Cornforth and Haden-Guest, Klugmann would prove an instrumental figure in the development of left-wing radicalism at Cambridge in the early 1930s. Indeed, he would himself be brought into the Soviet fold by Arnold Deutsch in 1936.[10] Having helped found the student Communist group at Cambridge, he built on this early development by hosting a meeting of student Communist organisations, also attended by delegates from the CPGB, during the Easter vacation of 1932. The aim was to construct a national Communist student group, named the National Student Bureau, to rival the national student organisations of the major political parties. Soon the National Student Bureau established its own newspaper, *Student Vanguard*, which was edited by Haden-Guest, Cornforth and Frank Straus Meyer – an American postgraduate student at Balliol College, Oxford.[11]

★

In the meantime, Adolf Hitler's Nazi Party was making considerable headway in German elections, which only further exercised Britain's Communists. In Britain, measures to tackle the Depression, such as the Means Test – which determined the level of unemployment benefits an individual could receive – were hugely unpopular. Giving some idea of the problems caused by the test, the journalist, novelist and social commentator George Orwell wrote of it that, 'The most cruel and evil effect of the Means Test is the way in which it breaks up families. Old people, sometimes bedridden, are driven out of their homes by it. [...] It is happening all over England at this moment, thanks to the Means Test.'[12]

The students at Cambridge, though insulated from the ravages of poverty, were hardly unobservant and in March 1933 the Cambridge Union debated the abolition of the Means Test. The motion for abolition passed.[13] Looking back four decades later as a noted Marxist intellectual, Klugmann would write of the 1930s that, 'Life seemed to demonstrate in an early way the total bankruptcy of the capitalist system and shouted aloud for some sort of quick, rational, simple, alternative.'[14] Klugmann was hardly alone in holding such sentiments. As a contributor to the May 1933 edition of *Trinity College Magazine*, the college's student periodical, wrote, 'The most important question to-day is the destiny of our Western civilisation. Can capitalism recover from the present depression? Will it always be crippled by ever-worsening crises? Is our world of May Week, Ascot and Cowes to go on, or will we all be dragged down to the level of the working classes?' The author went on to add gloomily, 'Fifteen years ago the world revolution seemed inevitable; to-day, apart from Russia, the fires of revolt have been stamped out with an iron heel.'[15]

Meanwhile, other examples of radicalism were in evidence. The burgeoning Cambridge left was particularly exercised by anti-war sentiments, but also resistance by those in the university of the right, unwilling to allow the left-wing radicalisation of the university go without challenge. On Armistice Day, 1933, some students, including Julian Bell and Guy Burgess (and possibly David Haden-Guest), 'charged' groups of 'reactionaries' who had barraged anti-war marchers with eggs and fruit. They used an old Morris car (adorned with mattresses to serve as armour) as a battering ram.[16] In December, despite not being a Marxist *per se*, Bell would write to the *New Statesman and Nation* to inform its readers that:

> By the end of 1933 we have arrived at a situation in which almost the only subject of discussion is contemporary politics, and in which a very large majority of the more intelligent under-graduates are Communists, or almost Communists … It is not so much that we are all Socialists now as that we are all Marxists now. The burning questions for us are questions of tactics and method, and of our own place in a Socialist State and a Socialist revolution.[17]

In the same year Maurice Cornforth addressed the university's Moral Sciences Club and attracted an unusually large audience to hear his thoughts on the philosophy of Communism.[18]

The year 1933 was clearly a major one in the development of Communism at Cambridge. As Geoff Andrews, Klugmann's biographer, has noted, the rise of Nazism in that year preoccupied the university's Communists.[19] For instance, another May 1933 contributor to *Trinity Magazine*, writing under the initials D.G. (presumably David Haden-Guest), wrote a fiery condemnation of Nazism, including an attack on 'pseudo-Fascists' at Cambridge. He concluded the article with a call for Communist revolution: 'We must work to overthrow the power of Capital before ever a Fascist movement is able to develop, and in so doing avoid the terrible period of suffering which must otherwise be passed through.'[20] Clearly, the growing dangers posed by Fascism abroad and the dire situation at home – unemployment hovered at more than 20 per cent throughout the opening months of 1933 – had added major impetus to the Communist cause.[21] As Anthony Blunt would write:

> I had a sabbatical year leave from Cambridge 1933–1934, and when I came back in October, 1934, I found that all my friends – that is an enormous amount of my friends and almost all the intellectual and bright undergraduates who had come up to Cambridge – had suddenly become Marxists under the impact of Hitler coming to power and there was this very powerful group, very remarkable group of Communist intellectuals in Cambridge of which Guy Burgess was one, James Klugmann was another, John Cornford another.[22]

It was in this increasingly radical atmosphere that Philby, Burgess, Blunt, Maclean and later John Cairncross found themselves while at Cambridge. It would, however, be a mistake to assume that the radicalism of their environment was the source of their conversion to Communism. In fact, it was they, particularly Burgess along with Klugmann, Cornforth, Haden-Guest, Bell and a few others, who helped to radicalise the university. As Eric Hobsbawm, the famous Marxist historian, would note in his 2002 memoir, *Interesting Times*, the student cohort he found on his arrival in 1935 'was the reddest and most radical generation in the history of the university'.[23] This was in no small part a result of the activism of the Cambridge spies.

★

Harold Adrian Russell 'Kim' Philby was born on New Year's Day 1912 in India to Harry St John 'Jack' Philby and Dora Philby. Jack had been an adviser to the British Government on the Arab world and a desert explorer. Such was his love of adventure, he adorned Harold with the nickname 'Kim', after the eponymous boy-spy from Rudyard Kipling's famous 1901 novel. Throughout much of Kim's childhood, Jack was an absent figure, exploring his beloved deserts. He was an unconventional man who, despite despising the British establishment and its politics, never relinquished his membership of his London clubs and sent his son to his own *alma mater*, Westminster College. Where Jack parted company with the British establishment was in its policy towards the Arab world, over which he defied his orders, resulting in his sacking from the Colonial Office in 1924. Eventually he would convert to Islam and marry a Saudi woman. He was nearly interned during the Second World War as a result of his approving comments on Hitler's Nazi regime – a fact that worried Moscow.[24] Jack died in 1960, three years before his son defected to the Soviet Union. Such was Jack's distaste for the British establishment, Kim believed 'he would have been thunderstruck, but by no means disapproving' of the revelation that his son had been a Soviet mole.[25] After his schooling, Philby the younger once again followed in his father's footsteps and attended Trinity College, Cambridge.

With his unconventional view of the world and disdain for the establishment, perhaps partially inherited from his father, Philby arrived at Cambridge in 1929 with already established left-wing views. Among his first political acts was to join the Cambridge University Socialist Society, whose meetings he attended regularly during his first two years of study. Before long, in 1932, he became its treasurer.[26] At that time he was a supporter of the Labour movement and the Labour Party. In the 1929 General Election, Ramsey MacDonald's Labour Party won an impressive 287 seats, but in 1931 the party was reduced to a rump, winning a mere fifty-two seats. For Philby, the destruction of Labour 'threw serious doubt on the validity of the assumptions underlying parliamentary democracy as a whole'. The result of this 'doubt' led to 'a slow and brain-racking process; my transition from a socialist viewpoint to a Communist one took two years.'[27] He left Cambridge in 1933 a committed Communist.

His further transition from Communism to Soviet mole, however, required outside intervention. On completing his studies he asked Maurice Dobb's advice on how he, Philby, might 'devote' himself to the 'Communist cause'. Dobb pointed him towards Louis Gibarti, an agent of the Comintern in Paris, who then introduced Philby to the Austrian underground Communist network in Vienna, which he promptly joined. In 1934, while in Austria, he met and soon married a committed revolutionary with links to Soviet intelligence, Alice 'Litzi' Friedmann. Soon after, the couple returned to Britain and Litzi promptly arranged for Philby to meet Arnold Deutsch, by then operating under the code name 'Otto'.[28]

★

After Philby, the second of the five to be recruited was Donald Maclean. The son of a Liberal MP, Sir Donald Maclean[29] and Gwendolen Margaret Maclean, the younger Donald, like Philby, was brought up in a highly privileged environment. Born in 1913, he was educated at Gresham's School, where he was a friend and contemporary of James Klugmann. Unlike other public schools, not least Marlborough, where Blunt was educated, sports were not prized above intellectual endeavours, and, though Maclean was a keen sportsman, he was not discouraged from pursuing academic excellence in equal measure. Moreover, corporal punishment was used only very sparingly.[30]

Nevertheless, the political environment of the school was certainly conservative, at least with a small 'c', as was his family. Both of Maclean's brothers, doubtless on the instruction of their father, participated in minor strike-breaking activities during the 1926 General Strike. One of Maclean's brothers, Ian, put forward a motion in the school debating society that, 'In the opinion of this House the tyranny of Fascismo [sic] is preferable to that of Trade Unions.' The motion lost by a mere four votes from forty-eight. A motion placed later that year, 'A Conservative Administration is best suited to a British temperament' won decisively and a similar motion, advocating a Labour government, was heavily defeated.[31]

As a teenager Donald had, however, to develop his own political sensibilities and it is clear that he was already developing a keen distaste for Fascism and Nazism. During the summer holidays he was sent to France and Germany to improve his languages. While in Germany, the tall, blond, blue-eyed Maclean was, in the words of his biographer Robert Cecil, 'to his disgust', approached by a group of Nazis who wished to be photographed with 'the perfect Aryan'.[32] By 1931, Maclean, and indeed the debating society, were shifting leftward. In a motion condemning socialism, he spoke in opposition and the motion was narrowly defeated.[33]

When Maclean arrived at Trinity Hall, Cambridge, in 1930, the university's shift to the left was already under way, only to be further catalysed by the two new arrivals from Gresham's – Klugmann in particular. Once at Cambridge, Maclean began to leave his father's politics behind him and to associate with Communists. This soon led to direct activism, including participation in a demonstration for the unemployed in London, at which he was arrested by the police. This did not go down well with his mother, who was forced to collect him from the police station. The death of his father in June 1932 led to a relaxation of parental authority and Maclean was able to increasingly give full voice to his new-found political beliefs. While at Cambridge he also befriended both Kim Philby and Guy Burgess, the latter of whom is said by Robert Cecil to have introduced the otherwise heterosexual Maclean to 'homosexual practices in a way that Gresham's had not done'.[34]

Maclean also joined the Communist Party and undertook, in the words of Deutsch, 'a wide variety of Party work, from distributing the newspaper to picketing factories that were on strike. He came to us out of sincere motivation, namely that of the intellectual emptiness and aimlessness of the bourgeois class to which he belonged antagonized him.'[35] When Philby returned from Vienna, tasked by Deutsch with recommending potential recruits, young radicals from Britain's elite educational establishments, Maclean's name was at the top of his list.[36]

★

If Philby's conversion from conventional, albeit already left-wing, politics to becoming a lifelong Communist, took two years and the collapse of the Labour Party, Guy Burgess' transition was rather more rapid. Guy Francis de Moncy Burgess was born in 1911, the son of Malcolm Kingsford de Moncy Burgess and Evelyn Burgess. Malcolm, a naval officer, died of a heart attack when Burgess was 13 years of age. Since the age of 12, Burgess had attended Eton College, the highly prestigious public school, but shortly after his father's death he was transferred to Dartmouth Naval College, with the expectation that he would follow in his late father's footsteps and pursue a naval career.

His stay at Dartmouth was, however, relatively short-lived. Though he was removed from the college on medical grounds (poor eyesight) at the age of 16, it seems likely that his homosexuality was the real motive for his dismissal. According to one of his biographers, Andrew Lownie, Burgess then returned to Eton, increasingly lonely and showing evidence of already developing left-wing political inclinations.[37] Eton was far more agreeable to Burgess and he did well both academically and in terms of building contacts that would endure long after his school days.[38]

In 1930, Burgess went up to Trinity College, Cambridge, to read history. By this stage his sexuality was well in evidence and he made little, if any, effort to hide it. This was in spite of the fact that homosexual intercourse was illegal, as it would remain until 1967. He also enjoyed the trappings of wealth and Etonian privilege, with membership of the exclusive Pitt Club,[39] where he indulged in a bottle of expensive German wine daily with his lunch. However, by 1931, when the global economic and political situation was worsening, Burgess was becoming increasingly politically aware.[40] One of two principal developments in Burgess' political awakening was the arrival at Cambridge of Jim Lees, an ex-miner and member of the left-wing Independent Labour Party, who 'taught' Burgess 'a lot and troubled his conscience'. The other was befriending other left-leaning individuals, not least Kim Philby who was already gradually transitioning from Socialism to Communism.[41]

As we have seen, Burgess from 1931 became increasingly militant in his left-wing activism, which included the politicisation of the Apostles, an elite debating society, as well as escapades, such as charging pro-war students in a mattress-clad Morris on Armistice Day with Julian Bell. He, like Philby, graduated from Cambridge committed to the Communist cause. However, unlike Philby, Burgess did not smoothly transition into the world of espionage, despite a summer vacation to the Soviet Union in 1934, during which the NKVD considered approaching him as a potential agent.[42] Instead, it was Philby's return to Britain in May 1934 that proved pivotal. Philby, having been enlisted by Deutsch, had considered other potential recruits and Burgess was discussed 'at length'. First, however, came Maclean, who, after his recruitment by Philby and Deutsch, promptly constructed a façade of abandoning his Communist views. Burgess didn't believe this ruse and promptly guessed the truth. In the meantime, Philby had also met with Burgess and talked with him about what he had seen and done while in Vienna – though Philby's new role as an agent was withheld. Towards the end of the year, Philby and Maclean arranged for Deutsch and Burgess to meet in a London pub.[43]

★

Anthony Frederick Blunt was born in 1907 in Bournemouth, the son of the Reverend Arthur Stanley Vaughan Blunt and Hilda Violet Blunt. Like Philby and Burgess, he enjoyed a privileged background, attending Marlborough College – a then minor, yet still exclusive, public school founded in the mid-nineteenth century for the education of the sons of the clergy. The school was, at that time, particularly awful – children were subject to regular beatings for minor infractions – and it prized games far above intellectual pursuits. A bright young boy, academically gifted but physically less suited to sports, Blunt endured a ghastly time during his school days at Marlborough, which were marked by isolation, bullying and dreadful conditions. Nevertheless, Blunt excelled in his academic endeavours and, towards the last few years, he began to make friends, particularly among the brighter boys. It was, in those years, that Blunt developed a lifelong fascination with art, but also a dissatisfaction with the British establishment. He and his friends founded a school magazine, *The Heretick*, where they expounded their developing beliefs. These were deemed sufficiently shocking that the magazine was abolished by the school after just two editions.[44]

In 1926, Blunt went up to Trinity College, Cambridge. His first year was a disappointing one in which he read a subject, Mathematics, to which he was unsuited. However, in his second year he switched to Modern Languages and began his first sexual relationship, the first of many during his Cambridge days, both as an undergraduate and beyond. Importantly, this sexual awakening included a relationship with Julian Bell.[45]

James Klugmann was another important individual to cross paths with the young Blunt, by then a lecturer. Blunt was one of Klugmann's tutors and the two got to know each other well over the course of 1934. In addition to his teaching duties, Blunt discussed European history, culture and art, which helped to develop his understanding of Communism and Marxism. As Geoff Andrews explains, 'Though he had been his tutor, Blunt was in fact a typical Klugmann target for recruitment.'[46] Aside from Klugmann, another major influence on Blunt's conversion to the Communist cause was Burgess.[47] Blunt introduced Burgess to the secretive and exclusive Cambridge Apostles. In no small part, Burgess was responsible for the politicisation of the Apostles and between 1927 and 1939, fifteen of thirty-one members elected were on the radical left.[48]

Nevertheless, Blunt was not necessarily sold on every aspect of Communism and would, years later, describe himself as only a 'paper Marxist' until 1936 – this in spite of a visit to the Soviet Union in 1935.[49] More important to Blunt was his loathing of fascism. It was in 1935, and perhaps as late as 1936, that he was approached by Guy Burgess to initially act as a talent spotter for the NKVD.[50] In an autobiographical missive Blunt submitted to Moscow in 1943, he wrote of this phase: 'During my last years at Cambridge roughly from 1935 to 1937 I knew a great many of the Party members among the students. ... [I was] in the closest contact with left-wing students in order to spot likely recruits for us.'[51]

★

It was into this increasingly Communist, radical and anti-fascist university community that John Cairncross would arrive in 1934. He did not come politically unprepared. His understanding of the working classes and poverty was certainly far more advanced that the vast majority of his fellow Cambridge undergraduates. Meanwhile, as we shall see, he had already seen the ugliness and brutality of fascism at first hand.

But, if induction into the shadowy world of espionage for the NKVD was the route chosen by Philby, Maclean, Burgess and Blunt, what happened to those other young Communists at Cambridge? Several of them also found themselves drawn into militant political activism. The Spanish Civil War saw the forces of the radical left, backed by the Soviet Union, wage bloody battles with General Franco's forces of the radical right. For several of the young Communist idealists of Cambridge, the conflict was an opportunity to directly fight for their cause and against the evils of fascism sweeping Europe. For a number of them, the decision to travel to Spain, to assist the Republican government, proved a fatal one.

John Cornford, a poet and another young Marxist intellectual, perished in 1936 on the Cordoba front, shortly after his 21st birthday.[52] Julian Bell also travelled to Spain, where he drove an ambulance. He was killed in 1937 in the Battle of Brunete.[53] David Haden-Guest was killed in 1938. As the son of the Labour MP Leslie Haden-Guest, his death received international media coverage and *The New York Times* reported:

> David Guest, brilliant young Cambridge mathematician and son of Dr. Haden Guest, Labour politician, was killed fighting with Spanish Loyalist forces ... Mr. Guest, who was 26, joined the Communist party after leaving Cambridge and left a teaching post at Southampton College in June to fight in Spain.[54]

3

A Foreign Country

While Cambridge University was rapidly radicalising over the course of the opening years of the 1930s – its Socialist Society would reach 1,000 members of an undergraduate population of 7,000[1] – Cairncross was beginning his own undergraduate career. Despite Cairncross' fame (or perhaps infamy), as the so-called 'fifth man' of the Cambridge spy ring, his early life remains shrouded in mystery. Surviving papers and records that document his life are, in this early period, few and far between. This is particularly true of his early university career until he reached Cambridge. In fact, he attended two universities before he arrived at Cambridge, spending two years at the University of Glasgow, where he arrived in 1930, followed by two years at the prestigious Sorbonne in Paris, before a final two years at Trinity College, Cambridge, beginning in 1934.[2]

*

Founded in 1451, the University of Glasgow was, by 1930, a prestigious if poor relation of Britain's other civic universities. In some ways this mirrored the wider fortunes of the city in the aftermath of the First World War. By the end of the nineteenth century Glasgow had become one of the most important industrial centres in the world. It had accumulated a number of key heavy industries, including iron, coal, steel, engineering and shipbuilding. In 1913 the city produced more than 750,000 tons of shipping. However, after the First World War, industrial and population growth gave way to decline, unemployment and poverty. By time the Great Depression arrived, shipbuilding and coal production had halved from their pre-1914 levels. This, of course, led to a knock-on effect to other industries. Steel, a key component in shipbuilding, and thus an industry in demand during the war, rapidly fell into decline as peacetime saw a collapse in orders. The industry also had major problems in terms of importing raw materials, which became increasingly expensive, a factor further exacerbated by geographical isolation relative to foreign competitors. The natural result of these fundamental challenges was the rationalisation of the industry and the laying off of staff.[3] This was, of course, catalysed by the Great Depression. In 1927, fewer than 47,000 individuals were unemployed. By 1931 that tally had risen to above 105,000.[4]

Social conditions in the city were also poor. The fashion for garden cities, which dominated urban planning in the early twentieth century had, in Glasgow, led to the creation of high-value housing stock – semi-detached bungalows with modest gardens in the suburbs – which was out of reach of the urban poor. They, instead, languished in overcrowded tenements. The result was, in the words of Peter Reed, Professor of Architecture and urban historian, 'With the blackening of time, Glasgow's uniformity of appearance descended, in the eyes of some, to grim monotony, while simultaneously much of the tenement property declined – through overcrowding, inadequacy of services and neglect of maintenance – into slums.'[5] The city's overcrowding, which had become epidemic by the 1930s, prompted the further building of housing for the urban poor, often cheap and of low quality. As the Lord Provost of Glasgow made clear, in a strongly worded rebuke to an audience of architects in 1935, 'We have built something-like 35,000 houses. Some of you who are architecturally minded will say that that this is 30,000 abortions and 5,000 houses.'[6]

The university itself had also been undergoing significant change, as well as experiencing problems, throughout the period. The university opened a new union in 1930, with the ceremony performed by its rector, the former Prime Minister Stanley Baldwin. This represented yet another investment in student facilities, one of many that would take place between 1922 and 1931. The result was that the students now had facilities of a much higher quality than could have been expected by their predecessors before 1914.[7] These improvements, however, masked significant problems. In the 1913– 14 academic year, the university had a student population of 2,916 (fewer than a quarter of whom were women), yet by the time Cairncross was at Glasgow the number had risen to in excess of 5,500.[8] However, despite undoubted improvements to facilities, wider university investment had collapsed. As a relatively recent history of the university makes clear, 'The years between 1922 and 1936 were essentially fallow years in the development of the University's physical plant, which failed to keep pace with the growth of student numbers, particularly on the Arts side, and failed to keep pace with the national trends in investment in labs and equipment on the Science side.'[9] The central problem was insufficient money; only one year in the five before Cairncross arrived had the university not operated under a budget deficit.[10]

★

The result was that when Cairncross came up to Glasgow in 1930, he found himself in both a city and university besieged by vast economic problems. The character of the university was, itself, particularly parochial. Comparatively few students lived in halls of residence – a mere 3.4 per cent of the student population. This was a small portion as compared to Edinburgh, which housed 13.9 per cent of its students and to St Andrews, which accommodated some 24 per cent, which was more similar to England's civic institutions than other Scottish seats of learning.[11] Instead, Glasgow's students tended to be sourced from the local Clyde region and typically travelled into the city during the day before returning home in the evening. Cairncross, and his brother Alec, were in that respect different. They chose to take up digs in Glasgow itself, rather than commute from Lesmahagow – some 20 miles from the city.

When the young Cairncross arrived at the University of Glasgow in 1930, his siblings had already forged something a reputation for excellence. Two of his brothers were already present at the university. His eldest brother, Andrew, was in his eighth and final year of study, having already obtained his Master's Degree and, a specialist in Shakespeare, was in the final stages of completing a Doctorate.[12] Alec, meanwhile, was in the third year of his degree and had also made quite an impression, winning prizes for outstanding performances in Logic, Moral Philosophy and History. In his third year, he would take the prize for his performance in the Political Economy Exams and become the Macer for the Dialectic Society – the university's debating club.[13]

Yet, though he had large shoes to fill, John Cairncross impressed immediately. His results in the bursary exams, held in 1930, were nothing less than intimidatingly high. He scored 92 per cent and 99 per cent in the English papers, 88 per cent and 100 per cent in French, 99 per cent and 94 per cent in German, and 82 per cent in Latin. His only relative weakness was in Mathematics, where he scored 68 per cent. In fact, at the age of just 17, he achieved the fifth highest score of all bursary applicants to the University that year, with a remarkable overall score of 900. With these results in hand, like his brother Alec before him, he was awarded both a Carnegie Trust Grant and a university bursary.[14] Once enrolled, he did not disappoint, winning the prize for highest achieving student in his year group in both French and German and did so in each of his two years at Glasgow. In his first year he also came fourth in Political Economy and, in his second year, came runner up in English.[15]

In terms of the diet of education he received, Alec Cairncross' university lecture notes for Political Economy, which John later sat, reveal a dense course covering dozens of economists, political theorists and ideas. These ranged from the work of seminal thinkers of previous centuries, such as Adam Smith and John Stuart Mill, to modern luminaries, such as William Beveridge and John Maynard Keynes.[16] Similarly, English introduced students to the literature one would expect: Chaucer and Shakespeare, Wordsworth and Keats, as well as literary criticism and theory. However, less obviously, they also studied the great Whig historians of the nineteenth century, Lord Macaulay and Thomas Carlyle.[17]

The political, social and economic ruptures of inter-war era Britain, which in many ways were to affect the Clyde Valley more acutely than many other regions of Britain, would have a serious impact on the university. The politics of the institution, at least where staff and students were concerned, was fairly conservative. The 1926 General Strike provoked alarm; rumours circulated rapidly that there would not be consequences for either staff or students who joined the Special Constabulary. When the strike broke out, Edward Provan Cathcart, Professor of Physiological Chemistry, denounced two of his colleagues, both philosophers, exclaiming, 'Now those bloody fools, Hethington and Bowman, are learning what is the result of their socialism.' Robert Campbell Garry, another physiologist, recalled of the period that, had the strike extended longer, most 'would have clamoured for authoritative leadership. Of the Right or of the Left? I think that I would have been the odd man out. I could not stand at any time stomach the self-ish, middle-class, snobbish social attitudes of the majority of my contacts.'[18]

Similarly, Alec Cairncross, who had been at Glasgow from 1928 to 1932, and thus had seen the onset and deepening of the Great Depression there, reported a conservative student body. Unlike Cambridge, which was rapidly turning Communist red during the same period, in Glasgow 'the predominantly lower middle-class students … were intensely conservative, or at best liberal, and certainly did not idealise a working class that they knew first hand.'[19]

★

When they finished their second year of the five year honours degree language students would spend at university, they were encouraged to take their third and middle year studying abroad. Cairncross planned to move to Paris for a year to take up a teaching post before returning to Glasgow for his final two years. However, he was assigned to spend his year at Clermont-Ferrand, 'a pleasant but unexciting city', so instead his parents lent him some money to spend his year in Paris instead, to study at the Sorbonne.

Before Cairncross went to Paris, however, he went on a cycling holiday to Austria. He travelled to Hull where he caught a ferry to Ostend and then continued on to Vienna. This was his first trip away from Scotland. While in Vienna he indulged in the high cultural pursuits that the city had to offer; the opera, theatre, palaces, and music all beckoned. What he also noticed, however, was the poverty of the Great Depression, the beggars and the unemployed. Following his holiday, he continued on to Paris and his studies. In Paris, he lived in the Latin Quarter. His budget only afforded him cheap rooms and he ate in the student's clubs and inexpensive restaurants. Yet the cultural experience was an eye-opener; for instance, where in Scotland he had rarely tasted wine, in Paris it was served with every meal. He clearly, however, expected the city to be a hub of sexual experience, but was soon disabused of this notion; he was strictly forbidden from bringing young women back to his lodgings.[20]

At the Sorbonne, Cairncross found himself surrounded by members of *Action Française*. This was an anti-Communist, anti-Parliamentary, nationalistic and anti-Semitic movement, described by the historian James F. McMillan, as a 'cult of violence'. Though not fascist, 'it belonged to the same family as Italian fascism or German nazism'. By 1934, the year that Cairncross left Paris, *Action Française* had 60,000 members, some 7,000 of whom were in Paris.[21] Cairncross was unimpressed and would later describe them as 'a reactionary monarchist movement which I found anachronistic'. Otherwise, he claims to have been largely unaware of politics during his first year at the Sorbonne, 'wrapped in a kind of academic cocoon'.[22]

Instead, Cairncross was far more interested in the cultural insights and literature he could absorb while at the Sorbonne. He enjoyed the cinema of Jouvet, the poetry of Baudelaire, and the seventeenth-century playwrights and poets who would, in later years, dominate his life. These were Molière, Racine, Corneille and La Fontaine. By the end of his first year of study, in July 1933, he had earned a certificate in both French Literature and Philology. Rather than return to Scotland, he instead elected to remain in Paris for a further year and to switch his scholarship from the University of Glasgow to the Sorbonne, so that he could pursue a *Licence-ès-lettres* degree. Once again, before returning to Paris, he spent the summer in Austria, indulging in high literary and dramatic culture.

Upon his return to Paris, in the latter months of 1933, Cairncross found the Sorbonne very different. In Germany, Adolf Hitler and the Nazi Party had come to power, and now the students at the Sorbonne included a considerable number of Jewish refugees who had fled the virulently anti-Semitic regime emerging at home. As a group, Cairncross recalled that very few of them were willing to discuss what was happening in Germany, instead opting to keep their heads down and avoid the 'painful subject of politics'. There was one exception to this, a Communist, François Bondy, who would later go on to earn fame as a journalist. From Bondy, Cairncross began to understand what was happening in Germany.

In the summer of 1934, after he had achieved his *Licence-ès-lettres*, having achieved a further two certificates in German, Cairncross cycled to Germany and saw for himself, 'with alarm', the influence of Hitler's rise to power. This ranged from the increased anti-Semitism and militarism of the people he encountered, one stating that, 'Poland is making things difficult for us. There must be conscription. Yes Germany must be armed.' The same individual expounded on 'the evils of the Jews. They are atheist, immoral, dishonest in business and anti-national. The Jews must go.' Meanwhile, the economic problems Germany had faced since 1929, as well as the stigma of defeat in the First World War, loomed large in Cairncross' analysis of what had occurred in Germany. Cairncross' own disgust was recorded in his diary, and described 'Hitlerism', as 'distinctly reactionary and militaristic, though it has no real programme.'[23]

This period would have a profound influence on Cairncross; though he had already seen poverty first hand in his native Lesmahagow, the reactionary, anti-Semitic extremism of Nazi Germany was something else entirely. In his own accounts of his life, he consistently presented opposition to Nazism as the basis for his espionage activities for the Soviet Union. This was plainly the case.

★

If Cairncross' experiences of British university education at the University of Glasgow and the Sorbonne had been one thing, his experiences at Cambridge were quite another. After his two-year stint at the Sorbonne, he decided, with prompting from his brother Alec, that rather than return to Glasgow he should try his luck and apply to complete his studies at the University of Cambridge. Luck, it transpired, was not necessary. His already advanced grasp of French and German, complete with his love of European literature, particularly Molière, ensured that he impressed in his exams for Cambridge. The entrance exam called for an exposition on Molière and he was able to supply a fifteen-page answer, and during his oral exam he over-heard an academic, William Stewart, proclaim, 'It would be difficult to get better than that.' He was admitted to Trinity College in the autumn of 1934 and, thanks to his *Licence-ès-lettres*, spared the first year of study.[24]

In the 1930s, Cambridge was a markedly different institution to its 'provincial' counterparts in Scotland and Wales. This clear distinction struck Alec Cairncross acutely, who had also made the leap from Glasgow to Cambridge, to undertake postgraduate work in economics. He first arrived at Cambridge in 1932 and described the experience in some detail years later when he wrote:

> Cambridge was almost my first experience of a foreign country. ... It was almost untouched by industry and the splendour of its quadrangles spoke of wealth, antiquity and learning. No greater contrast to Glasgow, that Victorian beehive, slummy, Philistine and warm, could be imagined. The university dominated the town where in Glasgow it was almost a thing apart.[25]

Like his brother, Alec, Cairncross also found Cambridge to be an alien environment. Though he was surrounded by interesting, bright, scholarly individuals, he was shocked by 'the prevailing authoritarianism', the curfew on students that demanded they be in their rooms by 11 at night, the constant requirement to wear their gowns and a 'system of fines [that] made me feel that I was back at school'. He also chafed at the lack of female presence at Trinity and the 'Sexual repression [that] thickened the air' that assured that his 'sexual experience remained nil'.[26] He was, nevertheless, an excellent student, a factor soon observed by his peers. The *Trinity College Magazine* noted in his second and final year, that Cairncross 'Learns a new language every fortnight'.[27] They weren't far wrong. He graduated with a First Class honours degree in modern languages.

The Communist influences that were largely absent in Glasgow and the Sorbonne were already well established in Cambridge by the time John and Alec arrived in 1932 and 1934. At Cambridge John met Roy Pascal, a German language scholar, and E. Herbert Norman, both Communists, the latter of whom Cairncross said was to be rumoured to '"brush his teeth" with Communism'.[28]

Perhaps the most significant figure he met, however, was Anthony Blunt, 'A well-known Communist', who occupied the rooms immediately below him. According to Cairncross, the two did not get on:

> He struck me as a typically English case of someone whose good knowledge of the French language ... supposedly guaranteed an understanding of French literature. ... It was not clear to me on what Blunt based his claim to rank as an expert in French literature, for he had no reputation or standing of any kind in French literary circles.[29]

Similarly, in his later, albeit unreliable, interviews with MI5 he told his interrogators that:

> He knew him [Blunt] quite well and whilst he believed that he was thoroughly Communist in his outlook, it was a Communist Party slant on art and letters rather than upon matters of politics. BLUNT was always something of a patrician, very stand-offish and not very accessible to undergraduates outside his immediate circles.[30]

However, Blunt ran the Modern languages Club and hosted many of its meetings in his rooms, so the two, like it or not, interacted extensively.[31] To Blunt, it was soon to become clear that there was potential in his new student. Cairncross plainly loathed the Nazi regime and was open to the idea of Communism, if nothing else than as a bulwark against fascism and Nazism. This made him a ripe target for ideological development. Indeed, Cairncross would reveal as much years later in his statements to MI5:

In Cambridge I came under Communist influence very gradually and ultimately attended two or three Party Member meetings, but thereafter I was repelled by the unrealistic and conspiratorial aspects of the doctrine. I should add that I was attracted to Communism in the first place by its clear desire to secure a line-up against Germany and also by its approach to the study of literature and philosophy whereby social developments were linked with the evolution of thought and art. While at Cambridge I was studying French and German and my studies brought me into contact with Anthony BLUNT (who occupied the room below mine) and James KLUGMAN [sic] – both at Trinity. Without any open breach with the Communist Party I dropped my association with it. I graduated in French and German in June 1936.[32]

According to the historian Christopher Andrew, Cairncross' Communist views were well known while he was at Cambridge. The evidence for this, the *Trinity College Magazine* described him as 'The Fiery Cross', said to be a reference to his ardent Communist views.[33] This, however, seems unlikely and is more probably a reference to his red hair and spiky demeanour. That is not to suggest that he did not travel in Communist circles; his own statement to MI5 and his autobiography reveal as much. For his own part, however, Cairncross denied ever joining the Communist Party.[34] His statement to MI5 noted that he had been attracted to Communism, but made no mention of membership of the Community Party of Great Britain. Similarly, his brother, Alec, recorded in his diary in 1979, 'I am positive that [John] had no Communist leanings in 1934–35 when we shared rooms and am very doubtful whether he was ever in the strict sense a Communist.'[35] Nevertheless, an investigation into his activities by MI5 in 1952 suggested that he had, in fact, 'belonged to the Communist Party when at the University'.[36]

Whatever the truth of the matter, once Cairncross had graduated in 1936, Blunt recommended him to Guy Burgess as a potential recruit. The two met in 1937, after Cairncross had graduated, at a weekend event at Cambridge thrown by Blunt. Burgess informed Moscow that Cairncross was 'lower middle class … speaks with a strong Scottish accent and one cannot call him a gentleman'; further he was a 'petit bourgeois intoxicated with his own success' and 'never a member of the party in the real sense of the word, but I think we should work with him and involve him'.[37]

4

The Third Secretary

Following an outstanding educational career, including his time at the University of Glasgow, the Sorbonne and a First Class degree from Cambridge, the next step for Cairncross was to get a job. His initial instinct was to build a career in academia, the first step in which was to obtain either an academic post or a research position. Unfortunately, neither were offered, despite his excellent academic record and interest in such work. His mistake, he would later conclude, was that, unlike others, he failed (to use modern parlance) to 'network': that is, he did not talk informally to the right people and to make his intentions known. The upshot was that any hope of an academic job was dashed. This, of course, stood him in stark contrast to the likes of Burgess, who, with his easy charm was, to borrow from the title of the recent biography on him by Stewart Purvis and Jeff Hulbert, 'the spy who knew everyone'.[1]

Instead, Cairncross took his sad story to a Trinity modern languages don, who promptly suggested a career in the Civil Service. With this advice in mind, Cairncross spent the summer months cramming for the Foreign Office and Home Civil Service exams. His preparations included consulting past papers, supplemented by lengthy study sessions fuelled by Horlicks. This preparation, combined with some luck and his talent with languages, primed him well. During his studies he consulted a history of the 1848 Revolution in France, a topic that happened to come up in the history element of the exam. Similarly, his study of the theories of the Cambridge economist Hans Singer also prepared him for the economics paper. With the exams completed, he returned to stay with friends in Germany and awaited the results. He came top in the exams for both the Foreign Office and Home Civil Service. The next challenge was to take an oral examination.

The oral exam proved to be a greater obstacle. He was to produce answers that he assumed were 'blunders' – his fault, he believed in both cases, was speaking his mind rather that producing responses he believed the examiners would have preferred. This was a fault that would dog him throughout his life. Nevertheless, he once again found himself situated at the top of the listings and was duly recruited into the Foreign Office as a Third Secretary in October 1936.[2] The world appeared to be at Cairncross' feet. A lifelong career in a highly prestigious branch of government beckoned.

★

As late as 1992, John Dickie, the journalist and specialist on the Foreign Office, was able to write with confidence that the members of the service 'are the *crème de la crème*: they know it, and rarely let an opportunity slip to ensure that other lesser beings realize it.'[3] This elitism is not a modern phenomenon, from its foundation in 1782, the Foreign Office was socially exclusive to the core.[4] During the Victorian period this exclusivity translated into the ministry being, in the words of an 1880s onlooker, 'a fraternity of gentlemen clerks, born and brought up in the official purple'.[5] At that time, few recruits had attended university or even Britain's public school system. Instead they received a private education, typically from establishments abroad, and were largely drawn from a relatively small, elite social sphere. By 1914 this social elitism continued to remain dominant and the products of Eton College in particular dominated recruitment. However, efforts had been under way to encourage recruitment from the universities and reforms in the opening decade of the twentieth century ensured that a good degree was to soon become an essential entry requirement.[6]

In 1955, Lord Strang, the diplomat, Foreign Office mandarin and Permanent Under-Secretary of State for Foreign Affairs from 1949 to 1953, contended that by 1918 '"birth" had ceased to be a criterion for the selection of entrants; and so had wealth'. His justification for this claim was that the Foreign Office recruited those 'who had managed to work their way through university education on scholarships'.[7] Of course, this optimistic assessment ignored the fact that the scholarship entrants into the university system from the working classes or even the lower middle classes were a very rare species indeed. It must be remembered that in 1930, only 9,129 people were awarded a first degree.[8] The universities remained exclusive institutions and were dominated by the offspring of the professional and managerial classes – the wealthy upper and middle orders of society. Indeed, even by the time that Strang was writing in the 1950s, only 4.5 per cent of children (and mostly boys) from the working classes received a university education as compared to 16 per cent from the professional and managerial classes.[9]

In fact, the Foreign Office of the inter-war period was particularly averse to change and resisted efforts at modernisation or improvement. The Foreign Office, and especially its diplomats, remained an extremely exclusive breed. It was dominated by products of the elite public school system, and 'personality' was prized over intellect when it came to recruitment.[10] As Strang noted, even the entrance examination system of the 1930s 'tended to exclude many people who might have made good diplomats, but who lacked the financial means to prepare for the examination'.[11] Though Eton College had lost its dominance and university degrees had become ubiquitous, the public schools remained a key stepping stone to entry and few grammar school boys were recruited.[12] Indeed, Strang himself presented something of an oddity for a Foreign Office official in the 1930s. A grammar school boy and the son of a farmer, he went on to study at University College, London, and was on the way to conducting doctoral research in Paris before his studies were interrupted by the First World War. He entered the then under-staffed Foreign Office in 1919, when it opened its ranks to former soldiers.[13]

The fact was that even with exceptions such as Strang, by the mid-twentieth century the Foreign Office was 'seen as an Establishment pinnacle'.[14] It was still socially exclusive and populated by university-educated men – itself typically a sign of a privileged upbringing. This was not lost on Cairncross when he first arrived for work in 1936. Even after his induction into an environment of wealth and social elitism at Cambridge, he was 'impressed', he would write in his memoirs, 'by the whole aura of tradition and influence' that the Foreign Office 'exuded'.[15] His lack of familiarity with the customs, traditions and unwritten rules of high society and his modest social stock was instantly observed – including by the porters, who recognised him as being of a socially 'lower rank'. When it came to his induction he was informed that he need not call his colleagues 'sir'.[16]

★

Cairncross' first posting was to the American Department, where he worked as a minor official, kept far from high-grade policy. His initial work consisted of dealing with Honduras' claims to British Honduras (modern-day Belize) and similar territorial claims from Venezuela over what Cairncross dismissively described as the 'surrender of a rock off the coast of British Guyana'. He was also tasked with the important duty of purchasing tea supplies and making cups for his colleagues.[17] He was soon transferred to the Western Department and its Spanish section in February 1937, before eventually being moved to the Central Department by the time the year was out. This move to the Spanish Department was, no doubt, partly a result of his familiarity with the language and his travels in Spain earlier in 1936.[18] This transfer clearly offered work of far greater interest than the minor border squabbles to which Cairncross had previously been assigned in the American Department. Spain was, at that time, in the midst of its bloody civil war, which would continue to rage until 1939 and had thoroughly divided the international community.

Both Mussolini's Italy and Hitler's Germany intervened on the behalf of General Francisco Franco's rebellious Nationalist forces, while the Soviet Union was the primary backer of the Republican government. The British and French, however, adopted a position of passive-aggressive neutrality that favoured Franco's Nationalist forces. Powerful members of the British political establishment, not least Sir Maurice Hankey (the chairman of the Committee of Imperial Defence), were staunch anti-Communists who saw the radical right-wing forces emergent in Europe as a firewall against the rise of Communism. The dangers of left-wing militancy in Britain fuelled by high unemployment – the General Strike of 1926 still fresh in their memories – and the threat of a resurgent Labour movement were similarly at the forefront of their minds. The last thing that such Conservative men wanted was to energise left-wing forces in Britain by aiding the Spanish Republican government. However, it was the Spanish Republican government that held democratic legitimacy in Spain. Diplomatic norms dictated that the British and French recognise the Spanish government.[19] The British position, as described by Conservative Chief Whip David Margesson, was 'to see the rebellion (of the Spanish Army officers) triumph. At the same time, we do not want to abandon our neutrality, for there is no other way of controlling Labour agitation.'[20] The result of British policy was, where possible, the prevention of the flow of arms to the legitimate government in Spain, while typically ignoring German and Italian shipments supplying Franco's rebels.[21]

For the British left, and indeed that of much of the wider international community, the Spanish Civil War rapidly became a totemic struggle in which the forces of the left battled those of fascism. As we have seen, several of the young men who were so influential in turning Cambridge red, including Kim Philby, were to travel to Spain, where a number of them were killed. By this time already recruited by and in contact with his Soviet handlers, Philby had undergone his public and wholly deceptive 'conversion' to the political right in an effort to better ingratiate himself with the British establishment.

In 1937, Philby travelled to Spain, nominally as a correspondent for *The Times* newspaper reporting from an obliquely pro-nationalist stance, but all the while working in secret for the Soviet Union. While covering the Battle of Saragossa in December, the vehicle in which he was travelling was hit by a Republican shell, killing three journalists. Philby, however, escaped with only minor wounds. His reporting of the event was carefully modest and he was received as something of a hero. Franco even awarded him the Red Cross of Military Merit.[22] The result was that he gained admission into the highest circles of the nationalist regime. This soon led his Soviet controllers to develop a plot that would not be out of place in a James Bond novel: Philby was to use his newly found access to assassinate Franco. The scheme, however, came to nothing when his handler, Theodore Maly, reported that, 'Even if he had been able to get close to Franco, then he, despite his willingness, would not be able to do what was expected of him. For all of his loyalty and willingness to sacrifice himself, he does not have the physical courage and other qualities necessary.'[23]

Meanwhile, Cairncross was back in London working on the war for the Foreign Office, part of which involved monitoring news coming out of Spain. This was to include seeing images of the mutilated bodies of Spanish Republicans, which he described as 'a ghastly set of pictures'.[24] One of his tasks was to handle prisoner exchanges – British subjects or those of value to Britain captured by the Nationalist forces. His job, which he conducted in conjunction with a highly efficient operative in Spain, Señor Milanes, was to negotiate the release of individuals in exchange for high-value prisoners held by the Republicans. One of the key individuals whom he helped to successfully escape Spain was the writer and journalist Arthur Koestler.[25]

In 1936, Koestler, like Philby, arrived in Spain as a reporter, in this case for the *News Chronicle*. He, again like Philby, presented himself as holding right-wing pro-Nationalist sentiments to mask his Communist sympathies. However, unlike Philby, Koestler's cover was blown when he was observed in discussion with a known Communist, and he was forced to flee.[26] His escape was short-lived. In 1937, the city in which he was then living, Málaga, was captured by Franco's forces and Koestler was soon arrested and only narrowly escaped immediate and summary execution.[27] If he was very lucky that he was not executed on his capture, he was equally fortunate that the British government intervened on his behalf, saving his life and securing his release. The British consul estimated that, between 1937 and 1944, Nationalist reprisals at Málaga saw some 20,000 people butchered.[28] According to Cairncross at least, Koestler's life was saved, in small part, thanks to Cairncross' own actions. 'I have no idea how the operation developed,' he informed readers of his memoirs, 'but at least I can claim to have pressed for action after the Department had rejected further intervention as hopeless.'[29]

★

The late 1930s were a difficult time for the British intelligence services. The rise of Nazi Germany, Mussolini's Italy and Imperial Japan, combined with their long-term efforts against the Soviet Union, made for a challenging landscape filled with dangers and threats. It was during this period, while working for the Foreign Office, that Cairncross was recruited as a Soviet agent. The precise route he took into the world of Soviet intelligence has been the subject of much speculation. In an early account by the journalist and prolific author of espionage histories, Chapman Pincher, published in 1981 and clearly based on at least some access to then still classified files or at least an individual highly familiar with them, it was suggested that Cairncross was recruited earlier still, while at Cambridge. Pincher contended that Cairncross 'suddenly' changed career ambitions, from academia to the Civil Service, in 1935, suggesting that his recruitment had already taken place by that point. Then, in 1936, Cairncross, gave up formal ties to Communism and applied to the Foreign Office on the instructions of Arnold Deutsch.[30] A similar claim was made in 1987 by Nigel West (the pen-name of the spy-writer and former Conservative Party MP Rupert Allason, who, as we shall see later, had at least some personal access to Cairncross) who wrote that Cairncross was 'recruited by Burgess in 1935 while still at Cambridge', a claim then repeated by Andrew and Gordievsky in 1990.[31]

In his 1994 memoir, Yuri Modin, Cairncross' one-time handler towards the end of his espionage career, produced a somewhat problematic account of the Scotsman's recruitment by the NKVD. Modin contended that it was not one of the illegal spies in residence who made the first move, nor indeed was it any of its spies at Cambridge. Instead, the task fell, on the orders of the head of the Communist Party of Great Britain, Harry Pollitt, to Cairncross' friend, James Klugmann. That is not to say that the Cambridge agents did not play a role; in fact Modin contends that they were asked to fill out a questionnaire on Cairncross.

In their responses to this questionnaire, 'they took a fairly dim view' of the prospective candidate; he was a man who 'hadn't a clue how to behave in company, nor any idea how to get on with people socially'. He was, on the other hand, 'both cultivated and highly intelligent, though he would never be part of their world'.[32] Plainly, the NKVD knew precisely what kind of individuals could reach the heart of the British establishment – well-connected networkers. It is here, however, that Modin's account falls into less compelling territory. For instance, it seems unlikely that Philby, said by Modin to have filled out the questionnaire, had even met Cairncross by that point. The two men were not, after all, contemporaries at Cambridge – Philby had departed in 1933, the year before Cairncross arrived. By Modin's admission, the original four Cambridge spies travelled in very different social circles to Cairncross and 'may only have known him by sight'.[33] As such, even if Philby did complete such a questionnaire, it is difficult to imagine it would have been particularly helpful. Certainly, Cairncross' autobiography suggests that the member of the group he knew best while at Cambridge was Blunt; the others only knew him, at most, peripherally.

There is also some chronological confusion in Modin's account. On the one hand, he asserts that Cairncross was ordered by his new spymasters to 'publicly break' with Marxist theory, afterwards working single-mindedly to attain a first-class honours in modern languages in 1936. The clear implication was that he had been recruited prior to leaving Cambridge. However, Modin later suggests that Cairncross' collaboration with Soviet intelligence came as a result of a dislike of snobbery he received at the hands of colleagues in the Foreign Office (more on which in the next chapter).[34] Clearly, only one of Modin's claims can be correct.

At this juncture it is worth returning to the timelines presented by Christopher Andrew. By 2009, Andrew had gained access to the vast archives smuggled to the West by the Soviet defector Vasili Mitrokhin and also had served as the official historian of MI5. In his later works, Andrew updated the timeline to state that Blunt had acted as a talent scout, Burgess had been left to sound out Cairncross, and Klugmann made the formal overtures and introductions to 'Otto' – the code name of Arnold Deutsch. It was in April 1937 that Theodore Maly was able to report happily to his Moscow bosses that Cairncross had been recruited and allocated the code name 'Molière'.[35] Andrew and Mitrokhin state that Cairncross was soon able to start passing information to the NKVD; this included documents he described as 'a wealth of valuable information on the progress of the Civil War in Spain'.[36]

For his own part, Cairncross wrote at length regarding his recruitment by Soviet intelligence. Following his admission into the Foreign Office, he had met with Burgess a number of times. This was in spite of an unsavoury reputation Burgess had accumulated during his Cambridge days. None other than James Klugmann warned Cairncross to keep his distance from the reputedly 'brilliant, effervescent but unreliable' Burgess. Having bumped into each other at a party, the two met on several further occasions and Cairncross came to recognise that he was indeed being groomed, though he had little idea for what.[37] Decades later, in now often quoted interviews with the journalist Barrie Penrose, he would describe his talks with Burgess. 'Burgess was fascinating, charming and utterly ruthless. But he never told me he was a Communist, let alone a Communist agent. Like me he hated appeasement, fearing that it was a disastrous strategy and, of course, it was every bit as disastrous as we had believed.'[38] In one meeting, at Anthony Blunt's rooms back in Cambridge, ostensibly to introduce his new friend to the poet Louis McNiece, Burgess used the train ride back to explore the question of politics:

I said that unless Britain pressed on with re-armament and formed a military alliance with at least France and Russia, we would find ourselves waging a war for which we were ill-prepared in every way, and would not be able to stand up to an aggressive and militarist Germany. Burgess nodded sagely, but made no comment.[39]

This, Cairncross claimed, was the first political conversation he had conducted with Burgess. In 1952, while being interrogated by MI5, he recounted the same story:

> I made the trip back to London in Guy BURGESS's company. I remember he asked me whether I thought there was any glamour in being attached to the Foreign Office. I told him that, as far as I was concerned, it was solely a case of doing a job, on questions which interested me. We also discussed the role of Communism, particularly in this country – apparently because he knew of my previous association. I expressed the view that Communist agitation, particularly in this country, was perfectly futile and the only thing that counted was to get as many Powers together, whatever their political views, to resist Nazi aggression. He agreed with this.[40]

Rather dangerously, Burgess then bragged to Goronwy Rees[41] that he had recruited Cairncross. This appears to have been a fiction on Burgess' part. According to Cairncross, they arranged again to meet at a Parisian homosexual café called *Le Sélect* – an embarrassed Cairncross failed to show up. This was again, in essence, the same account of Cairncross' relationship with Burgess during this period that he would later tell to MI5:

> I also had lunch at about March 1937 with BURGESS. The others present were BLUNT, Tom WYLIE and Helmut KATZ, a dapper young man who had been in Finland and spoke both Finnish and Swedish fluently. He was a German refugee. The atmosphere of the party was markedly and unpleasantly homosexual. Politics were not discussed. As some point thereafter, BURGESS was in Paris at the same time as I and left a message at my hotel asking me to contact him at the Select (a homosexual cafe). I did not go, as I had neither the wish nor the time to do so.[42]

Instead, Deutsch reverted to Plan-B and the task fell to James Klugmann. In a passage that would not be out of place in a John Le Carré novel, the two arranged to meet one quiet evening at seven o'clock at an entrance to Regent's Park. An unsmiling and unusually reticent Klugmann led his would-be recruit into the park where, from behind some trees, stepped 'a short, stocky figure' who was introduced as 'Otto'. This was, in fact Arnold Deutsch, the highly prolific recruiter and handler at the centre of the rapidly developing Soviet efforts to penetrate Britain's corridors of power. Klugmann departed without another word or look. Cairncross claimed he would not see his friend and 'betrayer' again for another three decades. However, according to KGB archives, James Klugmann continued to arrange meetings between Cairncross and his Soviet contacts after this first meeting.[43]

Indeed, the improved, if still selective, official access to the Soviet archives reveals a number of other important details to the story of Cairncross' recruitment. According to Nigel West and Oleg Tsarev, the files, at least those that were made available for inspection, do not recount the precise story. However, as noted above, Theodore Maly sent a missive to Moscow, dated 9 April 1937, stating: 'We have already recruited Cairncross. We shall call him MOLIERE.' The report continued by noting they had achieved this without revealing to Cairncross the work, conducted behind the scenes, by Burgess and Blunt in his recruitment. This, as Cairncross said, was accomplished by organising meetings between himself and James Klugmann. 'We shall,' Deutsch reported triumphantly, 'take him over by the end of May.'[44]

Importantly, these revelations also show that Cairncross, as he said, was not recruited by Soviet intelligence before he reached the Foreign Office. They also confirmed Andrews' later revised timeline of events and list of *dramatis personae* constructed with the aid of Vasili Mitrokhin's documents. Cairncross was recruited only after he had joined the Foreign Office: Blunt was the talent scout, Burgess tested the waters and Klugmann made the introductions to Deutsch.

5

An Unsatisfactory Probationer

By 1937 Cairncross found himself both in the Foreign Office and in contact with the Soviet illegals in London. This poses two key questions: why did he agree to continue his contact with the agents of a foreign power and how much material did he leak to them during his time at the Foreign Office?

In the case of the first question, there has already been much speculation on this point.

According to Cairncross, his first meeting with Deutsch apparently came as a great shock. When it became clear what was happening, he claimed he was 'appalled' at the situation in which he found himself. His 'first reaction was to fold-up inside … hot-headed anger gradually gave way to fatalistic calm and my survival instincts emerged'. By way of enticement, Deutsch suggested that, come the revolution, the services the Scot rendered to the Soviet Union would be met with rapid career advancement. Cairncross, by contrast, claimed to be more frightened by 'the cold-blooded tactical deception of the KGB … the KGB's reputation for ruthlessness … their treatment of statesmen such as Nikolai Bukharin and the cream of the Red Army'.[1]

Such fears were certainly not without justification. Just a few months prior to their Regent's Park meeting, the Bolshevik revolutionary and theorist Bukharin had been arrested, as were other senior figures in the Soviet Union. Executions soon followed, and Bukharin himself was executed some time later in 1938. These arrests, show trials and executions were widely reported in the West.[2] Certainly Cairncross was aware of them. When, later, his handler Deutsch was recalled to Moscow, Cairncross assumed he had been liquidated in Stalin's campaign of mass murder, the Great Purge.[3]

Whether or not Cairncross understood the scale of the bloody terror unleashed in the Soviet Union between 1936 and 1938 remains unclear.

Cairncross also came to the conclusion that he was being subtly blackmailed. If it were to come to light that he had been a Communist at university, let alone meeting in secret with Soviet illegals, his job would have surely been forfeit. Donald Maclean had faced a similar problem. In his Foreign Office interview he was able to pass off his well-known Communist sympathies at Cambridge as a youthful folly; adding, to demonstrate his 'honesty', 'I haven't entirely shaken them off.'[4] Cairncross, he was sure, would not be afforded the same latitude. 'Maclean was a member of the élite,' he reasoned, 'whereas I was the son of a modest shopkeeper.'[5]

Cairncross was therefore, he claimed, in something of a bind. On the one hand he was frightened of continuing an association with the famously brutal NKVD. On the other, both he and they knew that he was wide open to blackmail. There was also another factor; he was an 'idealist' and staunch anti-fascist. The threat of an impending war against Nazi Germany – a war that, without the aid of the Soviet Union would inevitably end in British defeat – required action. If the British government was not going to take it, opting instead for the policy of appeasement, it fell to men such as Cairncross to do so for them. Indeed, the argument he presented was a form of Churchillian-inflected Popular Frontism and he even cited the soon-to-be Prime Minister by name, 'Churchill did raise his voice to warn against the danger Britain was running into by its spineless policy *vis-à-vis* the Nazis, but … he was a lone figure.'[6] Thus, Cairncross the patriot agreed to meet with Deutsch again and eventually began to supply a small stream of carefully chosen documents. These omitted 'anything which did not concern the Russians directly or involved specifically British interests', the aim being nothing less than 'Britain's survival'.[7]

★

Others have suggested Cairncross was to turn spy for the Soviet Union as a result of somewhat less patriotic motives. According to Chapman Pincher, he was already a convinced Communist and had been since 1935, while still at Cambridge. Furthermore, Pincher asserted that Cairncross had been 'a scholarship boy from a poorly off home in Glasgow' and that his experience of poverty convinced him that, 'Soviet-style Communism was the only way of securing social justice.'[8] Andrew and Gordievsky presented a similar if more detailed origins story. Central to their account was his experiences of Red Clydeside and the Great Depression. They also speculate that during his time in Paris, he would have likely made contact with German Communists who had fled Nazi Germany – conjecture that Cairncross denied.[9] In his memoirs, he rejected that he had been a member of the Communist Party, though he did admit to attending Communist meetings while at Cambridge.[10] However, according to Barrie Penrose and Simon Freeman, he did admit in an interview to having been a member of the Party if 'only from January 1935 until late in 1936'.[11]

In Yuri Modin's view, the situation was rather more complex than to suggest that Cairncross was simply an ideological Communist, willing to sacrifice his country's secrets in the hope of establishing a new Soviet order in Britain. Instead, he pointed to the welcome that Cairncross received upon his arrival at the Foreign Office. Modin believed that the young Scot's character and lowly class were at fault. He would have been deemed, 'boorish, ill-dressed, arrogant, and scornful of either diplomatic or social niceties'. Furthermore, as we saw in the previous chapter, the Foreign Office was a particularly elite branch of the Civil Service. This was a point not lost on Modin, who wrote, 'Why he [Cairncross] was ever given a job at the Foreign Office at all has always baffled me.' Intelligence alone was rarely enough. 'Social background, good manners and good connections counted as much and probably more.' In short, they tended to recruit men like Donald Maclean.

John Cairncross, it is fair to say, couldn't have been more different and he spectacularly failed to fit in. 'To be perfectly frank,' Modin summarised, 'I think his collaboration with the NKVD was prompted by the boundless hatred their mockery provoked in him. John Cairncross had a sizeable chip on his shoulder, as the English would say.'[12] In short, he was hampered from the beginning by his lowly humble status and his own difficult personality. Spying for the NKVD was an act of revenge on a snobbish society he longed to be a part of but from which was unfairly excluded.

Cairncross' inability to fit in became apparent as soon as he joined the American Department. Even at this early juncture, at arm's length from the major decision-makers, he began to ruffle some feathers. His first mistake, one of many during his Foreign Office career, was to take issue with Sir Robert Craigie – a senior official and from 1937 to 1941 Britain's Ambassador to Japan – over Craigie's support for German colonial claims.

The venturing of such dissent by so lowly a figure, to a man many years and promotions his senior, was, as Cairncross was to admit, 'tactless' and he was duly 'hauled over the coals' for his insolence.[13]

It was also true that Cairncross' colleagues found him difficult to get on with. In 1939 the Assistant Private Secretary to the Prime Minister, John 'Jock' Colville, recorded in his diary 'lunching rather dully with John Cairncross' – described as 'a very intelligent, though sometimes incoherent, bore'.[14] As Colville explained to the journalist Simon Freeman in 1985, 'Cairncross was always asking people out to lunch. He was very brilliant but very boring. He ate very slowly, slower than anyone I've ever known.'[15] Donald Maclean was reported by Arnold Deutsch as stating that Cairncross 'considers himself more clever and better than all the others'. Deutsch also concluded in June 1937, after having met with Cairncross, that the Scot was 'politically deeply pessimistic', that he was 'very dissatisfied with his work', that he hated the elitist surroundings in which he found himself and that his colleagues 'behaved very untactfully towards him'. Deutsch further mused that a 'feeling of opposition puts him outside the ranks of his environment'. It was in no small part this hostility, the spy handler believed, that meant Cairncross 'was ready to start working for us at once'.[16] Even his own brother, Sir Alec, described in his memoirs 'a prickly young man, who was difficult to argue with and resented things rather easily'. He delicately further concluded that, 'John did not take to the Foreign Office, nor the Foreign Office to him.'[17] The problem lay, Cairncross himself concluded years later, in 'difference in background [which] was to constitute an insuperable barrier'.[18]

The result of all this, in Deutsch's words, was that Cairncross 'at once expressed his readiness to work for us and his attitude to our work is extremely serious. ... He trusts us absolutely and we carry great authority with him'.[19]

★

In 1938, Cairncross was transferred from the Foreign Office to the Treasury.[20] There has been some suggestion, not least from the former KGB officer Oleg Gordievsky, that Cairncross orchestrated this move on the orders of the Centre – the headquarters of the NKVD in Moscow. This was on the basis that the Foreign Office had already been penetrated by Soviet agents, while the Treasury had yet to be.[21] There is little evidence to support this claim. Though Cairncross described his time in the Foreign Office as a 'great experience', it is clear that he did not excel in either the work or environment, and his Foreign Office bosses had little time for him. He had simply never fitted into that socially elite world. As far as he was concerned, the fault lay with the snobbery of his colleagues and superiors and their attendant failure to see his value. His Foreign Office bosses, on the other hand, had a different view of the reasons for his termination.

In 1964, as Whitehall was beginning to come to terms with the fact that yet another highly damaging spy had operated at its heart for years, the Head of the Foreign Office's Security Department, J.E.D. Street, quickly compiled a report on Cairncross from his old personnel file. The summary of the Scotsman's time in the Foreign Office was withering. His boss at the Western Department condemned his work as 'slipshod, inaccurate and untidy', the result being that Donald Maclean had to examine, and presumably correct, much of it. Moreover, at the end of his first year, his probation report was similarly damning. The report's author doubted Cairncross' 'suitability for the Service' and that he displayed little evidence 'of sound judgement or ability to conform to office routine'.[22] A 1979 case history, written in the wake of Blunt's exposure, tersely summarised the official view in a mere five damning words: 'He was an unsatisfactory probationer.'[23] The result was that after just two years, Cairncross was out of the Foreign Office and sent to the Treasury.

The departure of a well-placed source in the Foreign Office created significant problems for the Soviet spymasters in London. Since the mid-1930s, the Soviets had already secured a man on their payroll inside the Foreign Office: a cipher clerk named John Herbert King.[24] His position came without either a pension or a particularly lucrative salary. King, however, craved a rather less modest lifestyle (which already came complete with an estranged wife as well as a mistress) than afforded by his humble means. In exchange for a sizable supplement to his income, he agreed to supply information to his handlers, though unaware that the destination was Moscow.[25] This arrangement continued until 1937. In 1939 King's past caught up with him and he was convicted of espionage and sentenced to ten years' imprisonment.[26]

Unlike many other spies, King was not recruited as a result of his ideological love of Communism, but for financial gain. Both King and his one-time mistress, Helen Wilkie, received considerable sums of money. Between July 1934 and June 1936 he paid her some £1,400, while between

February 1936 and May 1937 one of his own accounts received payments of some £3,010. These were sums far above his legitimate income of £420 per year.[27] The generosity of King's benefactors was well warranted and, if anything, understates the quality of his intelligence, some of which was sufficiently impressive that it may even have been seen by Stalin himself.[28] Important though King was, his significance by 1937 was limited by events beyond his control. In 'June or July' 1937, King's handler told him that he would be departing for a 'month or so'.[29] But rather than leaving the poor agent for a mere month, the handler, Theodore Maly, vanished without trace. Maly had been recalled to Moscow, and returned to face Stalin's purges.[30] As King reported to MI5 interrogators in 1939, 'Since then I have never seen or heard from him.'[31]

Inevitably, King's capture posed a major problem for the Centre – it had lost an important spy in one of Whitehall's most sensitive ministries. Of course, they had another key source in the Foreign Office, Donald Maclean. Cairncross was, at that time, being groomed as a substitute for Maclean, whom it was likely would soon be posted to an embassy abroad. As such, when Cairncross was unceremoniously booted sideways to the Treasury, Maclean was left without a replacement. More to the point, Cairncross' potential usefulness as a spy reduced accordingly. His work in the Western Department of the Foreign Office had allowed his access to a vast array of materials on a whole range of different topics, not least the Spanish Civil War.[32] Guy Burgess rated his access to important information on Czechoslovakia as the 'very best imaginable'.[33]

Even Cairncross himself, typically keen to downplay the significance of his connection to the NKVD prior to 1941, noted that his position in the Foreign Office was clearly an asset for his Soviet handlers. He recalled of his transfer that the move 'must have come as a shock to the KGB's *Rezidentura* in London, since they had been counting on me to replace Maclean'. He then further added that the move would have been still more disappointing for them as his Treasury work was of a 'non-secret nature' and constituted a 'sharp drop' in his 'potential usefulness'.[34] As Modin put it, 'We would certainly have urged him to stay in his post at the Foreign Office, which was naturally far more interesting to us than the Treasury.'[35]

Clearly then, it is highly unlikely that Cairncross' transfer was on Moscow's orders. In fact, evidence from the Soviet archives seen by Oleg Tsarev and Nigel West suggest that, although the transfer did not come as much of a shock, it was regrettable. They had already received word from

Maclean that Cairncross was unlikely to remain at the Foreign Office for much longer. Maclean assessed that Cairncross' position was 'very weak' but that, for a little while longer at least, he would keep his position. This did not last and word was soon sent that Cairncross was to be transferred.[36]

★

If a sense of profound isolation, brought about by a failure to adapt to the socially elite world of the Foreign Office, had driven Cairncross into the arms of Deutsch and Maly, the next question to address, posed at the outset of this chapter, is what damage did he do while at the Foreign Office?

Yuri Modin claimed that information provided by Cairncross was 'whatever he could lay his hands on'. This included 'a good deal of' material on Germany, all of which appeared in 'concise and well written' intelligence reports.[37] Cairncross had, by the final months of 1937, been transferred (within the Foreign Office) again, this time to the Central Department.[38] Unlike his previous department, preoccupied as it was the Spanish Civil War, his new placement positioned him at the heart of the action – the appeasement of Germany and its aggressive stance towards neighbouring powers. However, as we shall see, his ability to provide voluminous quantities of information was limited.

During the entire span of his Foreign Office career, Cairncross was to deny strenuously the extent of his espionage activity on behalf of Soviet Russia. What he did admit to providing to Deutsch were rare envelopes of information. 'These, in fact, were not very great', he explained, his 'department dealt only with Spain and no secret information arose at that time'. He also claimed to keep 'information to the minimum' and only offered material 'already available to the KGB through Maclean, duplicating material of no value'.[39]

The Soviet archives present a more mixed picture than that offered by either Modin or Cairncross. Cairncross, Deutsch explained in 1939, though willing to work for Moscow, was initially cautious. He lacked familiarity in tradecraft; that is, in this instance, the methods of the espionage world, to operate while avoiding detection. As such, when he first began, he refused to deliver documents. Eventually, however, Deutsch, by 'working on him', was able, 'to put this right'.[40] However, precisely what was supplied is, at least at present, impossible to gauge. As noted by Christopher Andrew and Vasili Mitrokhin, 'There are very few references to such documents [supplied by Cairncross] either in Mitrokhin's notes or in the material from KGB archives made available by the SVR for West and Tsarev, [in] *The Crown Jewels*.'[41]

Shortly after Cairncross had been recruited, a major crisis befell the NKVD's London *Rezidentura*. This was not a result of exposure or any other counter-espionage activities undertaken by the British authorities. Rather, Stalin elected to purge much of the NKVD. Theodore Maly, the head of the highly successful *Rezidentura*, was an early victim, recalled to the Soviet Union in the summer of 1937. He was sentenced to death on the ludicrous basis that he was a German spy, a brutal and ironic end to an illustrious career in the service of the Soviet Union. Meanwhile, Arnold Deutsch was also having problems. His legal basis for residence in Britain, study at the University of London, had come to a close in September 1937 and he was forced to depart for Paris. In November 1937, like Maly before him, Deutsch was recalled. Shortly before, he returned to London for a few days to place his house in order; after that he was gone. Unlike his former boss, however, Deutsch was fortunate enough to survive the purges.[42]

The purges of the NKVD had crippled the London *Rezidentura* and control of Cairncross passed to Anatoli Veniaminovich Gorsky (known by Cairncross under the pseudonym 'Henry'). To make matters worse, Gorsky, no sooner than he had made contact with Cairncross, was promptly recalled to Moscow for months of training. This left Blunt, Burgess and Cairncross without a direct point of contact to the NKVD for nine months.[43] In summary of this period of his life, Cairncross categorically claimed that, 'I provided no further data until after the Germans invaded Russia' in June 1941.[44] However, and though he had also recorded that he never spoke to James Klugmann again (at least not for three decades), the KGB archives suggest otherwise. With Deutsch out of the picture, he was still able to supply some material via Burgess and Klugmann.[45]

In the final analysis it is difficult to establish what material Cairncross provided to Moscow in his early days as a spy. The period in which he was in contact with Deutsch lasted a mere seven months before Deutsch was recalled, from May to November 1937. At first, as both Deutsch and Cairncross confirm, he was reticent to supply written material and had to be eased into his role as a spy. After Deutsch was removed from the picture, the Foreign Office material provided by Cairncross can only have reduced and there were few in the *Rezidentura* or Moscow in a position or mood to appreciate it anyway. Modin described the impact of the purges in stark terms: 'There were very few people left working at the Lubyanka and the survivors had other things on their minds than looking after junior agents in the West. Their main preoccupation was saving their skins.'[46]

In October 1938, less than a year after Deutsch's departure, Cairncross was transferred to the Treasury.[47] If the inter-war period Foreign Office was elitist, and presented, to use the words of the historian Lord Peter Hennessy, 'a determined resistance to any external suggestions for improvement', the Treasury was by contrast 'almost a citadel of progressive democratic virtue'.[48] For his own part, writing in his memoir, Cairncross claimed that his move to the Treasury was beneficial, and that the staff of his new Ministry 'were very much of my own type, forming a meritocracy'.[49] Nevertheless, even if the atmosphere was more to his liking, the work itself at the Treasury was clearly rather tedious. His time was spent 'toiling on uninteresting if formative work'. When later meeting with Gorsky, he described being relieved at not being asked to provide secret documents. Not that it would have been possible, 'unless the construction of new Post Offices could be regarded as confidential'.[50] Revelations from the Soviet archives, however, cast this period in the Treasury in a rather different light. Controlling the money, as it did, the Treasury was in fact a hugely useful place to insert a spy. It received documents from all facets of government, foreign affairs, defence, intelligence and so on. The result was, until Gorsky was again called away to Moscow in 1940, Cairncross was able to supply a rich stream of documents.[51]

★

A little earlier, however, in April 1938, during Gorsky's absence, the London *Rezidentura* was taken over by a new officer, Grigori Grafpen. This did not prove a lasting arrangement. Grafpen lacked the know-how to operate his station effectively and met his spies in Kensington Gardens, which were in the immediate vicinity of the Soviet Embassy. In terms of tradecraft and the security of his contacts, this was extremely foolish. Grafpen also failed to prevent Cairncross' transfer to the Treasury, ruining the plans to use Cairncross as a replacement for Maclean – though it is difficult to imagine what he could have achieved given Cairncross' considerable capacity to rile his colleagues and superiors. Perhaps fortunately for his charges, Grafpen fell victim to the purges, was recalled to Moscow before the year was out, and was promptly sentenced to five years' hard labour.[52]

A former cipher clerk, Anatoli Gorsky became Cairncross' new controller. Gorsky was short, wore spectacles and was adorned with 'angry eyebrows'.[53] Cairncross described 'a Russian with distinctly Slavic features'. The two men did not get on well. Deutsch had been a rather easy-going, intellectually minded and understanding controller, Gorsky was very different. He was described by Andrew and Mitrokhin as 'a grimly efficient, humourless, orthodox Stalinist'.[54] Anthony Blunt, years later in an interview with Maclean's biographer, Robert Cecil, similarly described the 'flat-footed' controller whose inflexible approach was an unwelcome change.[55] The 'orthodox Stalinist' immediately categorised Cairncross, who had far less time for Marxist theory than the other four Cambridge spies, 'as an unbeliever'. The result was that his new controller proceeded to keep him at arm's length. 'This change,' Cairncross wrote, 'significantly affected my relationship with the KGB.'[56] From the point of view of Moscow, this could only have been for the worse. The result was a detrimental impact on their mole's productivity. When Gorsky was eventually replaced as Cairncross' controller matters improved rapidly. 'The style of the new handler suited the Carelian [Cairncross] much better,' explained Yuri Modin, 'he consequently produced twice as much intelligence.'[57]

Also hampering the efforts of the otherwise highly useful sources, Cairncross among the most productive, was a lack of trust in their material in Moscow. Despite the myriad of successes racked up by its British agents, Soviet intelligence officials in Moscow were disinclined to take it seriously. Instead they suspected British deception efforts. This was down to the profound paranoia of the Stalinist regime. That the British were uninterested in Soviet intelligence (unlike the NKVD which was intensely interested in Britain) and not attempting deception was unfathomable. Such was the mistrust, Moscow communicated to their London man, Anatoli Gorsky, that a key task was weeding out deception. Another NKVD officer, Elena Modrzhinskaya, suspected strongly that the information being supplied by the five was British trickery. The fact that none of them had supplied the name of a single British operative in the Soviet Union was deemed significant evidence that they were double agents.[58] It would not be until 1944 that Moscow came to have confidence in its most productive British spies.

Yet, despite the shortcomings of a new controller, the absences and general confusion thrown up by the purges, and a lack of trust in Moscow, it was far from the end of Soviet espionage in Britain. In fact, things were only just beginning.

6

LISZT

In 1937 the Chancellor of the Exchequer, Neville Chamberlain, succeeded Stanley Baldwin as the Prime Minister. The situation in which he found himself was difficult to say the least. Germany under the Nazis had become increasingly aggressive: it announced a vast programme of re-militarisation in 1935 and sent troops into the Rhineland in March 1936. Both acts were expressly forbidden under the terms of the Treaty of Versailles. Italy too had succumbed to an extreme and aggressive fascist dictatorship under Benito Mussolini. In 1935, Italy invaded Abyssinia (the Empire of Ethiopia), which led to swift condemnation and sanctions from the League of Nations. Mussolini ignored the sanctions and withdrew Italy from the League. In east Asia, Imperial Japan had annexed Manchuria in 1931. In 1937 Japan then proceeded to launch a full-scale invasion of China, beginning the Second Sino–Japanese War, which lasted until Japan's surrender in September 1945. Each of these three belligerent powers directly challenged British interests. In the east, Japan posed a worrying threat to Britain's imperial possessions. Italy endangered Britain's strategic security in the Mediterranean and Germany threatened to overthrow the entire balance of power in Europe.

The situation was grim and the British Chiefs of Staff were keen to impress upon the government the extent of the danger. In December 1937, they informed the Cabinet that:

We cannot foresee the time when our defence forces will be strong enough to safeguard our trade, territory and vital interests against Germany, Italy and Japan at the same time ... We cannot exaggerate the importance from the point of view of Imperial Defence of any political or international action which could be taken to reduce the number of our potential enemies and to gain support of potential allies.[1]

A particular problem with this piece of advice was that suitable allies were few and far between. The nation with the greatest military potential on earth, the United States of America, was still reeling from the economic difficulties brought about during the Great Depression and had turned staunchly isolationist in its international outlook. The other alternative was the Soviet Union, a difficult proposition to stomach for a British Conservative Prime Minister. Moreover, the purges that had hampered the NKVD's ability to operate in Britain had also swept the Red Army, beginning with nine senior officers, resulting in its effective decapitation.[2] Looking on from Britain, the Chiefs of Staff concluded that in the wake of this calamity, the Red Army would present 'an embarrassment rather than a help'.[3]

Armed with this gloomy advice, Chamberlain continued his policy of appeasing the dictators. This culminated in the Munich agreement, where Britain, in effect, gave Hitler *carte blanche* to annex the Sudetenland. The Cambridge spies, by this juncture posing as pro-establishment conservatives, were, nevertheless, horrified. Guy Burgess believed that Chamberlain was 'an ignorant provincial ironmonger' – perhaps also providing some insight into how he viewed Cairncross – and the Prime Minister's French counterpart Édouard Daladier, a 'confused and panic-stricken patriot'.[4] In a letter to the future Prime Minister Sir Winston Churchill, Burgess called for collaboration with the Soviet Union:

> Hitler uses force only against fear, he has been right in that till now, for the odds were against him. Soon they may be against us. That is the simple truth of the crisis – he took what he could get … What is to be done? … you alone have the force and authority to galvanise the potential allies into action … The guarantee of the new Czech Frontier must be absolute & gun tight …. the French must reaffirm the Franco–Soviet pact & Russia must be induced to do this by the promise of consultations with us.[5]

Years after the events in question, Donald Maclean was bitterly critical of Chamberlain's 'peculiar pig-headedness', going as far as to suggest that the Prime Minister's appeasement policy was 'attempting to use Germany as a military counter-force to the Soviet Union'. He further described the policy of appeasement as an example of 'foreign policy catastrophes for which they [individual statesmen] were principally responsible'. Meanwhile, the objective of the Munich agreement 'was to persuade the victim [Czechoslovakia], as the police say, to come quietly.'[6] Soon enough the agreement lay in tatters as, on 15 March 1939, Hitler broke his word and German troops invaded the remainder of Czechoslovakia. The response of the British and French governments was to issue guarantees of support to Poland – the next target on Hitler's hit list.

Like Burgess and Maclean, John Cairncross was intensely contemptuous of appeasement and Neville Chamberlain's handling of foreign policy. Indeed, as will be discussed later, his autobiography initially began life as a deeply critical, polemical history of the policy.[7] In April 1939, though by that stage long departed from the Foreign Office, Cairncross kept in regular contact with his old colleagues. With this in mind, Guy Burgess asked him to collect information regarding the ongoing policy of appeasement. As Cairncross explained to his interrogators in 1952:

> In October 1938 I moved to the Treasury but continued in the normal course of social relations to see something of my Foreign Office friends. I also carried on the habit of making occasional entries on European events in my diary on the basis of my discussions with these friends. Round about Easter 1939, after the invasion of Czechoslovakia by Hitler, BURGESS and I had lunch together and the previous argument about Chamberlain's intentions came up. He asked me to substantiate my views and I made notes, both of recent conversations and some held immediately after seeing BURGESS, and let him have access to them.[8]

This note he provided to Burgess, would, years later, come back to haunt him – it being instrumental in his falling under the suspicious gaze of MI5. But for the time being, Cairncross' role as a Soviet spy was largely at a temporary end. He had been moved to an uninteresting job at the Treasury and, more to the point, the purges of the NKVD had reduced the *Rezidentura*, by the summer months of 1939, to a single officer – Anatoli Gorsky. In addition to being difficult to work with, Gorsky was particularly poorly briefed by the Centre in Moscow. Thus, when Philby returned to Britain from Spain, Gorsky had only a general idea of who he was.[9]

If the foreign policies of the British government provided little basis for the Soviet agents to revise their loyalties, a far more significant challenge would soon arise: the Molotov–Ribbentrop Pact.

★

The Molotov–Ribbentrop Pact, or the Nazi–Soviet Pact, was a non-aggression agreement between Nazi Germany and the Soviet Union. The agreement stipulated that neither side would wage war with the other or form an alliance with a hostile enemy power. In secret, the pact also divided Eastern Europe, delineating which areas would be controlled by each respective power. The impact of the agreement was immediately obvious in Britain. Without the threat of a potentially hostile Soviet Union to the east, there was little to prevent Hitler ordering the invasion of Poland – which, of course, he promptly did on 1 September 1939. The reaction of Louis MacNeice, the writer and school friend of Anthony Blunt, was to write a mournful poem full of trepidation, entitled 'Primrose Hill', published in *The Spectator* two days after the Molotov–Ribbentrop agreement was announced. In many ways it summarised many of the fears of those final days of peace. Its final lines read:

And the evil sirens call,
And the searchlights quest and shift,
And out of the Milky Way
The impartial bombs will fall.[10]

For many among the young radical intellectuals of the 1930s who had found Communism so attractive while at university, the Molotov–Ribbentrop Pact came as a real blow. For many of them, their attachment to the Soviet Union was born of a revulsion of fascism and the Nazi regime. Communism was the ideological antithesis of fascism, and the Soviet Union the great beacon of socialism. Yet here it was siding with the Third Reich. For Goronwy Rees, the Welsh-born journalist, Oxford graduate and close friend of Guy Burgess, it was too much. Rees had been a staunch anti-fascist and Communist while at university, he had even been persuaded, by Burgess, to work as an agent for the Soviet Union. From 1938 until the Molotov–Ribbentrop Pact, he supplied summaries of gossip accumulated from gatherings held at his *alma mater*.[11]

Years later Rees' abandonment of the cause still riled and Maclean accosted Rees, whom he had not seen for years, and gave him a tongue-lashing, 'You used to be one of us, but you ratted.'[12] Burgess evidently also took what he no doubt viewed as an act of desertion to heart. In 1943, Burgess described Rees to the MI6 man, David Footman, '"He's frightfully nice," Guy warned me, "but sometimes does most awful things." What he had done to shock Burgess is something I never discovered.'[13] Though Rees had promised to keep their secret, Burgess was worried by the extent of the knowledge that the Welshman possessed regarding his and Blunt's work for the Soviet Union. In 1943, Burgess even went as far as suggesting Rees' assassination and offered to do the deed himself, despite Rees being one of his closest friends and Burgess the godfather to one of Rees' children.[14]

If Rees was seriously phased by the new and shocking foreign policy direction by the Soviet Union, few of the other Soviet moles were. The prevailing view in radical left-wing circles was that the British and French governments sought to foster a war of mutual destruction between the Third Reich and the Soviet Union. This view was, no doubt, partly inspired by the long-standing bellicose attitudes of some Conservatives. For instance, the backbench MP Henry 'Chips' Channon believed that Britain 'should let gallant little Germany glut her fill of the Reds in the East and keep decadent France quiet while she does so.'[15] This, however, was not government policy and nor had it ever been. As the historian Wesley K. Wark has wryly observed, such theories are 'a wee bit difficult to square with the policies of a government that issued unprecedented guarantees to Poland, Romania, Greece, and Turkey in the spring and summer of 1939'.[16]

Nevertheless, many agents of the Soviet Union in the West celebrated the genius of Stalin. As we have seen, it was Maclean's view that the entire policy of appeasement had been designed to encourage Nazi Germany to become 'a military counter-force to the Soviet Union'. The American spy Michael Straight, another Cambridge-educated Soviet mole operating in the US Department of the Interior, wrote in his autobiography that his handler, Iskhak Akhmerov, was ecstatic at the news:

> The sense of optimism bordering on euphoria that Green [Akhmerov] felt on the outbreak of the war was apparently shared by my old friends at Cambridge. Stalin had foiled an anti-Soviet conspiracy by signing the pact with Hitler; the capitalist nations had blundered into a war against each other; the war would soon lead to mutinies and uprisings that in turn would culminate in world revolution.[17]

Cairncross, by contrast, at least by the time it came to writing his autobiography, had come to a rather different conclusion. The Molotov–Ribbentrop Pact was the inevitable result of Chamberlain's inept foreign policy decisions: rather than working with the Soviet Union against Nazi Germany, he had left Stalin no choice but to enter into an agreement with Hitler.[18]

★

On 31 August 1939, the fragile peace was smashed and German troops, dressed in Polish uniforms, seized a German radio station in Gleiwitz, in Upper Silesia. This ruse was used to create a pretext for a German invasion of Poland, which promptly began early in the morning of the following day. On 3 September, the British Prime Minister Neville Chamberlain, took to the airwaves and gave the most famous radio announcement of his premiership: informing the public that Britain was at war with Germany. He went to the House of Commons and told MPs, 'This is a sad day for all of us, and to none is it sadder than to me. Everything that I have worked for, everything that I have hoped for, everything that I have believed in during my public life, has crashed into ruins.'[19]

After a period of a little over seven months, the so-called 'Phoney War' (or as it was known at the time, the 'Bore War') came to a close with the German invasion of Denmark and Norway, beginning on 9 April 1940. British troops, composed of twelve and territorial battalions, were soon dispatched to Norway and landed on 14 April. The invasion was poorly organised, the troops ill-prepared, ill-equipped and their objectives were unclear and subject to rapid change. The perhaps unsurprising result was that the chaotic campaign soon ran aground. By the end of the month the British government had already taken the decision to withdraw.[20] Speaking in the House of Commons, Edward Turnour (Earl Winterton) said of the disaster that he could not 'imagine a greater abuse of language than to describe what happened in Norway as "a minor setback". It has,' he continued, 'been a most serious rebuff, the consequences of which we cannot yet measure.'[21] This proved wholly prophetic. The collapse of British hopes in Norway also saw a collapse of confidence in Neville Chamberlain and his government. On 10 May, while ministers were still reeling from the events in Scandinavia, Nazi Germany invaded Belgium and the Netherlands. Chamberlain was replaced by Winston Churchill that same day.

The German invasion in the West swept through the Low Countries and into France through the Ardennes region. By 16 May the German forces had thrown the Allies into disarray and had already penetrated 55 miles beyond Sedan.[22] Despite efforts at counter-attack, the Allies were forced into a rapid retreat. Already, such was the surprise and chaos by that stage, the political decision to withdraw the British Expeditionary Force was already being considered and Churchill instructed his predecessor to prepare the retreat to the coast.[23] As *The Spectator* reported on 31 May, in fact long after the Germans had already surrounded Calais, the BEF was 'fighting a desperate rearguard action in its endeavour to reach the coast'. The magazine also informed its readers that there was a 'reasonable hope that a large part of the BEF' could escape by sea at Dunkirk.[24] This was a well-founded hope. Despite official projections, which placed the tally at a meagre 40,000, in all 338,000 Allied troops escaped capture or death in occupied Europe during the Dunkirk evacuation.[25]

On 18 December 1940, Hitler formally commanded his generals to prepare an invasion of the Soviet Union. This might have come as a surprise to his generals, as only a little over a year earlier Hitler informed them in November 1939 that, 'We can oppose Russia only when we are free in the west.'[26] Yet in December 1940, though France had fallen, Britain had stubbornly refused to capitulate. Thus the order began by anticipating that objection, 'The German Wehrmacht [armed forces] must be prepared *to crush Soviet Russia in a rapid campaign* (Operation Barbarossa) even before the conclusion of the war against England.'[27]

The reason for this literal change of direction, from west to east, lay in the striking difficulties inherent in the German plan to invade Britain – code-named Operation Sea Lion. The Royal Navy, at that time still a vast titan of military power, kept close guard of the English Channel. No invasion could hope to succeed unless the Royal Navy's Home Fleet was removed from the picture. The Home Fleet was a formidable guard, comprised in part of five destroyers apiece stationed at Dover and Portsmouth, nine at Harwich and a further three and a cruiser at Sheerness.[28] At that time, German strategists believed that their best hope lay with the Luftwaffe – if its pilots could win control of the skies then the Royal Navy's ships would be left relatively open. This was a view shared in the highest circles of Whitehall. In 1940 the Foreign Office mandarin, Alexander Cadogan, wrote in September 1940 that winning air superiority was key to any German invasion, 'which he most emphatically has not'.[29] As instructed, the Luftwaffe soon turned their attention to the destruction of the Royal Air Force, which had retreated from Continental Europe along with Britain's other forces, suffering losses along the way. The Battle of Britain soon began.

★

While Britain's catastrophic induction into the Second World War was ongoing, Cairncross remained at the Treasury. This was not, however, by choice. In November 1939 he applied to rejoin the Foreign Office, failing that he asked if they might instead help him secure an alternative posting and, among other choices, suggested the Government Code and Cypher School at Bletchley Park – Britain's cipher-cracking bureau. His request was rejected and he was advised to stay in the Treasury. Many years later, in 1964, once the scale of Cairncross' involvement with the Russian intelligence services had become clear, it was concluded that this request was on the orders of the London *Rezidentura*.[30] Of course, given the secrecy surrounding Bletchley Park, it is surprising that he even knew of its existence, suggesting that the reach of his access in Whitehall was significant.

In September 1940 Cairncross finally got his wish; he was transferred from the Treasury to become the Private Secretary to Lord Maurice Hankey. Lord Hankey occupied an unusual position in government: he had been a career civil servant, rising to the very top of the service, acting as Cabinet Secretary from 1916 to 1938. Under Neville Chamberlain's government, he was appointed to the Cabinet position of the Chancellor of the Duchy of Lancaster, a position in which he remained after Churchill gained the keys to No. 10 Downing Street in 1940. Churchill did not, however, invite Hankey to his newly slimmed down War Cabinet.

This did not much diminish Hankey's extraordinary range of responsibilities. He was placed at the head of innumerable committees that covered everything from intelligence matters and wartime scientific research and development to the management of the Post Office. Moreover, all Cabinet minutes passed across Hankey's desk.[31] According to the NKVD's archives, this move was all part of the plan for Cairncross. Gorsky was keen to orchestrate his agent's move from the Treasury, with its limited access to sensitive information, to Lord Hankey, 'who was charged with particularly secret tasks'.[32]

His posting to Lord Hankey's office proved a happy time for Cairncross. His work was rich, rewarding and varied, reflecting the range of materials that came across Hankey's desk. The office was small, which was to Cairncross' liking, and consisted of Hankey, Lord Falmoth acting as a scientific advisor, Sir Hugh Clement Jones, who acted as the Minister's general assistant, and three secretaries including Cairncross.[33] Hankey himself was also an interesting character in his own right. The Conservative politician and ever witheringly rude diarist, Sir Cuthbert Headlam, described him thus:

> The latter [Lord Hankey] looked dirtier and sicker than ever and I wondered more than ever why he had been made a member of the War Cabinet – presumably he is of some use – knows a lot of precedents, etc. They say, too, that he can deal with Winston [Churchill] – if he really can do that, he is, indeed, valuable![34]

Cairncross, by contrast, even five decades later, remained somewhat star-struck by Hankey and he lavished his former boss with praise and compliments. He depicted a kindly, polite, good-humoured and above all considerate man, who was keen to offer advice to his young underlings and even invited them for weekends at his country house. Meanwhile, given the importance Hankey held within the government, many of the great and the good were in regular attendance at the office, including the future Prime Minister, Harold Macmillan. Doubtless, having spent much of his career as a disliked and socially belittled figure, Cairncross was at last not merely accepted but in regular contact with individuals who before 'had so far only existed … in books or newspapers'. 'I would,' he wrote, 'have been happy to stay with such an important and pleasant personality.'[35]

With his posting as Private Secretary, Cairncross was given an allowance amounting to around half his salary. This afforded him considerably greater financial means, which meant that he could move from his existing digs to a rather more elegant flat in Dolphin Square, Pimlico. This part of London, he recalled, was rather less formal than the world to which he had previously been accustomed:

> Dolphin Square was something of an innovation in conservative London. There was a certain aura of freedom from straight-laced society. I remember

a skit at the Great Theatre in which an innocent maiden was about to be seduced and murmured, 'O Dolly this is folly', while the sly young man uttered, 'O Rupert this is stupid'. He is finally assaulted by an entertaining lady who drives home her appeal with the cry that 'this is Dolphin Square where women are desperate'. It was not often my luck to run into such cases of despair. [36]

Nevertheless, despite largely being a happy time, the early phases of the war, in addition to advancement, also brought major tragedies – two of which struck in relatively quick succession. Shortly after Cairncross had moved in to his new flat in Dolphin Square, it was bombed during the London Blitz. Cairncross was in the building at the time and was extraordinarily lucky to survive. 'I heard the plane overhead,' he wrote of the alarming experience, 'the bomb dropping, and the falling debris in the room next door. When I looked around, there were no walls, but the staircase was sound, and I climbed down the four floors to safety wrapped in a blanket.' He was forced to move in with his brother, Alec. Yet no sooner than he had done so, the Luftwaffe struck again. 'A bomb hit the neighbouring house. We all spent the night in the open, and this was unfortunately at a time when my sister-in-law was expecting her first child, Frances. This was of course the nightly lot of Londoners during the Blitz, but in such things I have always been lucky.'[37]

The second tragedy was the death of Cairncross' elder brother, Bill. A private in the Royal Warwickshire Regiment, Bill fought at and was wounded during the Battle of Dunkirk, and he passed away on 30 June 1940. He was aged 35.[38] Cairncross and Alec made their way to Scotland for the funeral on the sleeper train. Alec recorded the moment the two arrived, 'I woke as we neared Beattock to see a morning of unbearable beauty, with a cloudless deep blue sky above the moors.'[39]

★

Cairncross' stint with Lord Hankey proved to be a particularly rich posting for the NKVD. Their agent was easily able to acquire 'secret papers' from Lord Hankey's office, including Cabinet minutes and other high-level documents. Cairncross, who often worked late, was simply able to take them in the evening. Provided they were returned before the start of the day's work in the morning, nobody was any the wiser.[40] One of the first documents he was able to supply was a lengthy report, penned by

Hankey, concerning the activities of MI5 and MI6.[41] During 1941 alone, Cairncross was able to supply some 3,449 documents. These materials covered a great variety of topics. Gorsky wrote to Moscow informing them that, via LISZT (Cairncross' new code name), he was sending them sixty films, which covered everything from Foreign Office and MI6 reports, counter-intelligence investigations, and even technical documents related to bacteriological warfare.[42]

It was this time, while working for Lord Hankey, that has without doubt become the most controversial period of Cairncross' life – it is alleged that he became an atomic spy.[43] In 1990 Christopher Andrew and Oleg Gordievsky, in their book *KGB*, asserted that the 'first warning of the Anglo–American decision to build an atomic bomb probably came from John Cairncross.'[44] The basis for this allegation was Gordievsky's testimony, seemingly confirmed by Cairncross' position as Hankey's secretary. Lord Hankey chaired the British Scientific Advisory Committee (BSAC), which discussed the potential development of atomic weaponry at length and that Cairncross acted as one of the committee's secretaries. Lord Hankey soon also joined the MAUD Committee and the Tube Alloys Consultative Committee – Tube Alloys being the British atomic bomb project, eventually subsumed into the US Manhattan Project. Cairncross therefore had the means to supply the secrets Gordievsky claimed he had leaked to the Soviet Union.

Cairncross, however, always rejected the claim that he had leaked any materials related to Britain's atomic bomb project. He denied that he had been the secretary at BSAC meetings, despite his name being listed as acting in such a capacity on the documents. This, he claimed, was merely an administrative error. Moreover, as he pointed out, all that proved was that he may have had access to such documents, it did not prove that he supplied them to the Soviet Union. In 1990 he appeared on the BBC's current affairs television programme *Newsnight*, where he outlined his objections to Andrew and Gordievsky's claims.

Interviewer: 'A new allegation in this latest book is that you were probably an atom spy, maybe the first atom spy.'

John Cairncross: 'That is ridiculous. He [Christopher Andrew] offers no substantiation for that. Simply because I had access to some, by no means all the documents which he has mentioned, and there was a great deal of confusion in his description of the procedures and structures,

[Cairncross shakes his head] it is a far cry from that to say that I was the first atom [spy]. It could be, he says that I was almost certainly, the first atom spy, well certain newspapers have gone further, even reputable ones and said I was. Well that, [breaks off] I want to see the evidence, that is a very, very grave charge.'[45]

In 1993, John Costello and Oleg Tsarev, with privileged access to the Soviet intelligence archives, seemingly corroborated Cairncross' firm denials. They claimed that Gorsky wrote to Moscow stating, 'I am informing you very briefly about the contents of a most secret report of the Government Committee on the development of uranium atomic energy to produce explosive material.' The source of this material was Donald Maclean.[46] The following year, the former senior Soviet intelligence officer Pavel Sudoplatov published *Special Tasks*, which instead asserted that the information attributed to Cairncross had, in fact, been supplied by an agent with the code name 'Leaf'. Leaf, Sudoplatov informed readers, was again claimed to be Maclean.[47] This, however, is a claim that few historians have been willing to believe for two reasons.[48] First, Maclean did not have access to BSAC meetings, Cairncross did. Second, 'Leaf', translated from the Russian 'List', appears to have been a mis-transcription of Liszt, which by that point was Cairncross' code name.[49]

Confusing matters further in 1994, however, was Yuri Modin. In the English edition of his autobiography, he claimed that, 'Lord Hankey's private secretary became the first agent to inform the NKVD that the Americans and British had been working since late 1940 on the joint manufacture of an atomic bomb.'[50] Meanwhile, between 1993 and 1996, Russian intelligence officials also granted one of its former officers, Alexander Vassiliev, access to its archives. Materials he saw were transcribed into several notebooks before being brought to the West. Details from these notebooks suggest clearly that Cairncross was indeed an early source of information regarding the atomic weapons:

The Amer. professors Urey (Urey) (Columb. U.), Bragg, and Fowler (Bragg, Fowler) are currently in London, where they are working on developing an explosive of enormous power they invented. They are currently working on the problem of adjusting the strength of this explosive so that an airplane would have time to fly a distance of over 200 miles after releasing it. ... Request for information from London. Assumption that the substance in question is uranium-235. Verify through 'Liszt'.[51]

Furthermore, in 1998, the Russian intelligence services granted further access to its old archives, presenting further evidence that it was indeed Cairncross who was behind the leak.[52] Though Cairncross might have been the first of the atomic spies, he was certainly not the last. Even among the other major Cambridge recruits, following the end of the war Burgess had access to atomic secrets in his capacity as Private Secretary to the Foreign Office minister, Hector McNeil. Similarly, Kim Philby, as the MI6 liaison with US intelligence, had even greater access.[53] As a secret damage assessment conducted in 1955, in the wake of the flight of Burgess and Maclean, concluded, 'In the fields of US/UK/Canada planning on Atomic Energy, US/UK post war planning and policy in Europe and all by-product information up to the date of defection undoubtedly reached Soviet hands probably via the Soviet Embassy in London.'[54]

If as the evidence suggests, Cairncross was indeed an early atomic spy, his justification for leaking materials to the Soviet Union – British survival – was a dangerous gamble. Had the Soviet Union fallen, its invasion by Germany a success, then those atomic secrets provided by spies in the West would presumably have fallen into Nazi hands. That risk seems to have little concerned Moscow's agents in Britain and the United States of America.

KURORT: Bletchley Park and Ultra Intelligence

While Cairncross was busy working for Lord Hankey, and leaking considerable quantities of information to Moscow, Britain was itself developing a hugely important source of intelligence. This was Britain's cryptanalysis operation, conducted by the Government Code and Cypher School (GC&CS), headquartered at Bletchley Park during the Second World War. From the beginning of the war, a high priority was placed on acquiring information from, or better yet arranging infiltration of, Bletchley Park by the Ring of Five. So what was Bletchley Park, code-named KURORT by the NKVD, and why was it so important?[1]

Founded in 1919, a merger of the Admiralty's cryptanalysis department 'Room 40' and its War Office counterpart, Military Intelligence 1b, the mission of the newly formed agency was two-fold. Its first and public role was 'to advise as to the security of codes and cyphers used by all Government departments and to assist in their provision'. Its second (and highly secret) purpose was to study the communiqués of foreign powers and to break any codes and ciphers shielding them from inspection.[2] This team of Admiralty and War Office cipher experts, under the leadership of the Room 40 veteran, Commander Alastair Denniston, were provided offices in London and set to work.

During the early period of its life, the major subject of the new agency's attentions was the Soviet Union, which had emerged from the turmoil of Russia's bloody civil war.[3] However, the rise of Hitler and Nazi Germany led to a major reassessment of the British intelligence community's priorities. As early as 1934 senior Whitehall officials and military figures had identified Nazi Germany as the 'ultimate potential enemy' threatening British interests and security.[4] By 1937, after Hitler had publicly revealed Germany's rearmament programme, Britain's military leaders were so concerned by the combined threat posed by Germany, Italy and Japan they, like the new Prime Minister Neville Chamberlain, advocated appeasement.[5] Given the increasingly dangerous situation in which Britain found herself in the last years of the inter-war period, the attentions of GC&CS's cryptanalysts turned back to Germany. However, these efforts were greeted with very little joy.[6]

In 1926 the German military had begun introducing a new, mechanised, family of cipher systems called Enigma. Now perhaps the most famous cipher systems in history, Enigma machines resembled a complex typewriter. Enclosed within an elegant wooden case, the machine outwardly appeared to be a keyboard, a set of rotating wheels and a lamp board, each bulb denoting a different letter of the alphabet. To encipher a message, an operator needed only to press a key, this created an electrical signal, which passed through the machine's wiring, which would light a different letter on the lamp board. The operator typed out a message and noted down the illuminated letters. This outwardly simple machine contained within it a highly complex enciphering system that, in the Luftwaffe's models, was capable of generating a cipher with 1,074,000,000,000,000,000,000,000 permutations. Other models, such as those utilised by the German navy, were still more complex and given the numbers involved the Germans were convinced by the invulnerability of the system.[7]

In this respect, the belief that Enigma presented an insoluble problem, they were not alone. Britain's code-breakers of the inter-war period were (almost exclusively) men of an academic, artistic temperament. They had, for the most part, cut their cipher-cracking teeth on the book ciphers of the First World War, where a first-class understanding of the mechanics of language was key. For the likes of the inter-war GC&CS's chief cryptanalyst, Dillwyn Knox, cipher breaking was first and foremost a scholarly exercise, not unlike his other career as a Cambridge don translating ancient Greek texts. Though Knox and his fellow cryptanalysts made good headway against Enigma in the years in the run up to war, including some success against less-advanced models used during the Spanish Civil War, it was ultimately deemed an exercise in futility. The industrial revolution of cipher making, which had occurred with the birth of Enigma in the early 1920s, had ensured that a similar revolution would be required in cipher breaking. Machine-made ciphers would require machine-based solutions, and despite recognising the problem, GC&CS did not have the personnel with the technical expertise, or indeed the inclination, to embark on such a profound change of direction.[8]

★

In Poland, however, which was even more acutely threatened by a resurgent and militant Germany than Britain, the story was very different. Since 1929 efforts there had been made to gather together a team of mathematicians to tackle the problem posed by Enigma. Headed by the brilliant Marian Rejewski, the Polish cryptanalysts adopted a technical, mathematically driven approach to the process of attacking Enigma in which they enjoyed considerable success. By 1938 this had extended as far as building a machine, which they christened the *Bomba*, to ease the process. However, this success did not last long after the invention of the machine and soon, before the end of the year, the Germans had improved Enigma's security, rendering the *Bomba* obsolete.[9]

The Poles had unequivocally demonstrated that the importance of both mathematics and machines in the newly mechanised world of cryptography was a game changer. Though GC&CS's cryptanalysts were aware that cipher cracking, in this new mechanised age, would require an automated response, the Polish example was nevertheless still revelatory. The example of the *Bomba*, the existence of which was generously shared with the British in a 1939 conference, demonstrated that such a mechanised angle of attack offered possibilities for success that had eluded GC&CS.[10]

The agency had not, however, been idle in the immediate years before the 1939 Nazi invasion of Poland. The head of MI6, Admiral Sir Hugh Sinclair, under whose ultimate responsibility GC&CS also resided, purchased the Bletchley Park estate for use by Denniston's team in 1938. The previous year, Sinclair also ordered Denniston to begin head hunting for the 'right type of recruit' who would be appointed in the eventuality of war; typically middle-class, well-educated young men from Britain's elite universities of a type that had proven to be so successful in the First World War. Given that the agency had strong ties with the 'Golden Triangle' (the universities of Oxford, Cambridge and London), many existing staff having graduated or worked in these institutions, these were (Cambridge in particular) the obvious first port of call.[11]

In this recruitment process a number of key mathematicians, including Alan Turing and Gordon Welchman, were brought on board. Both men

85

became influential and hugely important figures in the work of the agency.[12] Nevertheless, while the GC&CS was indeed stumped by Enigma because of its hitherto failure to adapt, this point is typically taken too far. For instance, in his seminal biography of Alan Turing, the mathematician cum historian Andrew Hodges suggests 'pre-war cryptography, fossilised and isolated by secrecy, was transformed as soon as any contemporary mathematical mind was brought to bear on the subject'.[13] In fact, mathematicians had been recruited for many years, since at least 1932, however the influx of recruits in 1939 did, nevertheless, certainly bring with them new inspiration.[14]

As his predecessors had already concluded, Turing soon realised that if there was to be any hope of cracking Enigma regularly and quickly enough to produce valuable intelligence, a mechanised response was required. Soon after arriving with the agency in 1939 he set about designing a machine, which he called the Bombe – named in tribute to its Polish spiritual (though not technical) ancestor. Though support within the agency was limited, he was able to garner the aid of two senior agency officials: Francis 'Frank' Birch (a Cambridge historian and Room 40 veteran) and the agency's second in command, a former Royal Navy officer, Edward Travis.[15] A budget of £100,000 was found to finance the project (a considerable sum of money in the late 1930s) and the specialist engineers of the British Tabulating Machine Company were contracted to build Turing's machine.[16] These machines, utilised together with other methods, did not merely render Enigma vulnerable. They ensured that Axis transmissions could be read day after day and that a steady stream of intelligence flowed from Bletchley at a rate not far off real time.

Assigned the code name 'Ultra', the scale and quality of the intelligence derived from Bletchley Park was extraordinary. By the end of 1941, Bletchley Park was regularly deciphering around 20,000 messages a month.[17] This included high-level secret traffic from all three of the German military services, but also other important organisations including the Nazi foreign intelligence service, the *Abwehr*. At Bletchley, teams of linguists and analysts worked around the clock to translate and prioritise this mass of information. Thousands of young women from the Women's Royal Naval Service operated cryptanalysis machines. Hundreds of other young women worked on communications equipment to distribute the intelligence to military commands and Whitehall ministries. Vast mechanised index systems were constructed to store and sort all of the information the agency had collected. By late 1944, more than 10,000 individuals were employed by the agency.[18] In short, the Second World War prompted an industrial revolution in cipher cracking.

★

The impact of this revolution on the Second World War was considerable, however the agency would have to travel a long way remarkably quickly to achieve it. At the start of the war, Bletchley Park's staff numbers came to no more than 200 individuals. Given that the task ahead of them was so great, this modest staff contingent soon proved inadequate in number, so the agency began expanding at an unprecedented rate. By early December 1940 GC&CS, including its satellite stations and offices in London, employed 674 people. Yet despite this expansion the agency struggled to keep up with the demand.[19]

The cryptanalysts had, by January 1940, made their first breaks into a military grade Enigma system.[20] Soon they achieved great success against Luftwaffe Enigma signals, but lacked sufficient staff to translate and analyse all the material which arrived on their desks. Moreover, the intelligence analysis and translation team had, since September 1939, effectively been forced to improvise a wholly new intelligence processing apparatus from scratch. The result was that they were initially unprepared, learning and developing their trade on the job.[21] The first real test for Bletchley Park came in April 1940 when Germany invaded Norway. It was then that the real cracks began to show and the lessons learned remained valuable for the rest of the war. However, the only real strategic advantage that Bletchley's work contributed was to outline the scale of German strength in the invasion. Similarly, during the Battle of France, which lasted a mere six weeks, Bletchley's major achievement was to further develop and refine its internal systems.[22]

The system to emerge, as regards Enigma, was the careful compartmentalisation of labour. Messages would arrive at the agency from intercept stations (Y stations) both in Britain and across the wider world. These messages were transported via dispatch riders on motorcycles and, in priority cases, cable. Once at Bletchley they were registered before being dispatched for cryptanalysis. Two main cryptanalysis sections for dealing with Enigma were formed. These were Hut 6 and Hut 8. Hut 6 was tasked with cracking German Army and air force Enigma ciphers and Hut 8 the breaking of German naval Enigma systems. Once the cipher had been broken all of the messages sent using that key could be converted into plain German text. By then readable, the messages were then sent to Hut 3 (Army and Air) and Hut 4 (Navy) for analysis and translation. A mechanised information system, using state of the art Hollerith machines from the British Tabulating Machine Company, was also created to store all of the information that Bletchley had captured. The intelligence derived from the messages was then passed to relevant Whitehall ministries and military commands.[23]

One of the first major intelligence coups derived from Ultra was to confirm that the Germans were utilising radio navigation technology in order to guide their night-time bombing raids. Recording devices had captured two German airmen in a prisoner of war camp discussing these devices, and the log of a downed Heinkel also referred to them. However, it was not confirmed for several months until, in June 1940, when an Enigma message noted that a Knickebein (crooked leg, the name given to the transmitters) had been built at Cleves. Following testing to put the issue beyond doubt, the existence of the German 'beams' was put to rest and the 'Battle of the Beams' began. Increasingly sophisticated jamming technologies were instituted to mitigate the German advantage.[24]

With the Battle of France over and the British Expeditionary Force licking its wounds in England following the Dunkirk retreat of May and June 1940, Hitler and his senior staff turned their attention to the conquest of the British Isles. As noted earlier, A plan, code-named Operation Sea Lion, was rapidly drawn up and its existence confirmed by Ultra in July. It was swiftly observed by the German planners that in order to successfully cross the Channel, the Royal Navy would need to be neutralised. Given the limitations of German naval power it was obvious that the Luftwaffe would have to fulfil that task. However, this would only be possible with complete control of the skies, which meant first destroying the RAF. The battle for air supremacy, the Battle of Britain, began on 10 July 1940 and ultimately the RAF was triumphant. The role of Ultra in that victory was limited, overshadowed by the contribution of radar, but the input it did provide continued to highlight its potential. Specifically, it helped contribute to the building of a clear picture of the Luftwaffe's order of battle. This, useful as it was, comprised the major contribution of Ultra to the battle.[25] It was not until later, when it had something to offer in the Battle of the Atlantic, that Ultra's real value came to be felt.

With the Battle of Britain over and Operation Sea Lion jettisoned, the greatest threat to Britain's survival was acquiring vital supplies. With much of continental Europe occupied, an increasingly large volume of British imports came from the US and Canada. The concern was that the ships carrying these vital materials had to navigate dangerous waters patrolled by German U-boats. This was a major problem and between March and June 1941 some 282,000 tons of shipping was lost. However, by successfully breaking German naval ciphers, the Allies were able to reroute convoys and bring the fight to the U-boats. Between July and December, following GC&CS's success in this arena, losses in shipping fell to 120,000 tons.[26] However, in February 1942 the Germans changed their naval Enigma system, which locked out the cryptanalysts. It would not be until December that Bletchley found a route back into the ciphers.

Despite the sheer scale of the operation under way, one of the most impressive of the agency's characteristics was that it remained hidden from the Axis powers. So seriously was secrecy taken that this major wartime achievement remained unacknowledged by the British state until 1974.[27] However, while the German High Command and the British public were left in the dark about the agency's activities, Moscow was not.

★

In fact, the Soviet Union had access to material produced at Bletchley Park from a number of different sources. As we have seen, during the early 1930s, the Soviet Union was able to successfully recruit a number of young men from the University of Cambridge, Anthony Blunt key among them. Blunt, a fellow at Trinity, was then able to talent spot likely young men. One such man was Leo Long.

Long, a working-class son of a carpenter and committed Communist, came up to Cambridge in 1935. Blunt, as one of his mentors, introduced Long to the Cambridge Apostles, and then, to the NKVD in 1937, which code-named him 'Ralph'. He graduated the following year and took up a teaching position in Frankfurt. With the outbreak of war, Long joined the British Army and, given his mastery of German, became a Lieutenant in the Intelligence Corps. He soon found himself working in Military Intelligence 14 of the War Office, which specialised in collecting intelligence regarding the German military. As such it was in receipt of Ultra intelligence material, which Long promptly reported back to Blunt and, when Blunt was unavailable, Guy Burgess. Soon enough, that information found its way to Moscow.[28]

Yet the real prize was actually controlling a spy at Bletchley Park. It appears that Anatoli Gorsky had enjoyed some success in this area. He had recruited an unknown source, code-named 'Paul', who worked at Bletchley Park. According to KGB archival material reproduced by West and Tsarev, the mysterious Paul, whose identity remains unknown, was able to ascertain considerable information regarding the bureaucratic structure and training operations of the agency.[29] Britain's most sensitive secret installation had been penetrated.

Another key source was Kim Philby, who had infiltrated SIS. As such he had access to diplomatic traffic. His recruitment, aided by his school, university tie and connections to Guy Burgess, who had also penetrated MI6 (more on which later), reveals the power of social connections. The long-term strategy employed by the Centre in Moscow, with the plan to recruit young men at Cambridge who would, one day, command positions of authority within the corridors of power, had come off brilliantly. These secret organisations infiltrated by the Ring of Five were, in some key respects, socially highly conservative and trust was an all important factor. Men such as Philby, and the other members of the five, were deemed trustworthy because they had been to the right schools and universities, they knew the right people and they travelled in the right circles. In brief, they were gentlemen and their patriotism could be relied upon. This, of course, proved to be a grievous miscalculation.

The cultural climate of the British intelligence community, in which gentlemanly credentials had been a permanent feature since the foundation of professional intelligence agencies, independent of the War Office and Admiralty, had been established at the beginning of the twentieth century. MI5 and MI6 were born in 1909, in the form of the Secret Service Bureau. The Bureau was the brainchild of Commander (later Captain) Mansfield Smith-Cumming and Captain Vernon Kell. With a military education at Sandhurst, Kell proceeded to become an interpreter for the army. He was a man of no small affluence, and had family ties to the aristocracy. Meanwhile, Cumming also had a military education, from Dartmouth Naval College, and his spouse was a Scottish heiress.[30] The concept of the 'amateur professional' was also core to the new intelligence community. Sir Paul Dukes, an MI6 spy, opined in 1938 that young men recruited into the world of espionage would be unwise to view their new occupation as a 'career'. Moreover, the qualities that made a good intelligence officer were not the product of professional, formalised training, but rather:

bred first in school and university life, in form room and lecture room, on cricket and football grounds, in the boxing ring, at the chess table, in debating clubs, in a thoughtful approach to the problems of the day that beset mankind, in studious observation of your fellows, and above all in your study of yourself.[31]

In short, the qualities that made a good spy were derived from being a *gentleman*, and gentlemen were not *professionals*. In the case of the Ring of Five, this oversight, based on crude assumptions regarding social and economic class, came back to haunt the British intelligence community.

8

A Semi-Monastic Life

Though Moscow was already in receipt of a steady stream of intelligence derived from, and indeed about, the Government Code and Cypher School, in May 1942 Cairncross was able to go a step further. He was assigned to the heart of the British secret community's nerve centre – Bletchley Park, the primary war station of GC&CS.

Before he arrived, however, he first underwent training in Bedford on simple cipher systems.[1] Though Bletchley Park was able to skim the cream from Britain's elite universities, and had done very well from its long-established connections with Cambridge in particular, new recruits still required honing. With this in mind Colonel (later Brigadier) John Tiltman, one of Bletchley Park's most senior and respected cipher crackers, instituted a training regime at Ardour House, the premises of a gas company, in a showroom above the shop. There new recruits were initiated into the world of ciphers and, for those working on Japanese material, language courses.[2] The course was, however, in Cairncross' view something of a waste of time. He had after all been recruited because of his thorough knowledge of German, not his ability to master the art of cryptanalysis, and the training 'never proved useful'.[3]

Once at Bletchley Park, from August 1942, the world that greeted him would have been very different from his previous experience as Lord Hankey's aide. As we saw in the previous chapter, Bletchley Park was one of the most secret installations in wartime Britain. This was very much reflected in its security; ringed off by fences, with armed guards manning the gates and on patrol, and the workers huddled in prefabricated huts, sipping their rationed tea, Bletchley was a different world to Whitehall.

★

Security came at a premium on all Ultra intelligence and careful steps were made to keep those who knew about the intelligence to a minimum. The reason for this was simple: if the Axis powers gained wind that their most secure cipher systems had been penetrated, they could implement relatively simple changes in order to restore security and, in doing so, lock Bletchley out.

Careful plans were developed in order to restrict Bletchley's product from all those that did not 'need to know' about it. This meant that those outside of the agency who had access to Ultra intelligence or knew how it was produced was a short list indeed. Initially, this sensitive material was attributed to a particularly effective spy, operating out of Berlin, code-named 'Boniface'.[4] Such was the secrecy, even John 'Jock' Colville, the Assistant Private Secretary to Winston Churchill, had no idea where secret material, landing on his boss' desk, originated from. As he explained, all he knew was that Churchill received 'mysterious buff boxes', the contents of which were for the eyes of the Prime Minister alone, 'sent everyday by Brigadier Menzies' the head of SIS. Later in the war, Churchill became forgetful and began showing his intimate staff interesting decrypts, but this was a significant security breach.[5]

Special Liaison Units (SLUs) were established, under the control of SIS and coordinated by the RAF officer and Ultra memoirist, F.W. Winterbotham, which were attached to military commands.[6] It was their job to maintain the security of Ultra and to ensure that commanders, typically of far higher rank than SLU officers, observed the rules for handling Ultra. Most significant, Ultra material was not to be taken to an area where there was a risk that it might fall into the hands of the enemy so, after use, the material was burnt. Those individuals who transgressed the strict rules regarding Ultra, regardless of their rank, were reported to London. Peter Calvocoressi, in his memoirs, recalled one occasion in which a four-star general broke the rules, 'The rocket he received by return was quite something.'[7]

As we have seen, information and knowledge within GC&CS was highly compartmentalised. Though this led staff, as Cairncross reported, to sometimes endure a fairly solitary existence, the situation was clearly deliberate. It was an effort to ensure that information was distributed on a need-to-know basis. No individual, however senior, could know every aspect of what was being worked on by the agency. As such, no individual could reveal the whole picture to an enemy, either by accident, under compulsion or by design.

Physical security was also present at Bletchley Park. All individuals who came and went from the site had to offer their passes to sentries and a password system was instituted in late 1939 in order to facilitate movement across the estate after dark. Staff were warned darkly that failure to comply with the sentries' instructions could 'result in unfortunate incidents'.[8] In a series of instructions provided to the sentries and circulated to the wider staff, individuals who failed to halt when ordered were to be informed 'Halt or I fire' twice. If the individual still failed to comply, 'the sentry will endeavour to seize and detain them by hand; if that is impossible he will fire his rifle to hit low.'[9]

Meanwhile, the agency inundated staff with regular reminders of the dangers of 'careless talk', and organised talks and film screenings further aimed at reinforcing that point.[10] Careless talk proved a perennial problem and the agency's security teams investigated numerous such infractions.[11] In one instance, the then Director of GC&CS, Edward Travis, wrote to his staff to inform them that two individuals had engaged in careless talk and only his personal intervention, to save the agency from 'public discredit', had saved them from prosecution. As he reminded his staff:

> It would be a reflection on your intelligence to suppose that you do not realise that spies may, and indeed do, exist in this country; and that an idle piece of boasting or gossip on the part of any one of you may reach circles outside your control whence it may be passed to the enemy and cause, not only the breakdown of our successful efforts here, but the sacrifice of the lives of our sailors, soldiers and airmen, perhaps your own brothers, and may even prejudice our ultimate hope of victory.[12]

Commander Travis was absolutely right, there were foreign spies in Britain. However, the true danger did not stem from Germany, Italy or Japan, but from home-grown spies working for the Soviet Union. Solving the problem of 'careless talk', serious though it was conceived to be at the time, would have made no difference to this, the most serious foreign penetration of Britain's most sensitive intelligence secret. As we saw in the previous chapter, prior to Cairncross' arrival, the Soviet Union had already discovered the existence of Ultra and Bletchley Park. Furthermore, it had already received highly sensitive material generated at Bletchley Park, courtesy of Leo Long.[13]

Cairncross, through his appointment to Bletchley Park, had gone an important step further and gained inside access to this most precious of British intelligence institutions. On his arrival he was informed that the Soviet Union had not been informed of the existence of Ultra or the work of Bletchley Park because 'we do not trust them'. In particular, they did not trust the security of Soviet military ciphers and just because Britain and the Soviet Union were allies in wartime did not mean that they would remain so indefinitely. This situation did not sit well with Cairncross – he claimed that on his arrival at Bletchley Park he hoped to sever his contact with his handler but that the British decision not to share the fruits of Ultra changed his mind. The basis for this shift in view, he contended, on the one hand was the preservation of Britain. If the Soviet Union were to fall, then Britain would be next. On the other, if security were a concern, then his own back channel via his handler, Henry, was likely the most secure route and unavailable to Churchill.[14]

Cairncross' KGB file, however, presented a rather different story. The military draft loomed large in his future by the end of 1941. It was only thanks to the intervention of Lord Hankey, delaying his call up until April, that he had not found himself in uniform by January 1942. Thanks to access to 'Paul', the elusive source already at Bletchley, Anatoli Gorsky already had some insight into the recruitment process utilised by GC&CS and those individuals to talk to. One such person, it transpired, was Colonel F.W. Nicholls, the head of MI8. Cairncross was ordered to get to know and butter up Nicholls, not least by introducing him to Lord Hankey. Once sufficiently ingratiated, Cairncross was to complain that he was not only good with languages but that he was due to be called up. While lunching with Nicholls at the Travellers Club in London, Cairncross did as he was instructed and with complete success. When his call up papers arrived, he served just one day in the army before being demobilised and transferred to Bletchley Park.[15]

★

By the time that Cairncross arrived at Bletchley Park in 1942, GC&CS was well on its way to becoming the most profoundly successful intelligence agency of its type. Shortly before that time, some months earlier in

February, a profound set of administrative changes had taken place. The 'old guard' of cryptanalysts, who had been with GC&CS since its earliest days, had been swept sideways or out. This began at the top; the first head of the agency, Commander Alastair Dennison, was moved sideways to oversee cryptanalytic work on diplomatic and commercial radio traffic. His former deputy, Commander Edward Travis, was promoted as his successor as head of Bletchley Park.

This overhaul marked a major transition in the development of the agency and indeed the science of cryptanalysis. During the First World War, practical machine ciphers capable of efficiently producing military grade ciphers simply did not exist. However, the commercial release in 1923 of Enigma, developed by Arthur Scherbius, changed all of that. After some initial teething problems, the machine went into mass production. By 1926, the German military had become interested in Scherbius' machine and began rolling various versions of the system out across its networks.[16] From the perspective of the British cryptanalysts, this came as little concern. Germany was a defeated power and the stretched resources available to British intelligence were directed at the rather more serious threat posed by the emergent Soviet Union.[17]

It was only after the rise of Hitler, and once the looming threat his regime posed had been recognised, that serious thought to Enigma began. These early explorations into the mechanised system led to the sober observation that, at present, the system was impenetrable and that to defeat a mechanical cipher system a mechanical solution would need to be devised. As the agency's own secret internal history, written shortly after the war, noted, the solution to Enigma 'might call for elaborate apparatus which had not yet been designed'.[18]

The problem was, in the late 1930s, that GC&CS had no such access to that kind of specialist knowledge. Though the agency had long recruited individuals with scientific and mathematical aptitude, the clear preference had been for graduates with an aptitude for language and text. This had made sense in the pre-mechanised age of cipher cracking, when spotting patterns with words, the ability to make sense of incomplete text or jumbled letters made for excellent skill-set for cryptanalysis. The new age heralded by Scherbius' Enigma rendered this approach obsolete.

During the early days of the war, the importance of mathematics and technical skills became increasingly apparent and more and more mathematicians and scientists were recruited for cryptanalytic work.[19] Many of these young technical specialists found themselves dissatisfied with the older processes and attitudes that remained from the pre-war days. Similarly, the service chiefs, who had poured considerable resources into Bletchley Park, expected results and when these weren't always readily apparent they put pressure on the agency. In October 1941, four senior cryptanalysts, including Alan Turing, wrote to Winston Churchill requesting greater access to skilled staff and resources. By February 1942, matters had come to a head and Denniston had been replaced.[20]

In addition to the influx of a new generation of cryptanalyst, a new wartime cadre of young linguists, editors and analysts were appointed. These individuals, usually but not invariably drawn directly from the universities, were brought in to translate the deciphered material and assess its value. John Cairncross was one such individual.

★

Cairncross, after his spell on the language course at Bedford, was appointed to Hut 3. The primary purpose of this section, named after the building in which it was initially housed on the Bletchley Park site, was, according to the senior wartime Hut 3 officer, Peter Calvocoressi, 'to translate the deciphered Enigma material received from Hut 6, to interpret it, and to transmit it to those who needed its intelligence'.[21] That 'material' was raw decrypts of traffic generated by the Luftwaffe (German Air Force) and the Heer (German Army). The section, as Calvocoressi noted, worked in heavily conjunction with Hut 6, which, among other things, handled the cryptanalytic aspect of this work. Meanwhile, a similar relationship, for naval traffic, existed between Hut 8 (cryptanalysis) and Hut 4 (translation and distribution) of naval traffic. Numerous other sections existed to deal with a wide variety of other forms of Axis traffic, while still others existed to fulfil technical, bureaucratic and administrative functions.[22]

Hut 3 itself was split into something of an information conveyor belt, in which information arrived at the section in its raw form. That is, it would be a message, composed of letter groups of five, which would need to be prioritised, translated and ultimately sent on elsewhere, such as the front lines. This was not, however, an easy task. The message could include incorrectly transmitted or intercepted letters. A bad signal could mean that entire letters or phrases were missed by the intercept operator or incorrectly transcribed. Translation was conducted by the Watch, which consisted of some dozen individuals sitting at a semicircular table. The head of the Watch would sit on the inside edge of the table, inspecting the work of his juniors, and acting as a 'schoolmaster' might. He would accept work when it was correct and would throw 'dubious' work back 'to its originator as if he were a bad boy and not, as might be the case, a person of considerable distinction in his pre-war vocation'. His other main job was to distribute work around the team, sorting work into trays based on the priority of the message and instructing his underlings which trays to tackle first.[23]

Cairncross himself described the job in similar terms. It was 'the correction and restoration of words blurred, distorted or omitted'. A usual task 'which needed,' he further added, 'a generous dose of imagination, and a corkscrew mind.' For this work he found himself eminently suited, as he found it being reminiscent to 'solving a crossword puzzle, or amending a corrupt text of a classical writer such as Molière'.[24] He also had a great deal of time for his team leader, presumably the head of his Watch. The unnamed officer 'was one of the finest men I ever met, and, thanks to his skilful and kindly guidance, tension was conspicuously absent'.[25]

Meanwhile, inside his section, which numbered at most 150, there were to be found a variety of different types of work. Once the Watch had done its business, the messages were sent to two other sets of individuals. These were subsections of Hut 3 designated the titles 3M[ilitary] and 3A[ir]. Their job was to dispatch intelligence directly to commanders, and they did so at a rate of one every four to five minutes. The task of actually transmitting priority messages was assigned to a team of young women, who operated Britain's own cipher machines and communications equipment, known as the teleprincesses. There were also others with even more unusual tasks. For instance, one individual, a lexicographer from Cambridge University, was assigned the task of 'prescrib[ing] the correct and precise word or phrase to use for every bit of German equipment from a Panzerlastkraftwagen to a nut or bolt' and record his translations in a 'well-thumbed index'.[26]

★

During wartime, Bletchley Park was an austere environment. The huts in which Cairncross and his colleagues toiled were poorly ventilated. During the summer months they became extremely hot, yet icy cold during the winter. Coal burners provided a little heat, but also smoggy conditions. Cups of tea were available from large urns kept in the huts, but rationing was such that these facilities were limited.[27] By 1942, meals were served in a cafeteria at different times throughout the day in order to reflect the twenty-four-hour-a-day shift system. The shifts would change each eight hours, the day shift beginning at 08.00, the next at 16.00, and the late-night shift at midnight.

The town of Bletchley itself was also relatively small. In the 1931 census, it was recorded as being the home of a mere 6,170 individuals.[28] Geographically centred around the local train station, a junction on the line from London to Birmingham and the Oxford to Cambridge line, over the course of the war Bletchley posed a number of serious logistical problems for GC&CS. Bletchley Park itself was a fairly large estate in the 1930s, spanning some 581 acres. In 1937, MI6 acquired some 58 acres of this estate, including the Victorian mansion and surrounding buildings.[29] While this provided ample room for expansion, and over the course of the war a network of huts and blocks sprung up across the estate, the town itself lacked accommodation.

When the first 200 GC&CS staff began arriving onsite in 1939 they took up residence in the local inns and hotels. However, by December 1940 the agency already employed nearly 600 individuals. Over the course of the war the number of staff employed by the agency increased to in excess of 10,000 people, the vast majority of whom were stationed at Bletchley. Clearly, the accommodation provided by the town, even with widespread compulsory billeting, was incapable of housing all of those individuals. Soon villages far and wide also housed Bletchley Park staff. Eventually a great many of the military staff were placed into purpose-built accommodation blocks.[30]

The result of this arrangement was, on occasion, a certain reluctance on the part of the local population to accommodate the incoming workers. As one veteran of the agency recalled, 'We were billeted in Aspley Guise [a nearby village]. The family treated us like dirt – they wouldn't give us baths and wouldn't feed us properly.'[31] Meanwhile, billeting officers often struggled to find accommodation and, on occasion, threatened to take local residents to court for their failure to cooperate. In May 1943 the Bletchley Urban District Council complained about the 'attitude of certain householders who had consistently refused to take any one into their homes'.[32] Complaints soon found their way to Bletchley Park's administrators, as one individual put it: 'You are considered extremely lucky if you are within 10 miles of Bletchley and have indoor sanitation and a bathroom, the general rule being a W.C. in the backyard and a cold tap.'[33]

Of course, many others suffered few problems, found their hosts kindly and hospitable, and ultimately enjoyed the experience.[34] Cairncross appears to have had limited problems with his accommodation and quickly settled into his digs, with a local family in a nearby village upon his arrival. This did, however, create its own issues. As Cairncross noted, the tendency among Bletchley Park staff was only to really talk to those colleagues within their immediate section. They arrived on site, did their consuming eight-hour shift and were then transported back to their accommodation. The opportunity for getting to know many other people at Bletchley was, therefore, limited.[35]

Indeed, given Cairncross' limited view of the world in which he inhabited, it is undoubtedly the case that he had little inkling as to the scale of the operation in which he took part. As noted, Hut 3 was a small team, numbering in the low hundreds, but was part of an intelligence apparatus that employed many thousands of individuals – the majority of them young women operating a vast array of machines, conducting bureaucratic and administrative work, and providing the auxiliary labour that facilitated the work of individuals such as Cairncross. Yet Cairncross would have known little, if anything, of this. 'We lived,' he wrote, 'a semi-monastic life' only punctuated by days of leave, which he spent in London. As such, he met few, if any, of the celebrities of the agency. Indeed, even within his own section of Hut 3, there were many people Cairncross never met – Peter Calvocoressi among them.[36]

★

Once in place at Bletchley Park, Cairncross elected to utilise his position there to pass Ultra material, in the form of decrypts, to his Soviet handler. From the outset, the materials he provided Gorsky, or as Cairncross knew him, Henry, were of considerable importance. First, they included two volumes of a training manual on cryptanalysis, which presumably were acquired during the brief and abortive cryptanalysis training he received while at Bedford. Second, he was also able to supply a document instructing readers how to read Tunny traffic.[37] Tunny was the code name given by the British to a family of machines and their traffic created by the C. Lorenz AG corporation. These were the Lorenz SZ40 and SZ42 machines. For their period these were highly advanced machine cipher systems, which were used to protect the traffic of the highest grade, between the Supreme command, including Hitler himself, in Berlin to commanders in the field.[38] Third, he provided a description of the machines used to break Luftwaffe traffic.[39]

These were significant intelligence contributions and clearly provided evidence that the British had broken both Enigma and other very high-grade systems, the Lorenz key among them. However, this was only to be the beginning of Cairncross' leaks of material from Bletchley Park. In Hut 3 he had access to processed decrypts, which according to him were left strewn around the floor awaiting destruction. Complete with these documents in hand, as well as his own translations, he would stuff the decrypts down his trousers and simply walk through the gates of Bletchley Park. He was never stopped and checked. With the documents in hand, Cairncross would meet with Gorsky in London, follow him to a quiet spot in the suburbs and hand over his package of illicit decrypts.[40]

The significance of his activities did not become immediately apparent to Cairncross until May 1943. When he met with his handler, the latter 'announced with a triumphant smile that the Russians had won a great air victory in which they had destroyed 600 aeroplanes. His superiors had been delighted with my information and had granted me a decoration. He even confessed that he dreamed of my decrypts.'[41] This was in reference to a series of air strikes launched by the Red Army Air Force on 6–8 May 1943, the lead up to the Battle of Kursk.[42]

The Battle of Kursk, which raged during July and August 1943, was one of the most famous actions on the Eastern Front. In essence, the Germans attempted to encircle and neutralise the Soviet forces at the Kursk salient; a bulge of Soviet-controlled territory that jutted out, peninsula-like, into the German lines. The German plan was to attack at two points, one at the north of the bulge and another in the south. The Germans, according to some estimates, poured vast resources into the operation, code-named Citadel, including more than 900,000 troops and some 2,730 tanks. The defenders similarly deployed in vast numbers of men and equipment, at least some 1,340,000 and 3,440 tanks and self-propelled guns. Over the course of the action, often described as the largest tank battle of the conflict, the Red Army was able to resist the Wehrmacht and proceeded to launch a devastating counter-offensive.[43] Citadel was a clear victory for the Soviet Union and proved to be the last major offensive that the Wehrmacht was able to launch at the Red Army.

Many years later, in 1944, Yuri Modin, who would be Cairncross' next controller, was similarly impressed by his contribution to Kursk. He wrote that Cairncross' information saw the destruction of 'Over 500 Nazi aircraft', but moreover he provided important intelligence regarding the disposition of German forces as well as important technical information regarding the Tiger tank.[44] Yet Cairncross was far from the only source of foreign intelligence available to the Soviet commanders. The British supplied information regarding German intentions in April. Meanwhile, the Soviets also had access to information from the Red Orchestra, anti-Nazi spies operating from central Europe, as well as partisans operating behind German lines.[45]

Clearly, significant though Cairncross' information was – for his efforts regarding Kursk he was later awarded the Order of the Red Banner in 1944[46] – he was but one source among a vast array of information pouring into the Soviet High Command. Meanwhile, as important as intelligence was, it did not win battles; soldiers did. As Evan Mawdsley notes, 'Ultimately the Russians were victorious because they had time to lay out their field defences and to assemble powerful forces.'[47] Intelligence, including that supplied by Cairncross, was important, but its significance should not be overstated.

9

On His Majesty's Secret Service

Successful though his time at Bletchley Park undoubtedly was, after a year of working there, Cairncross had had enough. He was beginning to suffer the ill-effects of shift work and his eyesight was being damaged by the constant pouring over decrypts.[1] In his memoirs, Cairncross explained that he 'had a slight [time] bonus at the end of every week and it was badly needed, for this was an exhausting, if rational, arrangement.' At the changeover of shifts, at the end of the week, he 'would sometimes sleep from twelve to fifteen hours. … I am very dependent on regular sleep, and large amounts of it.' Eventually, the constant changes to his sleeping pattern, with regular night shifts, took its toll on his health. Meanwhile, 'Henry', Anatoli Gorsky, expressed an interest in Cairncross transferring from the military sections of GC&CS into its Diplomatic wing.[2] In February 1942, the Diplomatic and Commercial Sections of the agency had returned to London with a staff of some 200 individuals under the command of Alastair Denniston.[3]

Such a move back to London suited Cairncross just fine and, more importantly, the suggestion from Gorsky indicated to him that his Soviet masters were no longer interested in the military intelligence he was able to supply. Instead, they wanted secret British diplomatic intelligence. As such, Cairncross obediently began sounding out his colleagues in GC&CS to see if he could orchestrate a move. This proved more difficult than either he or Gorsky had bargained on. While his move to the Diplomatic wing of GC&CS might have suited Moscow, it did not suit his British bosses, who needed skilled men and women in its military sections. Cairncross' request for a move was duly turned down and he was forced to improvise.[4]

As fortune would have it, Cairncross soon bumped in Professor Frederick Green, 'a fellow Scot' who had been a French language specialist at Cambridge. During the war he had, like many other 'men of the professor type' in academia, taken up an alternative form of employment in the intelligence world.[5] In this instance, he was the liaison officer between GC&CS and Section V of the SIS. Green, who did not get on well with Commander Edward Travis, by then the head of Bletchley Park, was willing to hear Cairncross out. He soon took the case to his superiors in SIS and emphasised that Cairncross was not only bright but an excellent linguist with a thorough understanding of German.

Bletchley soon got wind of what was afoot and the situation turned sour. As Cairncross put it, 'the situation deteriorated so badly that I was obliged, after receiving an assurance from Green that my application to SIS would be approved, to pull out of Bletchley altogether. Thus for a short time I was in a kind of vacuum and spent a brief but somewhat disturbing few weeks unattached to any organisation.'[6] Thus, with his bridges burned at Bletchley, Cairncross moved on to another highly sensitive branch of the British secret state. This was the Secret Intelligence Service, which he joined on 14 June 1943; specifically, he was appointed to the German sub-section of the Counter Intelligence Section – Section V.[7] Once again, Cairncross' Cambridge connection had opened yet another door into the clandestine world.

★

SIS, or as it is more widely known, MI6, as an organisation needs little in the way of introduction. As Britain's primary intelligence agency tasked with collecting information oversees, it enjoys a fame and public recognition far beyond any intelligence agency in the world, save perhaps the Central Intelligence Agency in the USA. John le Carré's George Smiley and Ian Fleming's James Bond have, through their adventures in print and on the silver screen, catapulted this secret organisation into global stardom.

During the Second World War, its major successes included the vital role SIS played in the distribution of Ultra intelligence and its collaboration in the MI5-led 'XX System' or 'Double Cross System', in which Abwehr spies in Britain were rounded up and forced to work for the British. Yet the organisation also received a severe bloody nose on more than one occasion. The first major setback was the Venlo incident in November 1939, a disastrous effort to forge links with a German refugee in the Netherlands, which saw two British agents abducted by the Abwehr. The most serious failure, however, was the recruitment of Kim Philby.

In the late 1930s, shortly before the onset of the Second World War, SIS was, like GC&CS, looking for new talent. One individual they approached in 1938 was none other than Guy Burgess. Since 1936, Burgess had been employed by the BBC to recruit high-profile figures to appear on its programmes. However, once he had been headhunted for intelligence, he offered his resignation to the BBC and left to join the SIS's Section D. Section D's task was to run covert operations, conduct sabotage, offer support to resistance organisations and anti-Nazi groups, and to distribute propaganda. Burgess, with his experience in broadcasting, was employed as a liaison between SIS and other bodies that dealt with propaganda, including Department Electra House (a black propaganda unit), the Ministry of Information, and the Joint Broadcasting Committee (JBC). The JBC was a Foreign Office outfit that broadcast wireless propaganda programmes to Germany, and it was primarily there that Burgess made his mark.[8]

Burgess' career in SIS was to be cut short prematurely. In September 1940, he was charged with driving while drunk and his section was subsumed into the Special Operations Executive, which soon let him go. However, before his departure he proved instrumental in recruiting Philby. After his return from Spain, Philby had been working for *The Times*, but that gave him little to do. This was not at all pleasing to Burgess, who viewed this form of employment as a wasted opportunity. 'Find yourself a decent job quickly,' he ordered Philby, 'otherwise before you know it you'll be at the front, God knows where, perfectly useless to the rest of us.'[9]

As such, he set about trying to get another job in Britain's intelligence community. His first port of call was a meeting with Frank Birch, a senior cryptanalyst at GC&CS. Unfortunately for Philby, he was rejected because (or at least so Philby claimed) an apologetic Birch felt that he could not offer the potential recruit enough money. Conversely, Modin claimed it was because Philby felt the sum was inadequate. If so, this nearly proved a dire error. With conscription already firmly in place, the National Service (Armed Forces) Act having been introduced in September 1939, he had already been summoned for a medical examination in preparation for his mobilisation.[10] However, the intelligence historian Christopher Andrew and Oleg Gordievsky cast some doubt on Modin's claim. They noted that Philby was offered a £600 salary by Birch, the standard rate of pay for Civil

Service cryptanalysts graded as 'senior assistants' within the agency, and that this was the same salary that he accepted from MI6. More likely, they suggest, is that Philby was actually turned down by Birch, his talents apparently not suited to cipher cracking. Nevertheless, he was soon asked to report to a meeting with Marjorie Maxse, a senior figure in MI6's Section D. Clearly this meeting went well and Philby was asked to report again, a few days later, for a second discussion. On this occasion, Philby was surprised to see that she was accompanied by none other than Guy Burgess. Soon enough, Philby had been recruited into Section D and handed in his notice to *The Times*.[11]

Philby's recruitment into MI6 remained a sore subject for some of his former colleagues in the agency for many years after his exposure as a Soviet mole and flight to Moscow in 1963. Speaking to Sydney Radio in 1977, Group Captain F.W. 'Freddie' Winterbotham, a liaison officer between SIS and Bletchley Park during the war, bitterly recalled that Philby:

> was recruited because one of the people who looked after security in MI6 knew his father! And apparently failed to go into his background because after all he had been a communist in university. I think if a little more care had been taken at that moment, we wouldn't have had all that trouble.[12]

Clearly, a similar attitude was taken by recruitment officials at Bletchley Park, who also did not realise or chose to ignore his 'past' political idealism.[13]

Nevertheless, his failure to access Bletchley Park aside, before long Philby was able to supply the Soviet Union with highly useful intelligence, including advanced warning that the Germans were planning an invasion of the Soviet Union.[14] Similarly, he was able, in November or December 1941, to provide Moscow with intelligence that the Japanese planned to unleash a wave of offensives across Southeast Asia, information the British had secured through deciphering wireless traffic from the German Ambassador in Japan. With the Japanese committed, it was clear that there would not be an offensive launched against the Soviet Union, which freed up Soviet troops who could be moved from defensive positions in the East to the war in the West.[15]

Of course, the significance of such revelations was undermined by paranoid fear of betrayal by the Centre in Moscow. The fact that Philby, and indeed the other members of the five, were able to supply such high-quality material, but not the names of (non-existent) British operatives working in the Soviet Union, was inaccurately deemed evidence of British deception.

The fact that the British had their hands full with Germany, Italy and Japan, and were not nearly as interested in the Soviet Union as the Soviet Union was in them was impossible to accept in Moscow. The failure of their spies in London to confirm their paranoia was deemed not to be a sign that Soviet intelligence assumptions were unsafe, but that the sources were.[16]

★

As such, when Cairncross arrived at SIS in June 1943, it was into an already penetrated agency. By that time, Philby had already been transferred from Section D to Section V, where he headed responsibility for its work on the Iberian Peninsula. The purpose of Section V, according to Philby, 'was to obtain advance information of espionage operations mounted against British territory from foreign soil'.[17]

The section was headed by Felix Cowgill, a hardworking, if stubborn and often belligerent, former colonial policeman. Tim Milne, a member of Philby's SIS entourage, recalled that while it was commonplace for senior officers to make enemies in the world of wartime intelligence, Cowgill 'seemed to go far out of his way to antagonise people'.[18] Eventually, in 1944, Philby was ordered by Moscow to attempt to replace Cowgill; a 'sour', Machiavellian campaign in which he was successful.[19] This saw Philby become head of an expanded Section IX, which worked on 'communist espionage and subversion', while Section V was taken over by Tim Milne.[20] Also present in Section V was David Footman, the son of a clergyman and veteran of the First World War. Footman was an expert on the Soviet Union who had, during the inter-war years, published on the Russian Revolution. Yet despite these credentials, he was not highly rated by his colleagues. Patrick Reilly, from the Foreign Office, noted that 'he was emphatically not the man to commission any study of Stalinist policies'.[21]

Despite misgivings about his only adequate competence, Footman was the head of the German section when Cairncross arrived, and the new recruit to SIS was placed under his auspices. Unlike at least some of his colleagues, Cairncross liked Footman, finding him 'always calm, balanced and equable'. Perhaps once again suggesting more about himself than his subject, Cairncross wrote that 'the Chief [Major General Sir Stewart Menzies] disliked him. This was perhaps because there was a sharp contrast between his intellectual personality and 'C's' foxhunting and clubland background.'[22] Clearly, Cairncross saw these qualities in himself. He too had long chafed against establishment notions of masculinity, which tended to look down on those with brains as effete, instead favouring those displaying gentlemanly brawn.

The role itself also proved to be positive for Cairncross. Gone was the shift system that he had discovered to be so debilitating while working at Bletchley. At that time Section V was stationed at Glenalmond, an Edwardian mansion in St Albans, Hertfordshire. This followed the established pattern of Britain's clandestine and intelligence units at the time, to find a home, away from the dangers of bombing in the leafy Home Counties. Part of SIS and GC&CS had, of course, commandeered Bletchley Park in Buckinghamshire; Section VIII of SIS occupied Whaddon Hall near Bletchley; the Radio Security Service was located in Hanslope Park, also close to Bletchley Park; and, among many others, the Political Intelligence Department, a Foreign Office unit that produced intelligence summaries, took over a number of picturesque sites in Bedfordshire.[23] St Alban's was convenient for Cairncross as it allowed him to commute from his flat in London. He was working with 'agreeable colleagues in pleasant country surroundings', he found the job interesting and his health soon improved.[24]

The task he was to perform was not dissimilar to the one he had been engaged in while at Bletchley Park. He worked on traffic produced by the counter-intelligence unit of the Sicherheitsdienst (SD), which was the intelligence agency of the Nazi Party and the Schutzstaffel (SS), and under the authority of the Reichssicherheitshauptamt (Reich Main Security Office).[25] The work itself involved examining original German decrypts, which had been broken at Bletchley Park, and editing and analysing the information they contained. Any mention of agents had been weeded and indexed already. This was important information; it revealed vital clues as to the identity and whereabouts of German agents in Britain. This was an essential component in the process of the Double-Cross system that would so successfully turn German agents operating in Britain. But that aspect of the process was not part of Cairncross' remit, his role was to extrapolate general policy from the remaining material. As Cairncross was himself to note, the excitement and adventure of popular imagination regarding intelligence work and the SIS did not apply to him and his colleagues. Rather than James Bond figures, the 'reality' of MI6 'was much better reflected by a cartoon in *Punch* as a crowd of small unimpressive bowler-hatted figures scurrying to their offices.'[26]

Though all certainly an improvement on his previous posting, Glenalmond still had its downsides. Though a little under 30 miles closer to London, which facilitated commuting, travel time did eat into his day. He was required to awaken at 6 a.m. each morning in order to be sure of arriving at work on time. In the opening weeks of his time at St Albans, while he was still recovering from his time at Bletchley Park, he would struggle to get up for work. This led to some testy conversations with his boss, Footman, who not unnaturally complained that not only had he not come into work but had failed to call. This was hardly an ideal start to his new posting, but little appears to have come of it and he soon found his footing in SIS.

★

While at SIS, Cairncross became acquainted with Kim Philby. The two had met briefly via Guy Burgess earlier in the war, but were not closely associated.[27] Philby, of course, had left Cambridge in 1933, before Cairncross arrived in 1934. Following his departure from Cambridge, Philby had lived abroad, travelling Europe and working as a journalist. All the while, Cairncross was still studying and forging his career in the Civil Service. While at SIS, the two spies do not appear to have forged anything other than an acquaintanceship. In his memoirs, Cairncross described Philby as a man 'unconventional in his manners', distant and difficult to read. He claimed that in their time working together they only lunched twice, which proved largely unmemorable occasions, in which Philby arrived in his 'usual old green military jacket'. On the rare occasions that the two talked politics, Philby flatly rejected Cairncross' notions that Nazism was becoming increasingly radical 'with a growing opposition to the upper-class Establishment'. Most importantly, Cairncross claimed to have never known that Philby was, like him, a Soviet mole.[28]

In this latter claim, that Cairncross had no idea that Philby was a fellow agent of the Soviet Union, he was almost certainly telling the truth. In September 1944, Philby wrote to Peter Loxley of the Foreign Office. The letter regarded and appended a memorandum, written by J.C. Curry, head of Section IX, which dealt with anti-Communism. The focus of the letter, as well as the memorandum, was 'the illegal activity of the Communist movement in other countries and to investigate cases of Communist or Soviet penetration and espionage'. The letter and memorandum plainly passed through Cairncross' hands and he ensured that the material was passed to his Soviet handler.[29] Of course, had Cairncross been aware that Philby was also operating in secret for the same masters in Moscow it is highly unlikely that he would have taken the trouble, and indeed risk, of stealing the document penned by his fellow mole. Without doubt, any information that was of use to the Soviet Union, particularly British counter-Soviet intelligence efforts, would have made their way to Moscow via Philby's hands.

During this period, the fears and distrust that had hampered Moscow's appreciation of the materials flowing from Britain came to an end. Since early 1944, Philby had been able to provide, among other materials, highly useful intelligence regarding the foundation of Section IX. Over the following months, much of this material was corroborated by other sources and plainly demonstrated that Moscow's best spies in Britain were, in fact, loyal. As the centre informed the then head of the London residency, Konstantin Mikhailovick Kukin, code-named 'Igor', this was 'serious confirmation of 'S's'[Philby] honesty in his work with us, which obliges us to review our attitude towards him and the entire group'.[30]

Towards the end of 1944, Cairncross also received a new handler; this was Boris Mikhailovich Krötenschield, who also went by the name of Krotov, and was code-named 'Kretchin'. On his arrival in Britain, Krötenschield was impressed by his new charge. He wrote to Moscow to inform them about Cairncross, 'As before he continues to work for us with enthusiasm and to show initiative.' This was rewarded in November 1944 with a financial gift of £250, complete with a message of thanks for all his work. Cairncross responded, 'I am delighted that our friends should have thought my services worthy of recognition and am proud to have contributed something to the victories which have almost cleared the Soviet soil of the invaders.'[31]

Doubtless, having established their British spies' loyalty, a reassessment of the years of previous intelligence work had taken place and reward was in order. As noted earlier, Cairncross also received the Order of the Red Banner for material he supplied regarding German preparations for the Battle of Kursk. It was only in the final months of 1944 when that reward materialised. Krötenschield met with Cairncross and informed him of his award. As Modin explained, 'Kretchin showed it to Cairncross in its velvet-lined box. ... Cairncross held the medal in his hands for a moment: his happiness was obvious.' This moment was fleeting, the medal was soon taken back and returned to Moscow for safe-keeping.[32] Of course, not being there at the time, Modin's description of the event doubtless includes significant dramatic licence.

What is clear, however, is that Cairncross' work at SIS on behalf of the Soviet Union was significant. This was in spite of the still more important Philby also occupying a more senior position within the organisation. While working in Section V, Cairncross was, among other tasks, responsible for the destruction of old intercepts. This gave him ample access to raw intelligence, some of which he dutifully destroyed, but also 'passed about 1,500 on' to his handlers. This material was significant as it included intercepts generated by German counter-intelligence units operating against the Soviet Union. However, his work in the sub-section providing him access to this goldmine of material ended and, much to the Centre's disappointment, he was transferred to work on the Balkans. The result was that he handled very little material related to the Soviet Union. The one exception to this was a message from Cecil Barclay, SIS's contact in Moscow, on German intelligence pertaining to a reorganisation of the NKVD. He was also able to provide a file on Abwehr activities in the Soviet Union that contained material on agents, but the information was already a year old, limiting its utility.[33]

The transfer to the Balkans section proved unfortunate for both Cairncross and his handlers. He had been highly productive for them, having supplied 1,454 documents in 1942. Yet in 1943, presumably excluding decrypts, he was able to supply only ninety-four documents. This was not, however, useless material. For instance, his information included intelligence on Operation Ulm, an abortive German plan to attack Soviet electricity generating plans in the Ural mountains.[34]

★

It was during his time at SIS that Cairncross was to make an important and lifelong friendship. That individual was the novelist, Graham Greene. Born in 1904, Greene attended the University of Oxford, from which he graduated in 1925. Even as an undergraduate, he had literary ambitions and wrote a volume of poetry entitled *Babbling April*, which was published in 1925. After his graduation, he began a career in journalism, which soon incorporated travel writing and the literary fiction that would make his name. However, his route into the intelligence world came not from his journalism or novels, but his travel writing and, in typical British intelligence fashion at that time, from familial connections.

In 1938, Greene's sister, Elizabeth had joined SIS, where she was posted to Bletchley Park. It was through her that Greene, as well as the writer and satirist Malcolm Muggeridge, came to the attentions of the agency. In the case of Greene, his travel writings took him to places across the world, not least Sierra Leone, which were of interest to SIS. This connection soon bore fruit in 1941 when Greene, otherwise libidinously engaged in London, was sent on an intelligence training programme before being dispatched back to Sierra Leone to work as SIS's representative in Freetown.[35] In 1943, Greene returned to London, where he took up a post as head of SIS's Portugal desk.

Cairncross and Greene first met on the train from St Albans back to London, not long before Section V returned to London on a permanent basis. The two men both vaguely recognised each other as colleagues, and both were familiar with Kim Philby, but had yet to be introduced and remained unaware of each other's identities. Yet on that particular commute, Cairncross happened to be reading *England Made Me*, a Greene novel that had been published some years prior, in 1935. Greene noticed the book, and offered his opinion that it was not 'a bad novel'. Cairncross, in an effort to be helpful, noted that the author of the work had published a number of better books, not least *The Power and the Glory* (1940). 'Yes', Greene agreed, 'it is a fine piece of work.' Cairncross, intrigued, asked if the man opposite him happened to know Greene, at which point the ruse was up and the author came clean.[36] In his future correspondence with Cairncross, which lasted until Greene's death in 1991, Greene usually referred to Cairncross as Claymore – a two-handed medieval Scottish sword.

This connection to Greene would in future years, throughout the remainder of Cairncross' own life, prove to be significant. Greene became a periodic source of advice, solace and assistance, when Cairncross' usually calamitous interactions with the intelligence world and law enforcement occurred. Greene, once his friend's own literary career began to take off, also read drafts and provided professional advice. By contrast, Cairncross could offer little to Greene. Nevertheless, the latter appeared to enjoy interacting with his old colleagues from his espionage days. Indeed, even after it turned out that two of these friends, Cairncross and Philby, had been disloyal his contact with them did not diminish. Indeed, the resulting scandal appeared only to provoke mild entertainment. For instance, in October 1967 after his defection, Philby re-entered the news cycle after journalists from *The Sunday Times* tracked him down.[37] Greene's comment on the matter to Cairncross was, 'What a fuss at the moment about Kim!'[38]

Important to Greene was a sense of loyalty. This did not necessarily apply to traditional objects of loyalty, such as monarchs or countries. As he wrote in the voice of the protagonist Wormold, in his classic 1958 comedy spy novel, *Our Man in Havana*, 'I don't care a damn about men who are loyal to the people who pay them, to organizations. ... I don't think even my country means all that much. There are many countries in our blood, aren't there, but only one person. Would the world be in the mess it is if we were loyal to love and not to countries?'[39] This was not merely true of his sentiments in his works of fiction. While his friends and former colleagues might have betrayed their country, this mattered little. What was more important to Greene was that they maintained a higher loyalty, to their ideals, and he to them. For instance, Kim Philby's memoir, *My Silent War*, was not a work of self-serving propaganda, penned by an unscrupulous ideologue whose betrayal had cost the lives of both his and Greene's SIS colleagues. Instead, as Greene explained in a bizarre foreword to the 1968 text, they were a 'dignified statement of his [Philby's] beliefs'. He further added, '"He betrayed his country" – yes, perhaps he did, but who among us has not committed treason to something or someone more important than a country?'[40]

Regardless, what was clear was that Greene liked Cairncross and Cairncross, untrue to his usually prickly form, rapidly came to forge an important bond with Greene. In addition to the amusing opening introductions, which Cairncross described as 'a veritable *coup de théâtre*', he was plainly impressed by Greene. This extended from admiration of Greene's literary prowess, and his stature in that world, but, also to his rebelliousness. But, perhaps most important to the nascent friendship, was Greene's lack of social and professional snobbery. As Cairncross would write, 'I was originally surprised that he should have taken to me back in 1943, for he was already famous and I was not in any way distinguished.' This not only incorporated Greene's willingness to accept Cairncross' lack of religion (Greene was a Catholic), but also his relatively lowly socio-economic, Scots–Calvinist background.[41] Greene was, as far as Cairncross was concerned, 'not just a superb writer, but a wonderful and loyal friend'.

This immediate warming to Greene perhaps offers, if viewed cynically, an important window on Cairncross' mindset as a young man. Greene, though a celebrity and relatively senior intelligence official, offered both friendship without judgement based on class or social status. This stood in stark contrast to Cairncross' experiences at Cambridge and the Foreign Office. This was a kind of recognition, from an individual whose accomplishments were considerable, that Cairncross had craved throughout his entire life to that point, but had been denied. Certainly, in his autobiography, he seems to have taken considerable pride in listing his various literary accomplishments on which his famous, novelist friend had lavished praise.[42] At last, a person Cairncross himself respected, reciprocated that respect.

10

The Venona Project

Though the Second World War had been a period of profound success for the Cambridge spy ring, its close also heralded the beginning of the end for the group. The seeds to their downfall were being sown, not in Britain but in the United States of America.

As we have seen, the work that the two powers had invested in the development of cryptanalysis had been considerable. Where Bletchley had taken the lead in the information battle during the Second World War, the US swiftly gained the ascendancy in the opening years of the Cold War. Since the outbreak of the Second World War in 1939, the USA had been collecting international telegrams that originated from or were sent to the US. Naturally this included the messages sent to and from Soviet officials in Washington and other American cities. It also included messages about, and information from, Moscow's various agents around the world. Reading these messages was, however, no easy matter.

Where the Germans, among others, placed their faith – with no small degree of hubris – in mechanised code systems, most notably Enigma, which produced staggeringly vast permutations, such machines had soon proven vulnerable to analysis by Polish, British and later US cryptanalysts. The Soviet Union, by contrast, had been stung by cryptanalysts in the past.

After the revolutions and civil war, Lenin's incoming Communist regime continued to operate the same cipher systems that had been used by officials under the Tsar. In the wake of the October Revolution, Ernst Fetterlein, a highly gifted cryptanalyst who had been on the Tsar's payroll, escaped to the West and brought with him his considerable expertise and knowledge of Russian cipher systems. He was soon able to begin work in Britain's cipher-cracking bureau, the Government Code and Cypher School (GC&CS), on the Bolshevik systems in 1919.[1]

Meanwhile, throughout the 1920s, agents of the fledgling Soviet Union were active in Britain. The existence of such individuals fuelled anti-Soviet hardliners in the British government, not least the Home Secretary, Sir William Joynson-Hicks, and the Chancellor of the Exchequer, Winston Churchill. The Soviets were also fomenting revolution in China and they also had designs on Afghanistan. The latter, given Afghanistan's proximity to India, caused particular disquiet in Britain. In 1926, the British cryptanalysts scored a coup having deciphered Soviet telegrams from Peking, which provided evidence of Soviet efforts to agitate in Britain. This material was utilised by the Prime Minister, Stanley Baldwin, to sever diplomatic ties with the Soviet Union. To the dismay of GC&CS's cryptanalysts, Baldwin made the disastrous move of reading these deciphered messages in parliament, as did the Foreign Secretary, Sir Austen Chamberlain, two days later. This naive use of signals intelligence provided the Soviets with incontrovertible evidence that their lackadaisical attitude towards cipher security was not merely dangerous but already subject to exploitation.[2]

The Soviets, having had their fingers burned and provided with a full, public account of precisely how and why, soon changed their code systems. The outcome was that during the Second World War they had introduced complex book ciphers utilising a one-time pad that is, a cipher key that is used once and then discarded. The way the Soviet system worked was that a cipher clerk would have a code book and a one-time pad book. The codebook was used to turn words, phrases and letters into five-digit numbers. The one time-pad book contained pages containing sixty random five-digit numbers. By adding the random one-time pad numbers to the code numbers it was possible to create an extremely secure cipher system. These pages of the one-time pad or cipher book would be non-repeating and used only once.[3] If properly utilised, with both discipline and care, a one-time pad is impossible to decipher by anyone who is not in possession of the key.

Such systems, however, came at a price. The realities of wartime meant that communication with embassies and staff in foreign lands was an essential requirement for the Soviet Union. The result was that cipher makers had to produce unique page after unique page of non-repeating keys in order to cater for the many thousands upon thousands of messages that would inevitably be sent. It was an arduous task and a vast undertaking. Meanwhile, it was a similarly laborious task for a cipher clerk to encipher the desired message before transmission. Well aware of these limitations, the other major wartime powers all opted for less secure, machine-generated cipher systems for their high-grade traffic. The British, for example, had developed a system, modelled on the German Enigma system, called Type-X. The other problem with such systems was the potential for human error and the cutting of corners.

In 1941, when Germany invaded the Soviet Union, the amount of Soviet traffic went through the roof. This placed huge pressure on the manufacturers of the code and cipher books to match demand. To generate such quantities of random material, it has been contended that a room of women simply called out any number that happened to pop into their heads. Another possibility is that random number mechanisms, similar to those devices that generate winning lottery numbers, were deployed.[4] Regardless of the mechanism, the pressures of wartime clearly overwhelmed the system. Whether as a result of deliberate policy or the response of overworked cryptographers, the cipher makers began to duplicate pages – some 35,000 of them.[5]

Though the security of the Soviet ciphers remained an extremely formidable obstacle to any would-be cryptanalyst given the task of unlocking the messages, the total security of the one-time pad, was, for thousands of messages, lost. In the meantime, the Soviet Union's ever mistrustful wartime allies had not been idle. The Signals Intelligence Service of the US Army, suspicious of their allies and correctly predicting that the détente between the USSR and the West would not outlive the war, began analysing high-grade Soviet traffic. Soviet trade traffic, in its enciphered form, had been collated by the cable companies and by the end of 1943 groups of messages were transferred onto punch cards. This material was run through an IMB machine and it transpired that there were seven pairs of matching messages. When examined next to the cargo lists of ships bound for Russia under the Lend-Lease programme, US cryptanalysts were able to make a number of small inroads into Soviet cipher traffic: identifying words and phrases. With this information at hand, painstakingly though its development was, they were further able to start identifying the repeat uses of one-time pad sheets.[6] From there, a project developed to read this high-grade Soviet information; that project was code-named Venona.

★

In 1939, while Europe was plunged into conflict, the United States remained at peace. In the wake of the First World War, the most powerful economy in the world shrugged off the mantle of international leadership and instead pursued isolationism. Just as the US intelligence apparatus was neglected, so too was her military. Over the course of the 1930s, the defence spending of the major powers all increased significantly. By 1937, Germany was spending a massive 23.5 per cent of its national income on defence, the British Empire, on the other hand, only invested a mere 5.7 per cent of its income on its defence. Yet the US was willing to part with only 1.5 per cent for this cause.[7] In terms of practical military matters, such as the production of military hardware, the US lagged behind. For instance, in 1939 British and German aircraft production stood at 7,940 and 8,295 planes respectively. The US, on the other hand, produced a mere 2,195 units.[8]

The inter-war period also proved a difficult time for the USA's cryptanalytic efforts. In 1919, Herbert Yardley founded the State Department's Cipher Bureau or Black Chamber, which itself emerged from the US Army's wartime cryptanalytic service, Military Intelligence Section 8 (MI8). In the course of its existence, the Black Chamber attacked the communications of some twenty different countries and solved more than 45,000 cryptograms.[9] This all came to an end in 1929 with the election of President Herbert Hoover. Henry L. Stimson, Hoover's Secretary of State, took the astonishingly naive view that, 'Gentlemen do not read each other's mail'[10] and that such work was 'highly unethical'. He shut down the Black Chamber.[11]

With its closure, the US War Department refounded the bureau as the Signals Intelligence Service in 1930.[12] The US Navy had also a cryptanalytic department, the ponderously titled Office of Chief of Naval Operations (OPNAV), 20th Division of the Office of Naval Communications, G Section/ Communications Security, or OP-20-G. During the 1930s, little love was lost between the two organisations. The Signals Intelligence Service's William F. Friedman bitterly complained later, in 1942, 'For each dollar that the Army was able to obtain for cryptanalytic and cryptographic work, the Navy was able to obtain three to five dollars.' Yet despite this disadvantage, 'While they [the Navy] were ahead of us in quantity, we were ahead in quality.' As he went on to add, cooperation was 'intermittent and at times very indifferent – the usual mutual suspicions and jealousies pervaded our relationship'.[13] It was in this difficult situation that the American cryptanalysts found themselves in 1939 at the outbreak of war in Europe.

In spring 1940, the news that German forces had shattered the armies of Britain and France came as a rude awakening to the American public and its politicians. A poll conducted the previous September showed that an overwhelming 82 per cent of Americans believed that Britain and France could dispatch Germany without American assistance. Though isolationism remained the order of the day, a change had occurred; when President Roosevelt asked Congress for a billion-dollar defence programme, they gave him $1.5 billion. Over the coming months Congress would approve a further $6.5 billion and voted to increase the size of the US Navy by 70 per cent.[14]

Just as there had been a fundamental shift in attitude in US thinking regarding the war in Europe, so too were there notable developments in the US cryptanalytic circles. In late 1940 the first halting American efforts were made on Enigma. Meanwhile, in January 1941, American cryptanalysts were invited to Bletchley Park. Though the British proved guarded, keen to hold back technical secrets, this was a first step towards a fruitful relationship that, over the course of the war, would produce a hugely successful partnership.[15] In 1942, the Signals Intelligence Service took possession of Arlington Hall, a former women's college in Virginia. It was here that much of the most significant signals intelligence work, primarily directed at Japanese traffic, was conducted during the war. It was also where the early work on the Venona Project would be conducted.

★

Though the Americans had been collecting Soviet messages since 1939, no sustained effort was made to read the material in the first years of the war. Just as the British had been reticent to waste resources on the problem of the German Enigma ciphers prior to 1939, on the basis that the system was thought to be unbreakable, the American cryptanalysts had taken the same view of Soviet traffic. Unsurprisingly, after 1941, the main thrust of American efforts were directed at the Axis powers, and the Japanese in particular. Also, the Soviets were allies in the war against the Axis powers. Nevertheless, the head of the US Army's Signals Intelligence Service, Carter

W. Clarke, took a highly jaundiced view of the Soviet Union. He argued that it was best to discover anything there was to learn about the new allies while they were friendly, because once they returned to being enemies the opportunity would be lost.[16]

With this initiative in mind, Arlington Hall directed some of its resources towards the problem of Soviet traffic. By 1943, the cryptanalysts had identified a minimum of five different sets of Soviet cipher. One was used by the Soviet Purchasing Committee and a second by Soviet diplomats. Importantly, they were utilised by the Soviet intelligence apparatus. By that point, some 10,000 pages of commercial and diplomatic material had been collected. Lieutenant Richard Hallock, who before the war been an archaeologist with an expertise in ancient languages, was tasked with dealing with this mass of material. His instinct was that the beginning of each message might pertain to the subject of its content and, therefore, might not be unique. As such, he ordered punch cards to be made containing the first twenty-five letters, or five, five letter groups. Once the results of these labours bore fruit, it was noticed that some of the one-time pads had been reproduced. A window had opened.[17]

Important though this was, it pertained only to trade messages. Another key flaw in the Soviet traffic was required. This was found due to the work of Cecil J. Philips, a brilliant young man who, by 1945, and the mere age of 20, would soon be in command of fifty individuals.[18] Based on Hallock's work on the trade messages, he was able to begin to unravel the material produced by the Soviet intelligence services. In his own words:

> From October, 1943 until November 1944, we had nothing but trade messages. The trade messages were not likely to be terribly important so we were trying to solve other systems. I began working on the KGB, which at that time we didn't even know was KGB, but I began working on it. In 1944, November '44, I found an indicator in the KGB messages which allowed us to pair KGB messages with the trade messages. Now for the first time we were able to solve something that was of interest.[19]

This early work on Venona was to be a starting point in defeating what should have been, had cryptological and best practice been maintained, an impenetrable collection of messages. As it was, the hurried and overworked staff who had produced the cipher books that shielded the Soviet Union's spies, in Britain, the United States of America and further afield, had placed those agents in serious danger of identification.

★

In 1942, a linguist named Meredith Knox Gardner, who would go on to achieve considerable success working on German and Japanese codes, was recruited to Arlington Hall. At that time still in his early thirties, Gardner had already proven himself a highly gifted young man. He was born in 1912 and by the time he reached university he had discovered an aptitude for languages. He read German at the University of Texas before proceeding to undertake a Master's degree at the University of Wisconsin-Madison, where he was also employed as a teaching assistant from 1938 to 1940. He gained a job as a professor at the University of Akron and it was from there that he was recruited by the Signals Intelligence Service.

In some small ways, Gardner's life mirrored that of John Cairncross'. Gardner was born in October 1912 and Cairncross was born a mere nine months later. Both of them would grow up to become among the most intellectually high-achieving individuals of their generation. Both men were extremely gifted linguists, both men went into the service of their state, both men would work in intelligence and both men would play a key role in the world of cipher espionage. Cairncross, as we have seen, was a master of modern European languages and over his lifetime would learn, among other languages, French, German, Spanish, Italian and Mandarin. Gardner was similarly talented, if not even more accomplished. Not only did he have an even more spectacular array of modern European languages under his belt, including Russian and Lithuanian, but also Sanskrit.[20]

Once within the Signals Intelligence Service, Gardner was set to work on breaking German ciphers. However, soon after he began to work on Japanese material as well. As such he took it upon himself to learn the language and had mastered it within the space of just three months. This added yet another language to the half-dozen he already spoke. By 1944, Gardner had directed his efforts towards the Soviet traffic.[21] Building on the work conducted by Hallock and Philips, Gardner was able to apply his extraordinary linguistic talents on drawing some meaning from the mass of Soviet intelligence signals he had before him. Soon enough, Gardner's careful work began to reveal results. Shockingly for America's security apparatus, it became apparent that the Soviets had agents in their most prized and secret programme; the project to build the atomic bomb. As Philips put it:

> The list of names of scientists which Meredith Gardner broke out in December of 1946, was one of the sort of key events in all of this. Before that, starting in the middle of '46, he had begun to see things that looked like spying. … It was clear that this was some sort of a surreptitious kind of activity. When the message, the long list of scientists, was broken out in December of 1946, why, that was perhaps a seminal event, I guess.[22]

However, for all of his brilliance, Gardner was painfully quiet to the point that his fellow cryptanalyst, Frank Rowlett, described him as 'a shy, introverted loner' who was difficult to get to know. This, however, did not prevent him from making significant, if slow progress against the Soviet material. As Robert Lamphere recalled, 'Little by little he chipped away at the messages,' with the aid of what were then still very basic computers. This involved deciphering a few words at a time, a problem made more onerous by the extensive use of code names by the Soviets.[23] As we have seen, both agents and handlers were awarded code names, names that would change over time. For instance, Klaus Fuchs was initially code-named 'Rest' in the material, only to later be called 'Charles', while Julius Rosenberg was 'Antenna', later replaced with 'Liberal'. Similarly, key politicians and figures were given their own designation. Robert Oppenheimer was 'Bill of Exchange', Winston Churchill was 'Boar' and President Roosevelt was 'Captain'.[24]

The Venona project continued for many more years after the 1940s, only being rolled up in 1980. In terms of the results, the scale of Soviet penetration was vast. Some 350 different code names were in operation, many of which pertained to individual spies.[25] Among the most serious of those entrapped as a result of the Venona net were Julius and Ethel Rosenberg, who passed highly secret scientific information to the Soviet Union. On 19 June 1953 they were both executed. Klaus Fuchs, a German-born physicist and British citizen, who supplied information regarding the Manhattan Project, served nine years of a custodial sentence for his acts of betrayal. Yet none of the Cambridge Five, all of whom were eventually undone by the Venona project, served a single day in prison.

★

While the seeds of the work that would, eventually, undo Cairncross were germinating in the United States, he was still working for SIS's Section V, which by then had returned to London. His move to work on the Balkans had, as we have seen, severely diminished the number of documents he could provide to Gorsky. However, soon enough, in 1944, which by the end of the year saw him handled by Krötenschield, he returned to being a highly profitable source. He had access to German efforts to create Nazi resistance groups, a plan formulated on Himmler's orders in October 1944. Other material that passed under his gaze included SIS reports on the Soviet Union since the beginning of the war.[26]

Despite having moved around SIS fairly widely, and having worked on a great deal of material, Cairncross never reached the kinds of heights that Philby did. As we have seen, Philby had risen rapidly to the top. He had begun his SIS career at first as an instructor training agents. Once Section D was subsumed into the SOE, he became a senior figure in Section V, rising to be its deputy head. By 1944, he had successfully deposed Cowgill and taken command of Section IX. The other members of the Five had also advanced in terms of career. Blunt had been promoted to major and held an important role in the deception efforts preceding the Allied invasion of Europe.[27] Burgess had acquired a job as an officer in the Foreign Office News Department.[28] Finally, Maclean had the ideal posting, not merely in career terms but also for his clandestine efforts on behalf of the Soviet Union, as the Second Secretary at the British Embassy, Washington DC.[29] Cairncross, by contrast, had led no sections nor even sub-sections – he remained a junior civil servant.

This should not, however, be taken to imply that he was not in useful positions as a spy. His career had taken him to the heart of Britain's clandestine state apparatus. In 1944, he was to supply the Soviet Union with some 794 documents. Though significantly higher than the ninety-four in 1943, it did not match up with the 1942 tally of 1,454.[30] Nevertheless, the number of documents was still enormous, which explained the considerable reverence that the NKVD held for him by 1944. With the exception of those documents he was able to smuggle from his employers, which proved easy in the case of materials destined for destruction, much of the material that Cairncross produced was his own reports or transcription of documents. This proved problematic for both his handlers and the Centre in Moscow, who complained that the volume of material being supplied was difficult to handle. Moreover, it led to the delivery of 'confused or incoherent material'. One solution to this, while he was still working for Lord Hankey, had been to buy him a Minox camera. This, however, proved to be an abortive solution at simplifying his task. For all of his considerable intelligence, Cairncross was plainly unsuited to such technology and simply could not operate the device, despite the best efforts of his handlers to show him.[31]

Indeed, Cairncross' relatively lowly position, in some respects, gave him access to materials he might otherwise not have seen. Indeed, as Tim Milne persuasively argued, there was a danger that the higher Kim Philby went in SIS, the less access to the run-of-the-mill material of use to the Soviet Union he would have. After he rose to the head of Section IX, he became a potential candidate to eventually head the entire SIS enterprise, to become 'C'. As powerful as his position would have been, he would have had less knowledge of individual agents and sources in the field, his operational knowledge would have been 'broad rather than detailed', and his ability to vanish off for clandestine meetings with his Soviet handlers would have become near impossible. 'You cannot have the chief of the Secret Service taking numerous zigzag bus and Tube journeys to get from A to B.' Moreover, it would have been increasingly difficult, within Soviet intelligence circles, to keep his name known to a minimum number of people, escalating the risk of a leak that might expose their agent. He was, Milne argued, best placed, from a Soviet intelligence point of view, no higher than he rose.[32] Doubtless, Cairncross could have been a more useful agent had he been promoted further, but his access was more than sufficient to make him extremely effective for the Soviet Union.

Towards the end of the war, in 1945, Cairncross' work began to slow down, as did his interest in it. His section, by then Section I, the political wing of SIS, was being wound down. He had been transferred to it in August 1944 and there he was tasked with dealing with material on Germany and Eastern Europe. The shift occurred after the head of the section was visiting Cairncross' office. Given he was losing interest in the work, this was a logical move, and he was transferred to the Political Information Unit. The next major question was what he would do following the end of the war? SIS approached him again about staying on. Cairncross, however, suspected that this would involve both a foreign posting and the running of agents, a task to which he felt unsuited. Instead, he opted to return to the Treasury.[33]

11

The 'Ealing' Spy

Cairncross' move back to the Treasury did not prove a difficult process. He only needed to get in touch with a personnel officer he knew, Harry Wilson Smith, of whom he asked to be 'winckled [sic] out' of his wartime role.[1] With that granted, Cairncross found himself back, after a two-month delay, with his old colleagues with the rank of Principal. The date was 21 June 1945, less than a month after Victory in Europe Day on 8 May 1945.[2]

This was the end of Cairncross' war. The argument he made consistently after the allegations first emerged that he was the 'Fifth Man' of the Cambridge ring was that, while he had been a spy, he had never deliberately jeopardised Britain's interests. His motivation was to defeat Nazi Germany, and the best way of achieving that was through aiding the Soviet Union. 'I never considered myself a traitor to Britain,' he explained, 'but a patriot in the struggle against Nazism.'[3] Yet, shortly before he left SIS, he was, according to West and Tsarev, able to supply his handlers with information on British agents in Scandinavia and the Iberian Peninsula. Moscow rated the material very highly and instructed that he be thanked and rewarded with a 'present'.[4] This revelation from the Soviet archives, though impossible to verify in the current political climate, once again firmly stands in contrast to Cairncross' own estimation of his contributions to Moscow.

★

Once back in the Treasury, Cairncross claimed that his willingness to continue working for the Soviet Union had diminished rapidly. His interest in 'the political struggle' had waned, he had no love of Stalinism and now 'almost regretted' his previous espionage work for Moscow. It is possible that the full enormity of Stalin's criminality weighed upon him, but there is no evidence to confirm this. The Soviets, however, had little desire to give up their connection to him. But his relationship with the NKVD had begun to turn sour, in no small part because of a new handler, Ivan Milovzorov.[5]

Milovzorov was, according to Yuri Modin, unfit to run Moscow's 'star agents'. For a start, he was incompetent, ignoring the basic rules of trade craft, such as meeting agents in pubs. Modin lamented the ineptitude and security risked by passing around secret documents in a busy pub in full view of the clientele. Milovzorov, 'a glum, ill-tempered lout at the best of times', was also temperamentally unsuited to the task of running agents. He gave orders in an 'offensive' fashion and was 'harsh', which characters such as Cairncross, Blunt, Burgess and Philby simply would not tolerate. The result was that Cairncross' output diminished markedly.[6] Cairncross further claimed that his return to the Treasury saw his access to secret material nearly completely disappear and that the little sensitive information to which he did have access, he did not feel obliged to pass on.[7] Again, however, West and Tsarev suggest that at least some material, including that told to him by former colleagues in SIS, did make its way to his handlers. This included British intelligence reports that the Soviet Union was planning to develop a site in Yakutsk for the testing of atomic bombs.[8]

In September 1945, Cairncross was temporarily stood down. Igor Gouzenko, a member of the intelligence staff in the Soviet embassy, walked out with hundreds of classified documents hidden beneath his clothes and supplied them to the Canadian authorities. At around the same time, in Turkey, another Soviet intelligence official, Konstantin Dmitriyevich Volkov, offered to defect to the British and to bring sensitive documents with him. This would be in exchange for safety for himself and his wife, and £50,000. Philby swiftly gained wind of this development and was able to get word to his handler, who promptly had Volkov abducted back to Moscow.[9]

The Gouzenko calamity and the Volkov near miss acted like an electric shock to Soviet intelligence, which rapidly tightened up security. Meeting with agents was to become less frequent, while in the case of Cairncross it was to be suspended for a number of months. In fact, contact did not resume until June 1948. But this was to be with a new handler. It had been communicated to Nicolai Rodin, code-named 'Korovin', the London resident from 1947, that Cairncross despised Milovzorov.[10] It was time, then for him to receive a new handler. This would be Yuri Modin, code-named,

'Karel' and known to Cairncross as 'Peter'. Cairncross denied that Modin had reactivated him, but he was soon, according to Modin at least, providing documents.[11]

Once contact had been resumed and business returned to normal, Cairncross' Treasury position proved eventually to be a goldmine of information. Initially however, his position was poor. Though he had access to important documents on military lists, the requirements of the armed forces, as well as Civil Defence, none of this was particularly spectacular.[12] As Modin conceded, Moscow had little interest in the Treasury, as Cairncross was more than astute enough to realise.[13] That did not mean that it could not once again be made interesting. After asking Cairncross to go through the Treasury's phonebook and room allocations, Modin was able to build a picture of the internal geography of Cairncross' building.

What Modin was after was atomic secrets. While Cairncross lacked access to such material, it was soon determined that he might be able to acquire it from a Treasury colleague, George Oram, who occupied a nearby office. Modin and Cairncross plotted a fairly daring act of theft. However, before Cairncross could go through with it he received word that he was to be internally transferred and that the theft would have to be rushed into action. However, in the interests of preserving his security, the operation was cancelled.[14] Soon enough, however, by January 1950, it transpired that he had been transferred to work on the provision of monies for defence research. Most importantly, he had been moved into the same office as Oram and shared a drawer with him – the same drawer in which Oram kept secret papers. For Modin this stroke of luck could not have been better, Cairncross now had direct access to at least some material on atomic research.[15]

But Cairncross' access was not limited to just Treasury documents on Britain's atomic project; he had access to a wealth of additional material. To give an idea of his reach, a contemporary at the Treasury, Geoffrey A. Robinson, described Cairncross as having access to details on high-grade weapons research – not limited to the atomic, but also to the chemical and biological. Also at his fingertips was research work in a wide variety of other areas, including signals intelligence, communications technology, radar and aeronautical research, and so on.[16] Modin was 'overjoyed' by the scope and detail of the material Cairncross could provide, which showed not just how much Britain was spending on armaments but also nuclear research.[17]

★

Cairncross' access to highly sensitive Treasury material was, however, short lived. By September 1950, Cairncross had fallen out with one of his superiors, E.G. Compton. With echoes of his complaints regarding his former Foreign Office bosses, Cairncross found Compton 'a despotic character' keen on 'fault-finding'. He was moved to the foreign currency control section and, by May 1951, to the Ministry of Supply.[18]

Revealingly, regarding Cairncross' working methods, Yuri Modin also found Cairncross extremely aggravating to work with. That was not to say that Modin did not get on with Cairncross, whom he 'liked ... best of all our London agents', rather that in many respects Cairncross was, despite his astonishing results, an utterly inept spy. He was, the journalist David Leitch wrote, 'a spy from the Ealing comedies so popular at the time'.[19] He was almost constitutionally incapable of keeping to schedule, consistently forgetting appointments with his controller and mixing up the date, hour or location. In the first months, Cairncross missed all of his meetings with Modin, necessitating the latter to improvise. In the end, Modin was forced to construct an elaborate system whereby Cairncross was provided at least two precautionary back-up meetings, fallbacks for when he missed the original allotted hour (and place).[20] Like an earlier handler, Modin attempted to provide his charge with a camera, which again proved a doomed exercise. Rarely could he get the document in frame and, when he did the image produced would be out of focus or overexposed. 'Cairncross was,' Modin wrote, 'the least mechanically minded man I have ever known.'[21]

In addition to almost comic ineptitude, Cairncross was also constantly afraid of being caught, a subject that he brought up in each meeting with Modin. The fact that his own forgetfulness and lack of technical ability to even operate a camera jeopardised his security all the more simply did not register. In an effort to improve security (against Modin's wishes, who preferred the security offered by foot), the Centre provided the money for Cairncross to buy a car. This initiative also proved doomed to failure. Initially, Cairncross forgot to make the purchase. When he finally did get round to getting a car, his mechanical ineptitude meant that he could not operate it. He simply could not pass his driving test, finding himself unable to negotiate the 'knobs and pedals'. When, after many months had gone by, Cairncross finally did acquire a vehicle and successfully learned to operate it, he nearly managed to get both himself and Modin arrested. When the two met and drove away for the first time, Cairncross with clearly marked secret files in the car, he managed to stall the vehicle in front of a policeman.

In his panic, while attempting to restart the car, he made matters worse by flooding the engine. In the end the helpful Bobby helped get the car started, while Modin sat silent and terrified in the next seat, afraid that his Russian accent would give the game away if he was asked a question or uttered a sound.[22] For his part, Cairncross denied that he was ever given a car, noting that petrol was rationed, and anyway he did not drive, only to contradict himself later in his memoir: 'I sold my car and to that extent the KGB enabled me to survive.'[23]

★

By 1951, the net around the ring of five had begun to close. Donald Maclean was particularly exposed. The source of his trouble came not from within the ranks of the Soviet spies operating in Britain and the United States, but from the work being done on the Venona Project. By late 1949, the cryptanalysts of Arlington Hall had begun to put messages together. It transpired that a number of telegrams sent from Washington to Moscow between 1944 and 1945 appeared to implicate a member of the British embassy staff. The Russians described the information as 'Material G'.[24] The hunt was soon on to determine who the mysterious source 'G' might be.

The British, when informed, were remarkably lackadaisical. There were too many individuals who passed through the Embassy, telegrams were circulated too widely, and investigation might reveal to the Americans embarrassing inadequacies.[25] When he heard the evidence that there was almost certainly a leak, Guy Liddell, the Deputy Director of the Security Service, took to his diary, writing:

> Hayter, 'C' and I discussed the Washington case of leakage from our Embassy there in 1945. ... certainly two top secret documents of a Cabinet level were sent to Moscow. We transmitted O.T.P. [One Time Pad] so it must have been someone inside the Embassy. ... Hayter finally agreed, somewhat reluctantly, that we should be in charge of the case in its wider aspects, particularly owing to its ramifications here and possibly elsewhere.[26]

The challenge seemed impossible. There were simply too many candidates: some 6,000 staff had worked in the Embassy, and the investigation made very slow progress. However, in August 1950, the cryptanalysts were able to provide some more information. The Soviet consul in New York had alluded 'to correspondence between Mr. Churchill and President Roosevelt in June 1944, to a British wartime Cabinet memorandum of May 14, 1944 and – in particular – to an (as yet) unidentified telegram from Mr. Churchill to Mr. Roosevelt.' Moreover, the message suggested that 'G' had deciphered the telegram personally. This narrowed the field considerably. So too did other titbits of information, 'G' had a wife and thus was male. People were interviewed, but 'G' remained elusive and the field of suspects stubbornly failed to narrow much further.[27]

In March 1950, there was a breakthrough that proved to be a turning point in the investigation. The cryptanalysts could now show that 'G' in fact stood for 'Gomer' or 'Homer'. Moreover, 'Homer' had met with a Soviet intelligence officer in June, in Washington DC. He had also arranged a meeting in New York on 30 July 1944. By examining the movements of Embassy staff, a shortlist of suspects emerged.[28] On 11 April 1951, Guy Liddell took to his diary: 'There are two people who might possibly fill the bill; one Donald MACLEAN and the other, John RUSSELL.'[29]

Meanwhile, Philby, who had been posted to Turkey as the head of SIS's Istanbul station from 1947, was posted to Washington DC in September 1949. His job was to act as the senior British intelligence liaison in Washington. Not unnaturally, Philby paid careful attention to the Venona work being conducted. He soon warned Burgess that the project was homing in on an atomic spy, which turned out to be Klaus Fuchs.[30] Given his position, Philby was provided access to the reports that were being sent back to London and it became obvious to him that 'Homer', whom he knew to be Donald Maclean, was about to be caught.

Maclean, after his first posting to Washington in 1944, was then posted to Cairo in 1948. There his double life as both a high-flying diplomat and a Soviet agent became too much for him. A Top Secret Foreign Office briefing written in 1955 described a rapid decline in Maclean's mental state in Cairo: he engaged in a drunken brawl; he was suffering from chronic overwork; and he was rapidly descending into alcoholism. His superiors, who still deemed him to be a highly valuable member of the service, but in dire need of rest, sought to find him a less taxing position. So when a London job, as head of the American Department, came up, he was transferred. The logic behind the move was that the American Department would 'provide a suitable niche for him since this is usually the least strenuous of all the political departments'.[31] Thus, Maclean returned to a London desk job in 1950. His period of recovery in Britain would, however, be short lived.

Guy Burgess had also been active throughout the early post-war period. After a period in London with the Foreign Office, he fell foul of his superiors while on a holiday to Tangiers in November 1949. His behaviour included, 'continuous' drunkenness, altercations with MI5 and MI6 officials during which he revealed secure information, and alleged homosexual 'activities'. It was concluded that he had 'certain undesirable habits which might be a danger to security', and that as 'certain of his less desirable acquaintances might take advantage of his indiscreetness, he should be severely taken to task'. He was warned that any further 'indiscretions would mean his dismissal'. In order to keep him away from trouble, his superiors elected to send him to a different posting where his access to secret information would be minimal. Doubtless thinking of his utility to the Soviet Union, Burgess threatened to resign if he were given a 'non-political' job, and he was instead transferred to Washington DC in the capacity of Second Secretary.[32]

In Washington, however, Burgess showed no greater restraint. Outside of work, his days were spent in New York clubs and affluent homosexual haunts. He also enjoyed fast cars, picking up a number of speeding tickets, and offending the local citizenry. At a party thrown by Philby and his wife, Burgess arrived drunk and behaved poorly, treating fellow guests rudely.[33] Then things are reported to have proceeded from bad to worse, because:

> then Burgess turned to Libby Harvey [the wife of Bill Harvey, a CIA officer]. He said to her, 'how extraordinary to see the face I've been doodling all my life.' She invited him to sketch her portrait; Burgess executed a caricature so lewd and savage that Libby demanded to be taken home immediately. Bill Harvey had to be restrained from physically attacking Burgess, and was walked around the block by [CIA officer, James] Angleton until he calmed down.[34]

In all, Burgess was not selling himself to his American hosts or his British colleagues. Yet, in the end, this proved very useful for him because while Burgess was drinking and offending his nights away, Philby was pouring over Venona decrypts in mounting horror. It would only be a matter of time before Maclean was discovered and with him potentially the entire Cambridge ring, Philby included. He promptly instructed Burgess to return to Britain with plans for Maclean to defect. By a stroke of luck, or as Modin had it by design, Burgess was caught again drunkenly speeding along the US's highways, and to add insult to injury, 'bellowing' at the police when they stopped him. This was the final straw and Burgess was sent home in disgrace, just in time to inform Maclean to escape.[35] On 25 May 1951, Donald Maclean and Guy Burgess vanished.[36] They drove to Southampton, boarded a ferry and defected to the Soviet Union. Neither set foot in Britain again.

Soon enough, as a result of tipping off Maclean and Burgess, Philby soon also fell under suspicion. As one December 1951 report produced by MI5 noted, 'The Security Service has been carrying out an exhaustive investigation of PEACH [Philby] as a sequel to the disappearances of MACLEAN and BURGESS. As a result, there has emerged a very great case of suspicion that PEACH is, and has been for many years, a spy for the Russians.'[37] Though there was insufficient evidence to prosecute Philby, or even definitively determine his guilt for certain, his career as an official was over, as was his sideline in spying – for the time being at least.[38] In 1956 he moved to Beirut working as a journalist and there he renewed his ties with SIS, only again to betray his colleagues. When his activities were discovered, like Burgess and Maclean before him, he absconded to the Soviet Union in 1963.[39]

★

While the trap was closing in on Maclean, John Cairncross' life was also changing. He had met Gabrielle (Gabi) Oppenheim, who was born in 1915 in Frankfurt, the daughter of a family of commodities traders.[40] How they met and how their courtship developed is unclear, but in 1951 the pair were married. In his professional life, his move to the Ministry of Supply was not going well. He found the work uninteresting and it offered no room for the formation of policy.[41]

Nevertheless, the work did offer some advantages. Cairncross dealt with British armaments, under the supervision of Elizabeth (Betty) Ackroyd, a career civil servant who had joined the Ministry of Supply in 1940.[42] There he had access to a whole range of papers produced by multiple departments, not least the War Office, as well as committees such as the Joint War Production Committee, all of which he was able to supply to Modin. Some of this material was of such significance that it passed under the eye of Stalin himself. In total, West and Tsarev contend that in June and July alone some 1,339 pages of Cairncross material were passed on to Moscow.[43]

When Burgess and Maclean disappeared, Cairncross' life was turned upside down. In his memoirs he claimed to have been 'incredulous' and 'shattered' that they had betrayed Britain in such a complete manner.[44] Yet his own part in their story had not gone entirely unnoticed by MI5. During the investigation into the 'missing diplomats', as both the press and MI5 had taken to calling the case, Cairncross' name was discovered in Maclean's diary. Meanwhile, in searching Burgess' flat, despite his best efforts to destroy evidence prior to his departure, a fourteen-page handwritten note was discovered regarding the Foreign Office and various officials – a note partly based on named and dated discussions with those officials.[45] One of those officials named in the document was John 'Jock' Colville. When MI5 interviewed Colville, he was able to look back in his engagement book to see whom he had been speaking to on the specific dates of the conversations listed. The author was John Cairncross.[46]

The investigators soon corroborated that the handwriting belonged to Cairncross and he became a suspect. Prior to the identification of his handwriting, Cairncross had barely featured in the investigation, not appearing on the list of forty-four contacts of Guy Burgess and nor was he one of eight suspects to have emerged in the case. But, after the discovery of the note, he had his phone tapped, which revealed an odd phone call to a mysterious man named Karl, who planned to make a film about the missing diplomats. Likely aware that he might be being listened to, Cairncross responded that the film 'should show a complete victory smashing Russian attempts to get hold of Allied secrets'. Nevertheless, he was soon approached by the security services, who wanted to know why an incriminating document had been found in the flat of a known Soviet spy.[47] Things did not look good for Cairncross, as Guy Liddell noted in his diary:

> There seems to be a strong case against John CAIRNCROSS, now in the Treasury and was at one stage in Section V.
>
> A piece of paper in his handwriting, giving notes on interviews in 1939 with various officials in the Foreign Office and other departments, was found among documents belonging to BURGESS. As CAIRNCROSS is of the same Cambridge vintage as BURGESS and MACLEAN and knew them both, it looks very much as if he was at one time an agent of BURGESS.
>
> He will be interrogated on the notes and asked for an explanation.[48]

According to Cairncross, he was initially approached by an MI5 officer, Arthur Martin, in 1951, who questioned him regarding an unsigned letter sent to him about German rearmament in 1939. The letter was suspicious because it concluded with 'Fraternal Greetings', a phrase common among Communists. Cairncross could not help Martin identify the author. Martin then brought up the fact that Cairncross' name had appeared in Maclean's diary shortly before his defection. For this, Cairncross had no explanation.[49] This addition to Cairncross' memoirs is unsurprising: the file containing summaries of his interviews with MI5 clearly note this meeting with Martin. However, the first interview summarised in the file was with W. Jim Skaron, not Martin, and dated 3 April, and Guy Liddell's diary entry for 3 April 1952 notes that same event. Liddell did not make mention of the earlier interrogation by Martin.[50]

Regardless, Jim Skardon, who certainly did interview Cairncross in 1952, was an MI5 officer of no small repute. A former Detective Inspector in the Metropolitan Police, Skardon was regarded as the foremost interrogator in Britain. He had been the man selected to crack the atom spy, Klaus Fuchs, and had successfully extracted a full confession.[51] Certainly when he interviewed Cairncross for the first time, in the Treasury, he blindsided his opponent almost immediately. Cairncross had begun the interrogation feigning ignorance; denying having corresponded with Burgess or that he had a reason to provide him with information; and, contended that their acquaintance had only ever been sporadic. Having walked Cairncross into a trap, Skardon played his trump card:

> I then showed him the 14 page document traced to BURGESS's possession. He asked to be allowed to examine it and as he did so it became apparent that he had suffered a major shock by the production of this document. He read the first page or two carefully and then passed quickly to the end, and he was practically speechless. I thought it was opportune at this moment to caution him, and I did so quite formally.[52]

More than forty years later, Cairncross remembered the moment vividly, 'I froze as soon as I recognised my own handwriting. ... I was thunderstruck and muttered that I was out of my depth. Skardon simply smiled at my confusion and commented that he was swimming nicely.'[53] Skardon then changed tack, becoming friendly, offering to provide legal advice and to proceed with the interview off the record, so as to avoid 'legal obligations'. Cairncross agreed and then claimed that the document had been penned in order 'to assist his own reasoning, for it was prepared in a style which he adopted when considering any academic subject'. He said it consisted merely of summaries of political discussions that were all the result of chance meetings. As for its appearance in Burgess' possession,

> He believed at the time that he talked to BURGESS that he had no idea that BURGESS was interested in obtaining this sort of information for the purpose of passing it on to any other power. He believed at the time that he talked to BURGESS that he was merely discussing political matters with an individual who was vitally interested in them on their own account. He was at a loss to explain why such words as 'my informant' should appear in this document and thought he would take a day or two to arrange his thoughts in a sufficiently orderly manner to give a cogent and reasoned explanation of the circumstances in which he passed the document to BURGESS.

At the close of the meeting, Skardon informed Cairncross that if he was telling the truth then there were no grounds for prosecution, but regardless in all likelihood his Civil Service career was over. While Cairncross' superiors made their decision regarding his future, Cairncross agreed to go on holiday. Later that day, he was suspended by the Treasury and his details were passed to the port authorities lest he attempt to abscond.[54]

Guy Liddell, in particular, was unimpressed. He took to his diary to dissect Cairncross' claims:

> Cairncross has been seen. He was extremely perturbed when confronted with the document in his own handwriting which had been found amongst the papers of BURGESS. His statement is somewhat contradictory; on the one hand he says that he gave BURGESS the information because he thought that he was working for some Government organisation and that it would be in his, CAIRNCROSS', interests to keep in with him. On the other hand, he says that he was extremely nervous when he tried to get his notes back and was told by BURGESS that he had either lost or destroyed them. A further point which is not in his favour relates to an incident reported by the Watchers. He apparently deposited in a waste paper basket in one of the Parks, a copy of the Communist Review of current date. This would have been understandable in the circumstances

if the copy had been an old one, but it is difficult to see how a man who describes himself as having given up his Communist ideas and as having become a Churchillian, would go on wasting his time reading such turgid material as the Communist Review.[55]

Cairncross had arranged to meet with Modin, but, as Liddell noted, he was being watched. Modin claimed that as he was approaching Cairncross, he spotted two individuals behaving strangely and walked away from the meeting.[56]

The ordeal for Cairncross was, however, only just beginning. In a second interview he was asked to give a formal statement, which was transcribed and signed. In it he repeated his primary claim that he had no idea that Burgess was a spy and that he had flirted with Communism while at Cambridge but was a reformed character. He presented himself as having been a naïve young man, 'much impressed by his [Burgess'] wide and apparently inside knowledge of what was going on and of the elevated and influential circles in which he moved'. Moreover, Cairncross 'was under the impression that he was in a secret department', so in his mind it amounted to nothing more than a friendly exchange of political information between colleagues. He further 'imagined that I was possibly ingratiating myself with someone in M.I.5 who might stand me in good stead if ever my Communist associations were brought against me'.[57]

In his summary of this second interview, Skardon noted that after his statement Cairncross mentioned that he had been worried that Burgess' 'possession of such a paper … would enable him to blackmail CAIRNCROSS into providing further secret information'. This was a blunder on Cairncross' part. As Skardon wrote, 'This I feel almost certainly betokened a knowledge of the sinister possibilities of this association with BURGESS. At the very least it demonstrates that whatever he may have heard about BURGESS being employed in a secret department, he was not completely satisfied that BURGESS was entirely loyal.' If Cairncross had no idea that Burgess was a spy, why was he suspicious that Burgess might use blackmail to extract still more information?[58]

In a third and final interview, Skardon attempted to resolve that contradiction, but found it 'quite impossible to shake him on this, and he seemed to be quite unaffected by the direct attack made upon him'. The rest of the interview was spent going over the various individuals that Cairncross had mentioned in his previous interviews and statement as well as individuals on Burgess' list of contacts. In the end, Skardon was 'eventually satisfied' that Cairncross 'was "coming clean" at every point ... I have the very pronounced feeling that he is completely under control.' Skardon might have been convinced, but not everybody in MI5 was. In perhaps one of the most perceptive pieces of marginalia adorned to a secret document, someone faintly inscribed 'of whom!' after 'he is completely under control'.[59]

Regardless, Cairncross had survived. He had stuck to his guns and aside from a few contradictions, he had given nothing away. The investigation continued, but the case against him did not progress. As a document, likely written around 1953, summarising the security case he posed, noted, 'He explained that he regarded it [the Burgess' note] as being in the nature of an interdepartmental exchange of information, but now realises the enormity of his offence in doing so.'[60] The only penalty Cairncross endured was that his Civil Service career was over.

12

New Careers

Following his departure from the Civil Service, Cairncross had cause for both celebration and no small anxiety. On the one hand he had escaped prosecution and had successfully pulled the wool over Skardon's eyes. After well over a decade spent spying against his own country, from an acutely sensitive vantage point at the heart of the Civil Service and intelligence community, there was nothing MI5 could do about it. They might have had their suspicions, but if there was any credible basis for prosecution it was evidently not available. To add icing to the cake, he had always been a nervous spy and that life was now behind him, as was his otherwise tedious Civil Service job with its limited prospects for promotion. Nevertheless, it was still *a* job and his resignation had left him bereft of an income. Unemployment presented a serious financial problem indeed. Several months earlier, he had married Gabi and the need for a steady income was all the more pressing. He was able to keep his head above water by borrowing money from his brother, Alec, and selling the car Soviet intelligence had bought for him. However, this clearly was not a long-term solution to his financial difficulties; he needed to find a new job. But besides the financial inconvenience, his most pressing concern was preventing Gabi from learning the truth behind his resignation.[1]

Not only had he spent his professional career wrapped in secrets, keeping his dual loyalties very much to himself, he had, at the same time, been keeping these from his family – Gabi would prove no different. This stood him in stark contrast to Maclean, who entrusted his wife Melinda with his secrets and even discussed with her the possibility of passing intelligence via the wife of a Soviet diplomat. 'Melinda,' Modin wrote, 'was quite prepared to do this.'[2]

Cairncross' initial plan was to acquire a university post, but his efforts to find an academic job failed. He had spent the previous decade and a half working in the Civil Service, which had limited his opportunity to engage in scholarly pursuits. Looking to bolster his chances, he wrote to his friend and long-time confidant, the novelist Graham Greene, to both update him of his tricky position and ask for a letter of reference.[3] A graduate from Oxford, one of the universities to which Cairncross had applied for work, and a major name in the world of literature, seeking Greene's support was an obvious strategy. Similarly, Cairncross turned to his old boss, Lord Hankey, for a reference. Despite the ready support of these influential voices and Cairncross' undeniable scholarly talent, it was not to be. Cairncross failed to win any of the three academic posts to which he applied.[4] Undoubtedly, his most significant problem was that, aside from his undergraduate degree, he had no scholarly credentials.

Instead, Cairncross looked to continental Europe for opportunities. He was, after all, a highly gifted and qualified linguist and set about looking for work as a translator. In the end, Cairncross and Gabi settled in Rome, where they moved into a villa in Via dei Pamphili. Gabi and Cairncross had met in London and formed a romance. However, shortly before they married, Gabi had moved to California. Nevertheless, she returned to Britain and the couple were wed on 26 January 1951 in the Kensington Registry Office.[5] Once in Rome, Gabi swiftly found work as a secretary at the Food and Agriculture Organisation (FAO) of the United Nations. Like Cairncross, she was a gifted linguist, which undoubtedly aided her in acquiring her FAO job. She had moved to Britain in the 1930s (presumably fleeing the recently empowered Nazis) and gained British citizenship in 1934.[6] Upon her arrival, she began to work with the Jewish Refugee Council and maintained contacts with the Anglo–Jewish community throughout her life. Indeed, during the 1960s, Gabi was the secretary of the Anglo–Jewish Association, retiring from that role in 1974.[7]

In Rome, Cairncross became a freelance translator and journalist. He was a correspondent for *The Economist*, *The Glasgow Herald*, *The Observer*'s International Service and did work for the Canadian Broadcasting Corporation.[8] Journalism was a job to which he was plainly well suited. He enjoyed the variety of topics that he could cover, which included his particular areas of interest – the cultural and religious. Of particular mention in his memoirs was travelling to Sicily to interview a young woman who professed to have witnessed a miracle. She claimed her statuette of the Virgin Mary had begun weeping. Soon crowds of people had congregated around her house to witness the marvel. Indeed, in the bizarre tale Cairncross related originally for *The Observer*, the 'tears' had allegedly been subjected to scientific analysis and proved to be genuine human tears. The story was, he contended, of 'an Italy that had almost disappeared'.[9] Adding to the drama, both the Vatican and the Communist Party involved themselves, the former to offer their approval of the miracle and the latter to disprove it. An atheist himself, and perhaps as an individual with a complex history with Communism, Cairncross added a slightly cynical comment that 'the financial situation of the family has been transformed'.[10]

Cairncross also covered a range of other subjects in his journalism; these included but weren't limited to topical pieces such as Italy's declining birth rate in the 1950s as compared with other European nations; the discovery of historical works of art and relics, as well as economic resources such as uranium and oil; and the brutal treatment by the Soviet Union of Italian prisoners of war, who had been forced to resort to cannibalism to survive.[11]

All in all, Cairncross had landed on his feet. His and Gabi's income was steady, sufficient even to afford the luxury of buying a car. He had an income from his flat in London, which he rented out, he had his money from journalism and the UN, and Gabi was also bringing in an income. The Mediterranean diet, which replaced fats with olive oil, had cleared up a liver problem with which he had been suffering and he found his work and intellectual pursuits both fascinating and rewarding. He further supplemented his income by taking translation jobs for the United Nations in Rome.[12]

Soon enough he further added to his repertoire by engaging in scholarly pursuits.[13] His first major project was a book on his favourite author, Molière – after whom the KGB had code-named him years before.

The one clear downside was that that his life in Italy separated him from his family in Scotland, and as a result he wrote lengthy, rambling letters, particularly to his brother, Alec. In one letter, to Alec's wife Mary, he beseeched her to 'write from time to time', and expressed a desire to keep closer contact with them and the children in particular.[14]

★

Cairncross' first real taste of academic work, after university, came from his elder brother, Andrew – an authority on Shakespeare who had completed a

PhD in English at the University of Glasgow. Shortly before John resigned from the Civil Service, Andrew had been working on a project regarding Shakespeare's finances, looking to discover how much the famous playwright earned from his work. However, the study had been commissioned for a French series. As such, he proposed to John that he, Andrew, would conduct the research and present the findings, while John should analyse the financial information and translate the work into French.[15]

At that time he was still considering university posts, and the problem of limited status in the academic world still remained. Even with his work with Andrew, Cairncross needed to build up his scholarly credentials. He required publications. As it happened, he had been writing, in his spare time, on Molière since his student days. The additional time afforded to him by his sudden change in career allowed him to complete a book manuscript. The problem he found, however, was that publishers were reticent to take it. This, he reasoned, was because again he lacked evidence of scholarly expertise in the form of published, scholarly articles.[16] Nevertheless, despite initial setbacks, his first scholarly appraisal of Molière, *New Light on Molière: Tatuffe; Elomire Hypocondre*, was published in 1956 in Geneva by Librairie E. Droz and in Paris by Librairie Minard.[17]

Jean-Baptiste Poquelin Molière was born in 1622 from a well-to-do family, his father being an upholsterer and valet to King Louis XIII, a post into which Jean-Baptiste would follow. However, as a young man, he decided to become an actor. He formed a company of actors and earned a living touring for twelve years. On his return to Paris, he appeared in a Corneille play and caught the eye of Louis XIV. By this time, Molière had begun penning his own comedic plays, and gained success with *Les Précieuses ridicules* (The Affected Ladies), a comedy of manners that premiered in 1659. Over the course of his career, he wrote numerous comedies that skewered and satirised a wide variety of groups and professions. In *Dom Juan ou le Festin de pierre* (Dom Juan or The Feast with the Statue), he took aim at religion, a dangerous topic at the time.[18]

New Light on Molière, was, in essence, a re-examination of the origins of *Tartuffe ou L'Imposteur* (Tartuffe, or the impostor, or the hypocrite), a five-act play and one of Molière's best-known dramatic comedies. First performed in 1664, *Tartuffe*, though appreciated by the public, proved inflammatory with the upper echelons of the French Roman Catholic Church. The central character, the hypocrite Tartuffe, was dressed in semi-clerical attire, which immediately ruffled feathers. The play was rewritten and performed in 1667 only once, before it too was banned. It was not until 1669 that Molière produced a version of the play that could survive the censor. The central problem that Cairncross tried to solve was establishing the content of the original 1664 play. This was no easy task because all traces of the original play had long been lost. The central argument presented in *New Light on Molière* was that the original was a complete play in three acts, which were acts I, III and IV of what eventually became the 1669 version. This conclusion placed him at odds with the general expert consensus. This was that the 1664 play was an incomplete work, comprised of the first three acts.[19]

New Light on Molière was a short book that comprised seventy-eight pages of advanced scholarship. Cairncross had first formed an interest in the question addressed by the book while an undergraduate at Cambridge, having been set an essay on the topic by his French tutor, Professor Henry Ashton.[20] The text itself was and remains a challenging read, which assumed expertise on the part of the reader and considerable familiarity with *Tartuffe*. Cairncross also deployed a dense style of prose, in which he inserted French liberally without translation, again taking no prisoners when it came to assumptions regarding the abilities of his readership. It also included a short preface by Raymond Picard, written entirely in French and with no translation.

Picard was a professor at the Sorbonne and noted expert on the seventeenth-century playwright Jean Racine. His preface was, as to be expected, a glowing account of the volume and concluded by noting that the quality of the two essays ranked Cairncross among the best scholars of seventeenth-century French literature.[21] Some years later, in 1970, Cairncross would repay the favour and translated Picard's own book, *Two Centuries of French Literature*.[22] However, as glowing as Picard had been in his preface, other scholars were, while generally positive, pointedly critical of some aspects of Cairncross' contribution to Molière scholarship.

A review of the book by Gustave Charlier in 1957 in *Revue belge de philologie et d'histoire*, was largely favourable, noting the detail and ingenuity of the argument, but ultimately found it insufficiently compelling to change his mind. In a similarly critical review, Marcel Gutwirth suggested that Cairncross' enthusiasm had led him to 'overestimate' the strength of the argument he presented and that the book was 'marred' by overstatement. However, Gutwirth qualified his criticism, noting that nevertheless *New Light on Molière* was an important contribution to the field.[23] Of course, the reviews were not negative, but their praise was qualified by serious criticism and misgivings. This, did not, however, prevent either Cairncross or the publisher of his later book, a collection of poems entitled *By a Lonely Sea*, quoting those reviews stripped of negativity.[24]

★

While Cairncross was busy building his life in Rome, the British secret services had not lost interest in him.[25] Foreign Office officials, and no doubt MI5, continued trying to build up a picture of his activities. In 1953, Sir Maurice Hankey's son, Henry (later appointed as the British Ambassador to Panama in 1966), was contacted 'for a word' about his knowledge of Cairncross. It is inconceivable that others were not also quietly questioned.[26] The authorities knew where he lived (number 6, Via dei Pamphili, Rome); that Gabi was working for the FAO; and that he had taken tests to qualify him to work as an interpreter for the United Nations. They were also aware that he was working on his Molière book. The Foreign Office considered asking SIS agents in Rome to keep tabs on their former employee and suggested that the British Ambassador and Embassy staff be warned of Cairncross' presence in the city.[27]

Far more significant for the intelligence community was the issue of the 'missing diplomats'. The embarrassing fact was that Britain's intelligence community had very little idea where Burgess and Maclean were and could not even confirm to their family members that the two men had indeed defected. That would change when, in 1954, the Soviet official Vladimir Petrov defected to Australia. Petrov had been the Third Secretary of the Soviet Embassy in Canberra. Under Petrov's command was one Filip Vasilyevich Kislitsyn. As luck would have it, in the 1940s Kislitsyn had been tasked with telegraphing Burgess and Maclean's most important documents from London to Moscow and in 1949 he manned the archive containing these documents.[28] In 1951, when the pair defected, it was Kislitsyn who orchestrated their safe passage across the Czech border.[29] Three years later, in 1954, when he was posted to Canberra, the unsuspecting Kislitsyn passed on this crucial information to Petrov who, in turn following his defection, told Australian intelligence.

It was not until the Australian government, their intelligence officers having interrogated Petrov, passed on summaries of his statements that the British became any the wiser regarding Burgess and Maclean's location.

By April the *Daily Express* had the story, but the British government did not publish its own report on the matter until 1955.[30] This created a headache for the Secretary of State for Foreign Affairs, Selwyn Lloyd. On 3 May 1954, the newly elected Conservative MP, Tom Iremonger, challenged Lloyd on what the government knew regarding the fate of the 'missing diplomats'. He was soon followed by a raft of other MPs who also demanded answers. The unfortunate Lloyd, put on the spot, was only able to respond that 'in security matters it is important not to let the other side know how much we know'.[31] In February 1956, Burgess and Maclean were back in the news again, this time because they had been granted permission by the Soviet authorities to give a statement to the press, something that the publicity-seeking Burgess had been attempting to achieve since his arrival in Russia.[32]

Indeed, the 'missing diplomats' case returned to the news cycle again and again throughout the 1950s. Another high-profile case, in the wake of Burgess and Maclean's statement, blew up yet again in 1956. This time a series of anonymous articles appeared in *The People*, a Sunday tabloid, in March and April. The articles not only linked the author with Burgess, but were also deliberately sensational. The angry commentary, directed largely at Burgess, included complaints of his 'unnatural vices' and the contention that he and Maclean escaped capture for so long because they had enjoyed the protection of powerful figures. The author of the articles was Goronwy Rees, a fact that interested parties did not take long to establish. Foolishly, he had allowed journalists to alter his rather less sensational narrative into the tawdry story that was eventually published. This was unfortunate, because at the time Rees sat on the government inquiry on the question of whether homosexuality should be legalised. Given the nature of some of the comments about Burgess, plainly that could not continue.[33]

On a professional level, the impact of *The People* articles damaged Rees significantly. Since 1953, he had served as the Principal of the University College Wales, Aberystwyth. His connection and former close friendship with Burgess fatally undermined his position. Despite an overwhelming vote of confidence in Rees from Aberystwyth's students, eventually he was forced to resign.[34]

★

By 1956, Cairncross and Gabi had relocated to Geneva.[35] At around that time, Cairncross had successfully applied for a visitor's visa to travel to the

United States but, for reasons unknown, chose not to go.[36] In 1957, a colleague, who worked for the United Nations in New York, recommended Cairncross for a role as chief editor for The Economic Council for Asia and the Far East (ECAFE) based in Bangkok, which he duly took.[37] Cairncross was immediately captivated by Thailand, its culture and its people. He enjoyed what he called the 'subtle blend of Indian and Chinese traits' and developed a variety of positive cultural assumptions regarding the Thai people. They were, by European standards he insisted, given to a remarkable degree of tolerance and friendliness.[38]

While in Thailand, Cairncross also continued with his literary endeavours. His long-term scholarly project, which also dated back to his Civil Service days, was as a translator of seventeenth-century French literature. The target of his efforts was the play *Phaedra*, by the great author of seventeenth-century plays, Jean Racine. Cairncross' earliest attempt to translate *Phaedra* into English was sent to the BBC, which rejected his effort as being 'staid'. This was published in 1958 by Librairie E. Droz. As with Molière, Racine was a quintessential seventeenth-century French playwright and historiographer, but unlike Molière, who largely wrote comedies, Racine was most famed for his tragedies, notably *Phaedra*. What Racine did have in common with Molière, however, was that he challenged contemporary French orthodoxies, notably the treatment of the poor and the corrupt judicial system.[39] Racine has long been noted as a playwright who has proved extraordinarily difficult to translate. As Patrick Swinden put it, 'There is something about the speed, pace, sound, and grammatical disposition of the words in Racine's hexameters that won't go into English.'[40]

Similarly, Cairncross noted in his own foreword to his 1958 edition of *Phaedra* that, 'It has often been declared that Racine cannot be translated,' however, 'My own feeling is that an English version, however far it falls short, is better than none at all.'[41] In 1966, Cairncross revealed his solution to the problem presented by Racine, the English translation had used blank verse of ten syllables. However, in the French medium 'the poet has twelve'. This created a problem, Racine needed to be condensed by a sixth and each non-essential syllable stripped away, 'or else abandon literal transposition and devise a concise formula which gives the gist of Racine's line.' Central to Cairncross' translations, he argued, was 'the need for accuracy. Racine is as precise as he is concise – and he is clear.' The key was to preserve Racine's 'subtle, taut, and exquisite verse'.[42] In this his finished product was plainly judged to have succeeded; the

Times Literary Supplement offered a glowing review, praising the effort to 'reproduce the conciseness and the succinctness of the French ... the sinewy tautness of the English blank verse rhythm'. The reviewer gushingly concluded that, 'It is not merely the best English translation known to the present reviewer: it is far more impressive than anyone could have dared to hope.'[43]

The successful effort to publish his translation of *Phaedra* soon generated additional offers of work. Cairncross had long been trying to engage major outlets for his translations. The BBC having already rejected him, he attempted in 1954, again without success, to interest Penguin Books. However, with a Racine play published and with a good review in the *Times Literary Supplement*, Penguin soon approached him regarding the translation of two further plays. Cairncross was both pleased yet also haughtily vindicated. 'This is exactly what I prophesied would happen,' he informed his brother, Alec, 'Get into print outside England and what the English publishers told you was impossible becomes possible overnight.'[44] Regardless of his annoyance at their earlier rejection, in 1963 Penguin Classics published his translations of *Iphigenia*, *Phaedra* and *Athaliah* in a single volume. This process was not all plain sailing. E. V. Rieu, the noted scholar, classicist, translator and editor of the Penguin Classics series, soon offended the prickly Cairncross with his editorial insights. 'Rieu intervened,' Cairncross wrote to Greene, 'to query such vital points as the omission of an *op cit* in the case of an author I had repeatedly quoted, and also to ask Who *is* Giraudoux? Such are the masters of our culture'.[45]

Cairncross' efforts were not merely restricted to his beloved French seventeenth-century playwrights. He also soon began a number of other projects. The most notable of these was the production of a collection of poetry, *By a Lonely Sea*, which was published by Hong Kong University Press in 1959. The collection includes translations of French, Italian, Spanish and German poets. These primarily range from Renaissance authors, not least the great Italian poet Gaspara Stampa, to Cairncross' contemporaries. The final section of the volume includes a number of Cairncross' own efforts. Selected over a quarter of a century, the basis for inclusion was 'simply because they sang with iterative compulsion in the memory'. Importantly from the point of view of Cairncross' developing professional career as a translator, the book included a personal philosophy when it came to the art of translation. 'For the essence of the craft,' Cairncross informed his readers, 'is surely to be as literal as possible but to reproduce the music tension and impact of the original.'[46] Certainly, a number of the translations and original poems reflected Cairncross' own favouring of blank verse, as a means of producing literal translation.

Cairncross also appears to have begun projects that never material-ised into published work. For instance, in a letter to his brother Alec, in December 1958, he made reference to a study on Phaulkon – presum-ably Constantine Phaulkon, the Greek merchant who became an advisor to King Narai of Ayutthaya – due for completion the following month.[47] He wrote about the text repeatedly over the following few years, but what became of that work remains a mystery.

While in Thailand, Cairncross was ideally located to travel across east and southeast Asia. This, Cairncross took full advantage of, attending conferences in Malaysia, Japan and Laos for his work with ECAFE. In Laos, he even gave a speech attended by significant dignitaries, including an unspecified Prime Minister.[48] While not working, travelling or writing, he and Gabi also took advantage of the local scenery, relaxing on deserted beaches.[49] Looking back, Cairncross described the period as 'four wonderful years working with delightful people of all nationalities'.[50]

★

By 1961 Cairncross and Gabi had moved back to Rome.[51] His inter-est in Thailand, however, remained and he was a member of the Siam Society from 1964 until at least 1983.[52] In 1963, his marriage on the rocks, Cairncross moved to Karachi to work on Pakistan's Planning Committee and, while there, was enjoying the 'local scene'.[53] This included what he would describe as 'private attractions'. This consisted of attending exotic parties where he interacted with the great and good, as he described in a letter to Graham Greene:

> Last night, I was at a dinner at the Sudan Embassy replete with Princess Amina (the best belly dancer in these parts) her husband (from the English Royal family 'but way down' -- hence the 'Princess') a couple of young Polish maidens, a young English couple (and the local Pole who is having affairs with about all the girls present), a Pakistani girl who turned Catholic and myself. I concentrated on the immediately preceding guest and had a most profitable conversation. However, when the inevitable suggestion was made that we should all go off to the local nightclub, she

declined. But I hope to continue the contact on religious–as well as non-religious–matters.[54]

However, the real purpose of Cairncross' letter to Greene, besides sharing tales of Princess Amina,[55] was, once again, to beg for a letter of reference (as he had done a decade earlier) from his famous friend. As he had attempted before, Cairncross was determined to land himself an academic job. Dr Lester Crocker, an 'old buddy' from Cairncross' Cambridge days, wrote to report he had been promoted to Dean at the Western Reserve University, in Cleveland, Ohio. This meant that the newly minted Dean had left behind a post as the head of Romance Languages. Cairncross, Crocker suggested, would be an excellent candidate to take up the vacant position and that he should apply forthwith. All Greene was required to do was to assure the learned members of the hiring committee that Cairncross was 'all right' and could 'be trusted with their students provided that they're not too attractive'. Greene, as ever, obligingly wrote to them:

> I have known John Cairncross for some twenty years both as a colleague and as a friend and I would like to support his application for the Chair of Romance Languages at the Western Reserve University. He has not only the qualifications of a scholar but also the ability to convey his own enthusiasm for the subject to others.[56]

Greene's letter, and no doubt Cairncross' genuine ability as a scholar, now confirmed by publications, impressed. He was duly appointed and Cairncross left the Old World.

13

Confession

If things were going well for Cairncross professionally, they were not going well personally. His marriage to Gabi had ended in separation shortly before his move to Karachi. Quite what happened to the relationship is difficult to establish. In his memoir, Cairncross skirted its collapse in less than half a sentence: 'I have always been lucky in the circumstantial things of life, if not the essentials – for my wife and I had by now separated.'[1] In the midst of the separation, Alec Cairncross recorded in his diary that,

Gabi came with us to Cambridge and dined with me the previous evening at my club. She was positive that John didn't go to Pakistan to get away from his mother-in-law and that the idea of making money was only part of the story. He felt that he owed her security (in the form of cash) but got through a lot of what he earned and didn't appreciate the kind of security she really needed.[2]

In 1964, after the separation, he wrote a letter of commiseration to Eunice Frost, formerly of Penguin Books, who herself was undergoing a relationship crisis. In his letter he revealed some of his own hopes and fears for the future, which as ever were tempered by financial fears.

I am sorry about [Frost's 'bad blow'] (as a matter of fact you mentioned this in your first letter). I am myself just moving into a separate flat, at vast expense, and hope ultimately to marry again, though goodness knows when since, quite apart from finding a future wife at my advanced age, the commitments I will have to meet in supporting my present one will take away any surplus cash there may be. At the moment it looks like a smashing deficit. … I hope that somehow things will get brighter on the personal side for you.[3]

The letter, revealed a sensitive, considerate and humanist side to his character. Where he could often be eccentric and occasionally combative, his letter to Frost was one of warm empathy. The self-assurance and assertive tone had vanished and instead he revealed his own fears and loneliness came to the forefront, matched only by a genuine concern for Eunice. In addition to regaling her with his own problems, he also offered his advice on suitable locations for a recuperative vacation in Europe, invited her to Rome and offered to be her guide around the city.

★

Given the situation, Cairncross' appointment to The Western Reserve University heralded what he hoped would be a new start. He moved to Ohio, passing through Britain on his way from Italy.[4] Obtaining work in academia, as numerous attempts made clear, had been a long-term objective and this was his third, and at last successful, attempt at achieving that goal. He was genuinely well suited to academic life, as his studies and translations of seventeenth-century French Romantic literature attested. Not only did he find the work rewarding and enjoyable, he also appreciated the intellectual company to be found in a university senior common room. Though he never noted it explicitly, he doubtless enjoyed the prestige that accompanied the post. In 1964, he wrote to Graham Greene to report his happiness and to thank him for his letter of recommendation, 'which impressed the powers that be and has given me great standing here. (I need it. A coloured porter asked me the other day, in my hotel: "Do you go to school here, Sir!").'

'I have excellent colleagues,' he further added, and 'the administrative side is child's play given a good secretary and my experience at the Treasury; and the Art Gallery, the Orchestra and other facilities are outstanding.' He also reported that his 'sex life' had also taken a turn for the better: 'American life is as rich as I had expected. I am now convined [sic] that the over developed countries are really far more exotic and amusing than the under developed ones, sex life included.' He had met a troubled colleague, undergoing an ugly divorce that had driven her to 'pseudo suicide' attempts and he quickly formed a relationship with her. She was, he reported to Greene, 'the nearest thing to genuine I've come across [read, thinks along Cairncross lines], the experience is extremely interesting'.[5] His happiness was to be short-lived.

His move to Cleveland had brought him squarely back to the attention of MI5. Having been successful in his application to the Western Reserve University, Cairncross duly applied to the United States for a visa. It was this that brought him back onto MI5's radar.[6] His 1952 'confession', though pulling the wool over Jim Skardon's eyes, had not convinced everybody in MI5. As J.E.D. Street of the Foreign Office noted in a secret report written in February 1964, MI5 had 'felt for some time that they never got the full truth out of Cairncross'. His move to the US provided the Security Service an opportune moment to have a second bite at the cherry. Cairncross was, Street noted, 'outside the jurisdiction' of MI5 and, as such, might be willing to talk. Presenting the entire affair as good fortune, Street went on to note that Arthur Martin, an MI5 officer, just so happened to be in the United States at that time and could simply drop by.[7] The central question for MI5 and the Foreign Office was what to tell the American authorities? There were two considerations:

(i) that we should not get into a position in which any American authority could accuse us of having concealed relevant security information from them;

(ii) that it might be momentarily embarrassing in public or Parliament here if a complaint was made that an American visa had been refused to a British subject because of information given by H.M.G. to the U.S. authorities.

2. I would hope that the first of these points would be considered more important and that we should therefore authorise the C.I.A. to give the U.S. Immigration Service as much information as they think necessary, adding a strong request that if a visa was refused this should not on any account be attributed to information derived from us.[8]

Of course, the point that MI5 suddenly had an opportunity because Cairncross was 'outside the jurisdiction', was doubtless partly true. His arrival in the US presented a golden opportunity for a new round of interviews. That said, Cairncross had been residing abroad, 'outside the jurisdiction', in various different countries for over a decade. Why was his move to the US significantly different? The answer to this question remains unclear. MI5 could have arranged to interview Cairncross while he was in Italy, as it would, in fact, later do.

★

The man sent to talk to Cairncross was Arthur Martin, who had joined MI5 shortly after the Second World War and shown himself to be a skilled operator. He had been involved in both the Fuchs and Maclean cases and, had Maclean not defected shortly before he was apprehended, would doubtless have caught him.[9] Martin certainly imprinted himself indelibly in the memories of those Soviet spies he interrogated. Michael Straight recalled him as 'sophisticated and urbane'.[10] Kim Philby wrote that he was 'a quiet young man … He remained silent throughout, watching my movements. When I looked out the window, he made a note; when I twiddled my thumbs, he made another note.'[11] Cairncross was similarly impressed, and described a 'trim dapper figure' with a 'quiet manner' who transpired to be 'one of the most effective intelligence officers I have ever met'.[12]

Certainly, that proved to be the case. In April he was doorstepped by an FBI agent, who had called to let him know that Martin would be dropping in to talk to him. The agent had obviously been well briefed, had known that Cairncross liked poetry and knew how to handle his man. He noted that his wife shared similar interests and a flattered Cairncross even gave him a book of poetry to pass to his spouse. Martin arrived a few days later and 'radiated intelligence and efficiency'. He conducted a systematic interrogation with a polite and professional manner.

He informed Cairncross that in 1952 he had withheld the truth, which immediately told Cairncross that the game was up. He recalled in his memoirs the moment that he knew that he was done for. It was clear to him that, once again, the life and career he had built was over. Even if he escaped prosecution, he would be dogged for the rest of his life by MI5 officials. As such he 'was determined to make an end of this cat and mouse game once and for all, and even briefly contemplated suicide'. Instead, he poured himself a whisky and gave a considerably fuller confession than he had provided in 1952.[13]

Precisely what Cairncross said in the interview, which he dubiously claimed in his memoirs amounted to a full confession, is unclear. As yet, Martin's report, if it still exists, remains withheld from the public. However, it seems highly unlikely that it was the full truth of the matter. It does not appear to have made mention of atomic secrets or any other form of military research and development. It was, however, certainly full enough to cause major alarm bells to sound in Whitehall. As Foreign Office official, J.E.D. Street, recorded:

> 2. The Security Service have now told me that Mr. Cairncross was interviewed in the United States by Mr. Martin and has confessed to having been recruited by the Russian Intelligence Service as a spy in 1936 and to having worked for them until 1951, when he was dropped after the flight of Burgess and Maclean. Cairncross said that Burgess was the only British collaborator with the R.I.S. whom he personally had known as such.*

> 3. Cairncross entered the Foreign Service in 1936 but was transferred to the Home Civil Service two years later. He subsequently worked for the Treasury, G.C.H.Q., M.I.6 and the Ministry of Supply; he must have been an extremely valuable agent for the Russians. Having made this confession, Cairncross will no doubt be careful never to enter British territory again.[14]

This summary of Cairncross reveals a number of important points. First, the claims in Cairncross' memoirs to having only been an 'agent for the duration' of the war, were contradicted in his confession to Martin. Second, the document may suggest that Cairncross had admitted to knowing that Burgess was a fellow spy; once again this contradicts his memoirs.[15]

Earlier, in 1961, the KGB officer Anatoliy Golitsyn, code-named 'Kago' by the British, defected to the USA. One key piece of information that he was able to reveal was that in Britain, during the 1930s, a highly important 'ring' of five spies had been recruited from Cambridge.[16] It was soon postulated that Cairncross might be one of the five. As a dossier on Cairncross, sent by the Director General of MI5, Sir Roger Hollis, to the Foreign Office's Sir Bernard Burrows, made clear:

---

* 'as such' was penned in later by J.E.D. Street.

KAGO has mentioned a British spy network known as the Ring of Five, of which BURGESS, MACLEAN and PHILBY are believed to have been members. KAGO understood that this was a ring of five young men who were all known to one another and possibly University students together who had been recruited to the R.I.S. [Russian Intelligence Service] in the 1930s. If CAIRNCROSS was a spy, it is possible that he was one of this Ring of Five.[17]

Of course, Cairncross had not attended university with either Philby or Maclean. But what if Golitsyn was wrong about that detail? While that difficult question was being asked, MI5, who unlike the Foreign Office had clearly not been keeping close tabs on him, scrambled to find out more regarding Cairncross' movements and activities since 1952. They had been under the impression that he and Gabi had been living in Italy the entire time, from his departure from Britain to his move to Ohio. When it was discovered that he had lived in Bangkok, working for ECAFE, and that the couple had 'a good deal of social contact with the Embassy and members of British firms', the immediate worry was that he might have served as a KGB talent spotter.[18] They were fortunate that he had not.

So, were MI5 also interested in Cairncross again in 1964 because they had been tipped off? The journalist Chapman Pincher argued in 1984 that Anthony Blunt threw Cairncross to the wolves. Blunt, Pincher alleged, 'continued to protect his high-level friends whom he admired but, being an arch snob, had no compunction about naming associate spies of humble origin whom he disliked,' and besides Cairncross was out of the game.[19] Pincher, however, was wrong. While Blunt might have named Cairncross in his interview with MI5 on 23 April 1964, they had already extracted Cairncross' confession two months earlier in February. Yet it is easy to see why Pincher got it wrong: his sources' memories played them false. For instance, according to Peter Wright, a former MI5 intelligence officer who had worked on two spies' cases and likely Pincher's source, Blunt had indeed named Cairncross.[20] Similarly, another one of Cairncross' interviewers was Dame Stella Rimington (who would later in her career achieve fame as the first woman to become the Director General of the Security Service, a position she held from 1992 to 1996) who noted that Blunt was MI5's source.[21] Yet, the archival evidence conclusively shows that Martin had interviewed Cairncross by 18 February 1964. They cannot have been interested in Cairncross because Blunt tipped them off.

But Cairncross did not know this and if his memoir is anything to go by, he and Blunt had never got on. Their relationship at Cambridge had been 'distinctly frosty'.[22] Moreover, he was also at pains throughout *Enigma Spy*, to blame Blunt (whom he described to be 'a snob *par excellence*')[23] for all of his misfortunes with MI5 and the KGB – those in the 1960s being no exception.[24] He was convinced that it was Blunt who had given him up, and this was only confirmed by the likes of Wright and Pincher. Blunt became for Cairncross a convenient scapegoat character, one upon whom he could pour a lifetime's worth of anger and blame. Cairncross was wrong.

★

Despite the revelation that Cairncross had been a spy for the Soviet Union, the British authorities never prosecuted him. The interest paid to him by the FBI and MI5 did, however, cause him to end his brief academic career in the United States and he soon returned to Italy, away from the prying eyes of the FBI. In recalling his departure, he mournfully confessed that he 'had been extremely happy in Cleveland and had never enjoyed a post so much'.[25]

Though sad to leave Ohio, Cairncross was happy to have avoided extradition and prosecution. Had he been tried and found guilty, he would likely have been sentenced to a lengthy custodial sentence. In 1961, George Blake, a post-war MI6 officer and spy for the Soviet Union, was sentenced to forty-two years for his activities.[26] Of course, despite his worries, there was little probability that Cairncross would ever have been prosecuted. His confession was not conducted by a police officer and nor was it under conditions that would be admissible in court. Moreover, senior members of the British government were briefed that, 'The offence was not extraditable; and the United States Government might therefore be reluctant to deport him to the United Kingdom, even if they had the power to do so (which itself is uncertain).'[27] The FBI, for their part, did not see Cairncross as a danger to American security and were unwilling to recommend deportation or removal from the United States. Cairncross also posed another problem, as was briefed to the Prime Minister and other senior figures in the government; if the story leaked it would be most embarrassing:

If we sent a police officer to the United States in an attempt to obtain from Cairncross a statement which would be admissible as evidence and subsequently discovered that the United States authorities were unable to deport him, we should have increased the risk of a leak and, if the facts become known subsequently, we should expose ourselves to criticism for having failed to seize the earlier chance to interrogate him when he passed through the United Kingdom on his way to the United States.

The only way out was to try to convince Cairncross to return to the United Kingdom, so that he could formally confess. 'Having taken these steps, we might feel that we had done all that could be reasonably expected of us; and we should be better placed to meet criticism if Cairncross finally evaded us but the incident became subsequently known.'[28] Unsurprisingly, Cairncross had no wish to return to Britain, make a formal confession under caution and leave himself liable to prosecution, so he rejected the suggestion.[29]

To make matters worse for the government, just a few months earlier in January, had formed the Security Commission, which was designated to 'investigate and report upon circumstances in which a breach of security is known to have occurred in public service'. Moreover, the Prime Minister, Alec Douglas-Home, when announcing the establishment of the Commission stated that, 'The Commission could be called upon to act if there had been a breach of security even though there had been no conviction – perhaps because the individual had fled the country.' Clearly, the Cairncross case fell under those terms. However, Douglas-Home was warned that submitting the case to the Security Commission only increased the probability of it receiving embarrassing publicity. This would also offend the FBI, who would be forced to explain why they were willing to leave a known alien spy working in an American university. In addition, Cairncross' brother, Alec, was by then the government's chief economic advisor. Not only would revelations about Cairncross cause Alec 'distress and embarrassment', but the government would be forced to answer unpleasant questions about why they were employing as their advisor 'a man who was the brother of a self-confessed Communist spy'.[30] Unsurprisingly, Douglas-Home agreed that the case was not to be submitted to the Security Commission.[31] Thus, the case of John Cairncross was swept quietly under the carpet.

In many respects, this was unsurprising. The early 1960s had been a period of devastating spy scandals, the Profumo affair being the most notable, which had helped contribute to the fall of Harold Macmillan's government in October 1963. Macmillan was, at the best of times, mistrustful of intelligence and its utility. He also hated spy scandals, believing that they were best left out of the public eye. John Vassall was a homosexual British civil servant in the British embassy in Moscow. His dalliances were caught on camera by the KGB, who promptly blackmailed him into supplying secret information. When he was eventually exposed in 1962, rather than praising MI5's Director General Roger Hollis, Macmillan was most displeased. 'When my gamekeeper shoots a fox, he doesn't go and hang it up outside the master of foxhounds' drawing room. He buries it out of sight. … You can't just shoot a spy as you did in the war. You have to try him … Better to discover him and then control him, but never catch him.'[32]

The message was clear: spies were to be turned in private; the dirty laundry of the intelligence services was not to be aired in public. Yet this wasn't the reason Cairncross escaped prosecution under Douglas-Home, Macmillan's successor. The overriding reason was that there simply was too little evidence available to the government that would have been admissible in court. Nor was it possible to extradite Cairncross and force him to confess. There was no establishment cover-up. Despite Macmillan's instruction two years earlier not to prosecute spies, if the evidence had been available, it is clear that the government would have attempted to prosecute.

★

With Cairncross' new 'confession', MI5 arranged to interview him repeatedly over the coming years. He had returned to Italy and had begun working with the UN's FAO, and his job required that he periodically return to Britain. In order to gain entry, MI5 insisted that when he did return to the country he had to submit himself to further interviews.[33] Peter Wright, the infamous MI5 mole hunter, whose paranoia and conspiracy theories regarding the continued existence of Soviet cells operating at the highest levels of the agency, spread discord throughout the Security Service, was one of the officers to interview Cairncross. Wright described a by then 'frail-looking' man, but was keen to note his 'brilliant intellect'. Wright was clearly taken in by Cairncross' story and he wrote that 'Cairncross tried his best to help'. His impression was that the former spy was keen to return to Britain permanently and, though still thoroughly wedded to his Communist beliefs, imagined that 'cooperation' (as Wright believed it to be) would 'earn his ticket'.[34] Yet, albeit with the benefit of hindsight, even in a charitable reading of Wright's own self-aggrandising and self-justifying narration of events, the warning signs were there that he was being taken for a ride.

According to Wright, Cairncross gave them six names but also pointed out that he had no 'firm evidence' against any of them – and nor did Wright name any of them. Two of these men were senior members of the Civil Service and Cairncross alleged that they, like him, had been Communists at Cambridge. One was hounded out of the service and the other was restricted from working on secret material. He also named another four men, all of whom had worked with Cairncross while he was at Bletchley, yet absolutely nothing came of anything he told them. The first man named had expressed a similar desire to Cairncross to share British secrets with the Russians. However, he had long retired and there was nothing to be done. A second man had also retired. Another had, according to Cairncross, been indiscreet about his code-breaking activities to his Oxford tutor and had been sacked by GCHQ anyway. The fourth and final man named was thoroughly investigated and completely cleared of any wrong doing. In short, Cairncross had provided the 'Spycatcher' with precisely nothing of value. Not everyone at MI5, however, was as convinced as Wright that Cairncross was being helpful.

One of the other officers tasked with the responsibility of interrogating Cairncross was Stella Rimington. In Rimington's memoirs, published in 2001, she painted an interesting picture of her experiences interviewing Cairncross. They would meet, after he had finished work, in the offices of the old Ministry of Defence and there she and fellow officers attempted to wrangle further information from a reluctant Cairncross. As Rimington explained, it had been clear from what they already knew about the case that his 'espionage involvement was greater than he had admitted'. By that point in his life, in his late 50s, he was, 'a thin, grey, stooping figure' invariably clad in a mackintosh. Yet, despite his age, he had certainly lost little of his argumentative and difficult personality, and he viewed the exchanges with MI5 as an opportunity to engage in 'intellectual sparring matches' with his interrogators and was 'quite determined' not to admit anything more.[35]

★

On his return to Italy, Cairncross, as noted, had a job as an editor for the UN's FAO. The job with the FAO provided him a 'fat salary', but he hoped that by 1969 he might be able to 'retire to a humbler mode of life', provided he could get editing and translation work on a freelance basis.[36] As it was he continued working for them formally until 1975, but kept 'being asked to work for them', presumably as a consultant.[37] This was primarily as an editor and he was credited as a contributor to the FAO's 1975 publication, *The Missing Half: Woman*, despite claiming to have written the majority of the text. He also wrote a number of documents published by the FAO. These included: *Things to Come*, in 1974, for the Sixth United Nations World's Food Conference; *An Approach to Food and Population Planning* in 1978; and *Population and Agriculture in the Developing Countries* in 1980. The 'valuable' work allowed him to put to use his considerable academic talents as an editor and writer.[38]

In his spare time he continued to produce academic work. In 1967, Penguin Classics published a second collection of three Racine plays, *Andromache*, *Britannicus* and *Berenice*. He followed this in 1975 with a translation of three plays by Pierre Cornielle, *The Cid*, *Cinna* and *The Theatrical Illusion*; and a second volume of Cornielle's plays in 1980, *Polyeuctus*, *The Liar* and *Nicomedes*. This was by no means without its financial rewards. His advance for his first collection of Corneille plays was £350, plus he received 7 per cent royalties on all sales in the United Kingdom and the United States of America and 10 per cent for library editions.[39] Each of his four volumes with Penguin went through multiple reprints. Indeed, the most recent reprint of his original 1963 collection of Racine translations was in 2004. These were not insignificant print runs, the 1974 UK reprint of his second volume of Racine plays was 10,000 copies, the book had been reprinted seven times by 1985.[40]

Cairncross' translations have split opinion in more recent years. Patrick Swinden, for instance, contended that, 'John Cairncross's "Athens revealed to me my haughty foe" induces sleep'.[41] More recently still, in 2012 in the *Daily Telegraph*, the translator and writer Alan Hollinghurst contended that, 'John Cairncross's versions for Penguin Classics are fairly accurate but not metrically pleasing or actable.'[42] This is, of course, not universal. As another Racine translator, Tim Chilcott, noted in 2000, 'The late John Cairncross' translation yielded many insights, to the extent of providing several phrases and, occasionally, even whole lines that could not be bettered.'[43] Also in the positive column of the ledger, Professor David Lee Rubin, of the University of Virginia, wrote to the *Times Literary Supplement*, noting that Cairncross' 'four volumes of Corneille and Racine translations are frequently recommended by experts and have remained in print for decades. Of these, the rendering of *Phèdra* is, by common accord, the best published so far in the English language.'[44]

The relationship between Cairncross and his editors was not always smooth. He proposed a book that he would write on food and population, based on a colleague's research in FAO. His editor, Will Sulkin, brought it to the attention of a Penguin colleague, who turned the idea down flat noting that there was already another book on the topic. An outraged Cairncross wrote back complaining that he was:

> filled with dismay ... since I've read everything on the subject, I can say that the proposed book is a real breakthrough, combining food popula-tion and development in a brilliant way never before achieved. To say that there is already a book on Food Resources (which has the advantage of being out of print) is not to realize that the book is only slightly more relevant to the world's present dilemma than my Corneille. I didn't know Penguin employed people like that.[45]

Cairncross wrote again and apologised 'for my outburst', but not before a bemused Sulkin wrote to a colleague that Cairncross 'is dotty'.[46]

By the mid-1970s, in addition to Racine and Corneille, Cairncross hoped to add La Fontaine to his collection of translations, this however didn't come to anything, Penguin Classics had already commissioned enough books to see them through to 1980.[47] Regardless, Cairncross pub-lished a collection of La Fontaine's fables, in a much expanded edition of his 1958 collection of translated poems and originals, *By a Lonely Sea*, retitled to *La Fontaine Fables & Other Poems*. The volume was published by Colin Smythe Limited in 1982. He also contributed seven poems, which he trans-lated from Chinese, and a foreword, to Shih Shun Liu's 1967, *One Hundred and One Chinese Poems*.[48]

While working on his translations in the early 1970s, Cairncross was also writing a book – a social history of Christian polygamy.[49] This was certainly Cairncross' most significant single-authored work, a 236-page scholarly work of history of no small merit. The book was well received and a glowing review appeared in the *Journal of Church and State* in 1978. The reviewer, the noted ethicist T.B. Maston, praised the 'remarkably thorough' research and added, 'Anyone who is concerned with a scholarly study of any kind will be helped by an analysis of the methods and the approach of Cairncross.'[50] Graham Greene called it 'the dirty book by Claymore', and in a later letter he wrote, 'I'm half way through your book which fascinates me. ... Above all I'm amazed at the mount [sic] of research you must have done.'[51]

Cairncross' other great love, Molière, had not however slipped his mind. In 1963, he published a second monograph on the writer, *Molière Bourgeois et Libertin*. The book was less well received than his previous effort. H. Gaston Hall found that the study 'exaggerates the recent trend along lines suggested by the title. Cairncross's valid points unfortunately are lost in a tissue of misinformation, mistakes, and misleading hypotheses.'[52] Another reviewer, J.-C. Tournand, found that 'the texts used to accredit this interpretation are too skilfully chosen to be quite convincing'.[53] The *Times Literary Supplement* also took Cairncross to task. His conclusions were 'not always supported by the evidence', his arguments were on 'dubious ground', his title was 'misleading', and that on the whole the book 'like some of Mr Cairncross's other work ... encourages the reader to bring in a verdict of "Not Proven".'[54] He also published a scholarly article in 1972 outlining his ideas and, in 1988, a final monograph on the playwright.[55]

Cairncross' retirement was clearly going well, he continued taking writing, editing and translating jobs from the FAO, his translations were well received and a source of additional income. However, once again his former life as a spy was about to unsettle his tranquil existence.

14

The Hunt for the Fifth Man

After 1964, following the fallout from Cairncross' confession, MI5's interest in him waned. They still continued to interview him, but it was clear that they were unlikely to extract much more from him. He had been an active agent of the Soviet Union and a particularly damaging one – perhaps, it had been suggested, even the 'fifth man' of the Ring of Five. Yet prosecuting him, if even possible given his only informal confession, might prove both difficult and embarrassing. They were happy to let the matter rest.

Yet, Cairncross' past would still, nevertheless, come back to haunt him. In 1979, the case of the Cambridge spies returned back into the headlines with a vengeance. The journalist Andrew Boyle had alluded, in his book *Climate of Treason*, to the 'fourth man', whom he dubbed 'Maurice'. 'Maurice' was, in fact, Anthony Blunt, by that stage of his career an eminent art historian who had received a knighthood in 1956 and had been Surveyor of the Queen's Pictures from 1945 to 1973. Until that point, Whitehall had buried the fact that Blunt was a known, confessed traitor. In Chapman Pincher's view this was to evade public embarrassment, yet as Christopher Andrew notes, Blunt was promised immunity from prosecution if he came clean. As it was, Peter Wright, a conspiracy theorist, spent years interrogating Blunt, driving him to drink demanding evidence to substantiate his madcap theories. 'Maurice', Boyle correctly asserted, 'had won such renown in his own field that he had been signally honoured. To drag him into court might fortuitously embroil many eminent people, perhaps even members of the Royal Family, in scandal and controversy.'[1] As a mask, 'Maurice', a reference to E.M. Forster's novel of the same name about a homosexual academic, was paper thin. Blunt, though unaware of the book's precise content, instructed his lawyers to attempt to block publication anyway.

Taking to the courts proved an unwise decision on Blunt's part. Richard Ingrams, then of the satirical magazine *Private Eye*, published what he would later describe as a 'titbit of legal news' that directly associated Blunt with Boyle's new book.[2] The new Conservative Prime Minister, Margaret Thatcher, in no mood to continue to shield former Soviet agents living a comfortable and distinguished existence at the heart of British intellectual life, took to the House of Commons and revealed Blunt's treachery. 'Sir Anthony Blunt,' the Prime Minister informed MPs, 'had acted a talent-spotter for Russian intelligence', 'passed information regularly to the Russians while he was a member of the Security Service' and 'came under suspicion in the course of the inquiries which followed the defection of Burgess and Maclean in 1951'. However, he had evaded prosecution because, aside from his own confession, there was insufficient evidence against him.[3]

Naturally the press had a field day and the spy scandal dominated the news cycle. Soon enough the story caught the eye of John Colville, who had played an instrumental role in partially unmasking Cairncross in the wake of the flight of Burgess and Maclean to Moscow in 1951. Colville cryptically informed the *Sunday Times* that there had been another man, 'one of the best brains in the Foreign Office', who had also been in league with the Soviet Union at the same time as Blunt. He would not, however, give the name of the man in question, but was willing to provide clues. The spy, Colville told the journalist Barrie Penrose, had also worked at the Treasury and the Ministry of Supply. After trawling through the Civil Service listings, Penrose was able to deduce that the suspect was John Cairncross.[4] Scoop in hand, Penrose then travelled to Italy to talk to Cairncross in person.

★

In his *Sunday Times* interview, Cairncross, by then 66 years old, repeated his familiar tale of naivety – that he was tricked into supplying information to Burgess in the late 1930s, unaware that his friend had been a Soviet agent or even a Communist. This was, in effect, the precise same story that he had so successfully deployed during his interviews with Jim Skardon in 1952. Indeed, Cairncross directly referenced those interviews, telling the journalist that, 'I was relieved that they believed what I told them, which was in any case the truth.'[5] This, of course, was very far from the 'truth', but once again, despite the sensationalist headline that accompanied the story, 'I was a spy for the Soviets', no such admission appeared at any point in the article, Cairncross had stuck to his guns.

The *Sunday Times* piece was soon followed by others[6] and it was not long until the question of Cairncross' involvement with Soviet espionage was brought up in Parliament. Bob Cryer, the Labour backbencher, asked the Attorney General, Sir Michael Havers, whether the government planned to prosecute the former spy. The answer was, 'No. Even if there were admissible evidence, which there is not, extradition is not available from Italy in respect of offences of this nature.'[7] Meanwhile, the Scottish Labour MP Dennis Canavan asked the Prime Minister if Blunt and Cairncross continued to receive their Civil Service pensions or any other similar benefits from the state, to which the answer was again negative.[8]

Meanwhile, these revelations created considerable astonishment in Cairncross' family. Sir Alec Cairncross received a barrage of phone calls from journalists, first from the *Sunday Times*, but soon after from across Fleet Street, asking for his brother's contact details and for comment on the breaking story. Much of what they had to tell him, that John had been interviewed by MI5 in 1951, that documents written by him had come into the possession of known spies, and that John himself was under suspicion, came as a complete surprise. After hearing all of this, Sir Alec recorded his shock. He was, he wrote, 'taken aback'. With the revelations regarding Blunt fading out of the news cycle, it was 'increasingly unlikely that anyone would point the finger at him'. Sir Alec was also shocked to discover that John had been a Communist while a student at Cambridge. 'It was also claimed that he had described himself as a member of a Communist cell at Cambridge while I am positive that [he] had no Communist leanings in 1934–35 when we shared rooms and am very doubtful whether he was ever in the silent sense a Communist.'

Despite John's name having come up when Sir Alec had been himself questioned by the security services years earlier in 1964 in the wake of his brother's confession, it is clear that Sir Alec had known nothing. He complained, 'What rankles now as it rankled in 1964 is that John should [have] kept this all from me and should have held political views even when living with me that he never avowed. To be so close and yet so far apart seems somehow a little obscene.' The rest of the family, however, took the news with an array of different reactions, these ranged from 'fits of laughter' to taking it in their stride.[9] Indeed, John's young nephew, David, took delight in the idea that his uncle was a spy.[10] What was clear, however, is that none of them had any inkling that John had held a secret, double life and done so for fifteen years.

As ever, Graham Greene was also on hand to offer solace regarding his friend's latest calamity. In February 1980, Greene wrote to Cairncross regarding the latter's misadventures in the press and remained as blasé as ever about the alleged treachery of one of his spy friends. 'I am so glad that you have survived events! I was a bit puzzled because none of the photographs looked in the least like you and only the address tallied. What puzzled me too was that the papers hadn't got on at all to your connection with Section V of MI6.'[11]

Overall, despite having come to the attention of the press, the extent of Cairncross' activities remained shielded from the public. The attention the press paid to Cairncross was as nothing to that subjected to Anthony Bunt, whose character was destroyed. He was stripped of his knighthood and honorary fellowship at Trinity College, and lost his position in the British Academy. On 20 November 1979, Blunt held a press conference where he expressed regret for his actions – though more likely because he was caught and then exposed – and his desire to resume a normal life and return to the world of art history.[12] This was a forlorn hope; he died just a few years later in 1983, stripped of his honours, his reputation in tatters and his contributions to scholarship vastly overshadowed by his treachery.

★

When the *Sunday Times* story broke, Cairncross had been holidaying in Switzerland and had not seen the write-up of the interview. When he returned, he was outraged to find that the carefully crafted story he had provided to the two journalists had not been presented as he had hoped. He contacted his by then long separated wife, Gabi, in some anger. She in turn telephoned Sir Alec, who reported the conversation in his diary:

John had returned to Rome, seen the cuttings and was raging mad. He wanted her to find a lawyer for him. Mary thought no good purpose would be served by a legal action and that it would all boil up again if it came into the courts. How could he sue if he couldn't come to the UK? I decided to speak to John and finally got him by phone. He had cooled down and was quite realistic. But he still felt strongly that The Sunday

Times had broken all their promises, made several errors of fact and completely misrepresented him.

Sir Alec advised his brother to make a complaint to the Press Council. Alec hoped that there might be a tape recording of the interview that might corroborate John's version of events, but the only recording was of a later conversation. It was, as Alec noted, 'his word against theirs'. Nevertheless, he provided a statement to the *Sunday Times* and demanded an apology.[13] A week later, John rang Alec personally.

> The letter says he denied espionage and this was converted by the S T [Sunday Times] to 'confessed'. He didn't know Burgess in Cambridge and by the time the war broke out had already moved to the Treasury without access to sensitive information. All this makes it the more extraordinary that M I [Military Intelligence] made the statement to me that they did in 1964 and I will have to get this cleared up one way or the other.[14]

John also further outlined his plan of campaign to rescue his reputation from the machinations of a hostile press. He had drafted a letter he hoped the *Sunday Times* would publish, if they rejected it then he would send it to *The Guardian* and, if they in turn rejected the letter, then he planned to contact the Press Council. The contents of that latter remain a mystery, but it certainly was not to Alec's liking. Some weeks later, John produced a second letter 'even sillier' than its predecessor which made 'irrelevant comments on John's association with Burgess (esp. that he was known to be a Communist) argued that many things on the tape were not in the account of the interview (without specifying any)'.[15] None, of this, however, came to anything, and besides, the press had already lost interest in him. This clearly came as something of a relief to Alec, who recorded in his diary in the March after the story had first broken, 'Nobody mentioned John in all my conversations.'[16]

★

Still living in Rome, after this brief intrusion, Cairncross was rapidly able to return to his everyday life. Yet he did not remain out of the spotlight for very long and soon again found himself in trouble with both the authorities and the press.

In 1980 Cairncross was otherwise consumed with efforts to purchase an unfinished house. This proved a more arduous process than he might have imagined. Problems with a third party and planning permission had turned the entire enterprise into something of a saga. He had been trying to buy a property for some time and, as early as 1977, had spoken of buying somewhere in Greece, yet that project came to nothing.[17] By 1980 he had given up on Greece and instead decided to remain in Italy, but in a new home. Yet this too had gone painfully wrong as he struggled to complete his deal. As he rather indignantly wrote to Graham Greene, 'I'm touched by your solicitude over the future of the sale, but I feel like replying that I only look terribly stupid. I'm not really.' He further complained that he 'could write a book (quite an amusing one) about all my experiences dealing with Italian authorities, lawyers and private persons re property since I came to Italy'. This was not all bad, however. One of the upshots was that he had made a profit, not a 'fortune', but 'quite a packet all the same'.

In the meantime, he continued with his literary career as a translator, scholar and poet. As noted earlier, Penguin Books had decided to publish a new volume of his translations of Corneille, which included the plays *Polyeuctus*, *The Liar* and *Nicomedes*. They had previously published an earlier series of translations, but, as Cairncross bitterly noted, had been sitting on the current collection. Also to his annoyance, they had reduced the royalties he received by a per cent, all the while 'continuing to pay the widow of a man who served as editor for about a year with conspicuous incompetence, no doubt on a charity basis'. Happily, he had 'never been dependent on book earnings' and was at that time clearly doing well from his other sidelines. He bragged to Greene that 'offers of work continue to pour in. I am accepting some cannily just in case. It doesn't do to turn down a pleasant job offering some $12,000 these days, and I can turn it to good account.'[18]

Cairncross' good fortune regarding his financial situation would come in handy two years later, in 1982, when he once again fell foul of the law. This time he came to the attention of the Italian authorities when he foolishly attempted to cross the Italian–Swiss border with a suitcase containing a large amount of currency, at least 52 million lire (£22,000). Back in Scotland, the long-suffering Sir Alec Cairncross once again took to his diary to record his brother's latest misadventure. 'He was within a few miles of the Swiss border with a [illegible] case full of notes and claimed that he was on his way to Milan to invest the money but had wanted to pick up medicine in

Switzerland that he could not obtain in Italy. The penalty is forfeiture of the cash and a fine of up to 4 times the amount.'[19]

The press, who now had Cairncross on their radar, also followed the story. The *Daily Mail* reported that he was 'arrested at the Swiss border town of Chiasso' and spent a night in the cells after customs officials discovered the large supply of cash on his person.[20] The *Daily Telegraph* was more detailed, noting that Cairncross was sentenced to a year in prison for currency smuggling. Fortunately for Cairncross, he was granted 'provisional liberty' and 'freed as soon as sentence was pronounced'. More disastrously for the former spy was that his money was confiscated (now reported as £26,000), he was fined a further £40,000 and told to pay the legal costs, which amounted to some £3,000. A 'very upset' Cairncross lamented that the confiscated money was his 'life's savings', the product of his sale of his villa in Capri, and he proceeded to provide to the press a complex and bizarre explanation regarding his misfortune. 'In Milan I changed the bank cheques into banknotes. I am a collector of ancient Roman coins, and I wanted to buy some in Milan. I knew that if I offered cash the purchase would be easier.' He took the train from Chiasso 'because I remembered there is a chemist's shop there where I could buy some medicines … when I got there I thought I was still in Italy.'[21]

As ever when in a tricky spot, Cairncross elicited the aid of his famous friend and stalwart champion, Graham Greene. In a rambling letter, outlining his problem, Cairncross relayed this innocence. He 'would, of course, never dream of crossing the frontier' from Italy into Switzerland, which was, he noted, 'one of the most closely guarded in the world', and certainly not 'with a huge bundle of Italian bank notes'. Yet error or otherwise, that was precisely what he had done. Despite his arrest, Cairncross felt that he had, at least, been treated well by the authorities. Nevertheless, both he and his lawyers thought it best to acquire a character reference highlighting that he was of 'advanced age, [of] blameless record (judicially speaking) and reputation for balance and prudence, totally unlikely to have indulged in anything so mad as circumstances appear to suggest'. Of course, the irony of such a statement, given that only a little over two years earlier he had been embroiled in a major spy scandal, was not lost on him.[22] Nevertheless, he beseeched precisely such a statement from Greene who, as ever, was forthcoming. 'I believe completely in your story,' Greene replied, 'and am only too glad to write in your defence.'[23]

The case itself, deliberately dragged on by Cairncross and his lawyers, lasted a further five years (with at least three trials) until the end of 1987. During the period, Cairncross' mood oscillated back and forth from the hopeful to the black. He feared that he would be faced either with a vast fine or a stint in prison complete with 'terrific publicity (bad for my relatives and friends)', and so he instead temporarily departed for Paris, away from the jurisdiction of the Italian authorities. In an effort to hinder the collection of his assets by the Italian government, he sent friends and family his most expensive possessions. Meanwhile, his claim that he had travelled to Switzerland in error was seriously undermined by the discovery of a pencil-written declaration that stated that he was en route to Switzerland. In order to explain this rather gaping discrepancy, Cairncross darkly hinted at forgery. The basis for this suggestion being that the 'sentence was completely illegible for an Anglo–Saxon, just as the reverse would be true for an Italian'.[24]

Eventually, he avoided prison time but was forced to pay a 'whopping fine', which he was able to pay through loans.[25] He was, however, fortunate enough to receive at least some of the money back from the authorities, though not without administrative deductions.[26] For all of his protestations regarding a desire to purchase collectable Roman coinage, his wife Gabi, surmised that, 'John had sold the land at Capri and, fearing a devaluation, was seeking to place the proceeds abroad.'[27] The full amount of money he lost as a result of the affair is unclear, but it certainly was the case that it could have been far worse. He had received a substantial part of his money back and, save a brief stint behind bars at the time of his arrest, had avoided a lengthy period of incarceration and had been allowed to remain in Italy.

★

In the midst of his various legal problems, court appearances and unwelcome coverage in the media, at least one aspect of Cairncross' life was going well and that was the romantic. Though the two still spoke and appeared close, Cairncross had long been separated from his wife Gabi. As noted above, throughout his exposure in the press during the winter of 1979 and the opening months of 1980, Gabi was in regular contact with him and the wider Cairncross clan, including Alec but also John's elderly sister, Elizabeth (Elsie) Cairncross.[28]

Aside from fleeting references to various women in the years since their separation in the early 1960s, there is little evidence available regarding his love life.[29] As noted above, while in the United States, during his stint as a professor at Cleveland, he showed some signs of trying to form a relationship with a recent divorcee. This did not, however, last beyond his brief stay in the country. But, as he wrote to Eunice Frost at Penguin, he did wish to marry again, but in 1964 he was already 51 years old and overburdened by work. His pessimism was however misplaced, he would remarry.

In 1984, Cairncross met Gayle Brinkerhoff, a young American opera singer, still in her late 20s at the time. In Rome, the two bonded over 'spirited conversation[s] over a dish of pasta'.[30] Soon enough he wrote to Graham Greene to let him know the good news: 'I'm happy to say that I now at least have a wonderful private life with a delightful young American girl who, when her training is over, will have a fabulous voice (as I have checked with impartial sources).'[31] Unlike Cairncross' other relationships following his separation from Gabi, the one he developed with Gayle would last the rest of his life and she soon became a favourite talking point in his letters, discussing her burgeoning career as a singer.[32]

15

Agent for the Duration

In 1990, the historian and specialist on the Cambridge spies, Sheila Kerr, wrote to Cairncross. She was writing a PhD thesis on Donald Maclean and involved in the production of a television programme on Soviet intelligence activities. She asked to interview Cairncross on what he knew about these topics. At the time he was living in Les Clos, St Antonin du Var, in France and despite declining the invitation, Kerr arrived in France to talk to Cairncross anyway.[1] With her she brought minutes of a meeting of the British Scientific Advisory Committee, which dealt with proposals to build atomic weapons. The minutes listed Cairncross as one of two secretaries at the meeting. With this, she hoped in vain to elicit more information regarding Cairncross' role as an atomic spy.[2]

Later in the same year, the University of Cambridge historian Dr Christopher Andrew arrived on Cairncross' doorstep. He too was interested in Cairncross' espionage activities and attempted to persuade the former spy to give an interview for a forthcoming book and an accompanying television series.[3] A tried and tested interviewee, Cairncross again gave Andrew nothing. However, unknown to Cairncross, Andrew in collaboration with the KGB defector Oleg Gordievsky, was on the verge of releasing a book, *KGB: The Inside Story of its Foreign Operations from Lenin to Gorbachev*, which saw the light of day later in the year. Based on Gordievsky's insider knowledge, the two contended that Cairncross had indeed leaked the information that the British planned to build atomic weapons. Of the interview, Kerr wrote that the 'document did not prove he handled atomic secrets, but it was the only document linking him to the SAC [Special Advisory Committee]. Cairncross was not impressed, and denied knowing any atomic secrets. He said there must have been a clerical error because he never attended this committee meeting.'[4]

Cairncross' denials to Andrew and Kerr did not, however, prevent *KGB* from being published to great fanfare. The central, great reveal in the book was that Cairncross had been the fifth man of the Ring of Five, and that he had been an atomic spy. Though it had long been public knowledge that he had been a Soviet mole, the claim that had been deemed of such significance and in such infamous company saw Cairncross plastered across the headlines and divided writers and historians interested in mole-hunting.[5]

★

Following revelations regarding his espionage career in the wake of the Blunt affair in 1979, numerous journalists had contacted Cairncross in an effort to win a new spy scoop. One of these individuals was the historian and, later, Conservative Party politician Rupert Allason, who wrote to Cairncross in May 1982. Allason, under the pen-name Nigel West had, with Richard Deacon, written *Spy*, in 1980.[6] By 1982 he had a second book on the way, a history of MI5, which would see the light of day later that year.[7] Given the recent exposure of Cairncross in the press, Allason was keen to add another insider's story to the book. Stressing that he was keen only to print 'facts' and that he would 'inevitably' be required to publish some reference to Cairncross, he nevertheless insisted that it would not bring further unwanted media attention to his subject's case. Moreover, Cairncross' own contribution to the book would be kept strictly confidential.[8] Over the next few years, in addition to being elected by the constituents of Torbay to the House of Commons in 1987, 'West' forged a remarkable career as an author of espionage literature, ending the 1980s as one of the leading experts in the field.

West was hardly alone in taking an interest in Cairncross. In 1981, Chapman Pincher published *Their Trade is Treachery*, which was published in March 1981. Pincher largely expanded on the details that had already emerged in the press in the wake of the Blunt affair in 1979. This created some headaches for the Thatcher government. The latest revelations regarding Cairncross, though little more serious than had already appeared, certainly could lead to embarrassing questions being asked: why had Cairncross not been prosecuted or extradited? What was more, in the early

1980s Cairncross still took occasional trips back to Britain. Indeed, he even rang the British authorities in April 1981 to propose just such a trip. If the press got wind that a former Soviet spy had arrived on British soil without being immediately arrested, then the coverage was likely to be less than favourable.

Fortunately for officials, Cairncross called off his April trip. But the prospect that he might return at some other point in the future was a difficult scenario to contemplate, without easy solution. A Cabinet Office official summarised the dilemma, 'Should he be detained for questioning by the police, either on or during his stay here? ... Might it be necessary to consider mounting a prosecution, even if admissible evidence constituted a slender basis for charges? I see all the advantages of doing that, but I also see some political disadvantages in appearing to take no action at all.'[9] There were no obvious answers to this, yet when Cairncross did eventually return to Britain permanently in 1995, shortly before his death, the state made no effort to prosecute him. However, at that point, he was aged 82 and in very poor health.

★

Following his return to the spotlight, Cairncross then in his late 70s, angered by what he saw as an official decision to throw him to the media wolves – in direct violation of the agreement he had made with MI5 in 1964 – began to plot his retaliation. Initially he took to talking to the press, which he soon regretted. In 1991, *The Mail on Sunday* reported that he had told its correspondents he 'was made one of The Five during the War. I hope that this will finally put an end to the Fifth Man mystery.'[10] In his autobiography, Cairncross claimed he had denied being the fifth man and described the article as being 'in the worst tradition of the yellow press'.[11]

Clearly, the press could not be relied upon to produce a narrative that pleased Cairncross. As such he decided to put his other writing projects on hold and to dedicate his time to the production of a book – this would eventually become his 1997 autobiography, *The Enigma Spy*. The purpose of the proposed work was to put forward what he argued was his side of the story and to put to rest the claims made by Christopher Andrew, Oleg Gordievsky and various other historians, spy writers and former intelligence officers, who had levelled accusations at him. Though the decision to write an autobiography was in response to the raft of allegations that emerged in 1990, Cairncross had in fact already begun to write a history of

Britain's diplomatic and military position in the late 1930s. As early undated drafts of notes for the autobiography, apparently written in the late 1980s, reveal, his interest and initial efforts to write about the Munich agreement had begun before the publication of Andrew and Gordievsky's *KGB*. It was around that same time that he and Gayle were planning to relocate to Paris from their Italian home.[12]

The working draft of his abortive Munich book was entitled 'Munich and After' and Cairncross had decided to write under the pen name David Jardine. The surviving initial drafts outline the central premise of the unfinished book. It was to be a highly critical exploration of the policies of Neville Chamberlain and the opening years of the Second World War. Appeasement, it would argue, was a grotesque failure, a mistake from the outset. It was only when the conflict reached global proportions, once the USA was involved, as opposed to being a European conflict, that British fortunes were transformed. Cairncross' own experiences in the Foreign Office during these years were to be the key underlying resource of the book and it was to be an insider's account. That was not to say, however, that Cairncross did not conduct research.

One of the most interesting aspects of the surviving early drafts of 'Munich and After' are the historians that Cairncross was reading as part of his preparations for the manuscript. The narrative would draw heavily on very different schools of historical thought. These included the work of Correlli Barnett, Paul Kennedy and, the famous controversialist historian, A.J.P. Taylor. Each of these historians took a markedly different interpretation of the origins of the Second World War. Barnett's work on the subject, for example, has become a standard bearer for 'declinist' historical interpretation of British fortunes in the twentieth century. Declinism, as a prism of historical analysis, is centred around the notion that Britain had been in a position of terminal decline from her great power status since at least the First World War. This decline had been exacerbated by poor policy decisions on the part of Britain's various governments. Though primarily a military historian of the First World War, since 1970 Barnett had turned his attentions to what he saw as the 'collapse of British power', a term that served as the title of his first major study of the topic, which saw the light of day in 1972. Over the following decades, he would publish four books on the subject, the key text in the period that Cairncross was writing being the 1986 work, *The Audit of War*, in which the economic policies of the Second World War loomed large.[13]

Declinism and Barnett were, however, a million miles away from the other inspirations behind 'Munich and After'. A.J.P. Taylor, as a public intellectual and leading historian of the origins of the First and Second World Wars, took the contentious view that Hitler had no clear plan to achieve his foreign policy objectives.[14] Moreover, those objectives were of the same character of other German politicians – not least Gustav Stresemann, who had served as the Foreign Minister in the 1920s and (briefly) as Chancellor in 1923. The other key inspiration for the book was Paul Kennedy, who has written extensively on modern diplomatic history. Kennedy's view is different again. The author of multiple works on diplomatic history, he has argued that appeasement was the product of British statesmen's understanding of Britain's position. This position was one of apparent weakness, and so the 'excessively gloomy' chiefs of the armed forces urged the government to pursue a policy of appeasement while Britain rearmed.[15]

These three key sources, Barnett, Taylor and Kennedy, each singled out by Cairncross, who intended to utilise their research as a supplement to his own experiences at the heart of the Civil Service in the 1930s, make for interesting and conflicting bedfellows. As noted, Barnett offered a declinist analysis of the appeasement era while both Taylor and Kennedy were more inclined to provide a generous reading of British policy during the period. As Cairncross was swift to point out, his own reading of appeasement was far more critical than that of the historians to whose work he found himself indebted. The introductory page of an early draft included witheringly critical condemnation of the Chamberlain government and the Prime Minister personally.

According to Cairncross, Chamberlain was animated by an intensely moral conviction and was unaffected by strategic considerations. He regarded the national interest as an unworthy aim and the balance of power as a wicked concept. And Hitler proved unappeasable. Thus, he embarked on a dangerous course, which led to the Munich agreement in 1938. It was this document that he brought back to London and waved to an applauding crowd and of which he declared triumphantly, 'It is peace in our time.' In this belief he was tragically mistaken, for hostilities broke out a year later. Indeed, by leading the German dictator to believe that Britain would always give in, Chamberlain blundered into a war that he certainly did not want and Hitler did not expect. The Allies (now reduced to Britain and France) were involved in a conflict at the worst possible moment. France was defeated in June 1940, and soon after Britain succeeded by the skin of its teeth in repelling an attack by the Luftwaffe, and thus narrowly averting the occupation of Britain by the German Army (since the country, after the evacuation of its troops from Dunkirk, had no army to speak of).[16]

The existence of 'Munich and After' presents important evidence in Cairncross' political and historical thinking, not only about the origins of the Second World War but also his own recruitment by Soviet intelligence in 1937. It was clear that he possessed strong and deeply held views on the subject and still bitterly resented Chamberlain's policies from half a century earlier. Crucially, he presented the book under a pseudonym. This rules out the cynical conclusion that the proposed history was a purely self-serving venture, designed to excuse his own actions in the late 1930s. After all, if he did not present himself as the author, then the conclusions he reached could not serve as apologism implicitly designed to justify his own actions. It is clear that by this late stage of his life, he genuinely believed in the Churchillian picture of the 1930s that he was painting. That is not to say that he accepted the argument in 1951 when he presented it to his initial MI5 interrogators – Arthur Martin and Jim Skardon. However, by 1989 he certainly did.

The publication of Andrew and Gordievsky's *KGB* put an end to 'Munich and After'. The work that had been conducted on the manuscript was instead adapted into Cairncross' response to his latest accusers. Inflections of the work can clearly be seen in those chapters of *The Enigma Spy* that addressed Cairncross' motives and the political situation in the 1930s. The new project was to be entitled 'An Agent for the Duration', the significance of the title being his claim that he had only been a spy briefly and that any actual espionage that took place was limited to during the Second World War.

★

'An Agent for the Duration' was initially designed to be a hugely ambitious project. Envisioned as a three-part book comprised of twenty-seven chapters, the first seventeen would cover his life and exploits as a spy; part two was clearly to be an adapted version of 'Munich and After' of seven chapters; while the third and final part of the book would be three chapters dedicated to Cairncross' literary life and scholarship.[17] During the course of writing, Cairncross once again came into contact with Rupert Allason in 1991. Allason and his wife curtailed a trip to Monte Carlo to visit Cairncross in France, where the two discussed espionage and the latter's career and the press revelations in detail.[18] In his capacity as a sitting Member of Parliament,

Allason took the opportunity to write on Cairncross' behalf to Sir Patrick Mayhew, the Attorney General, to enquire whether there were any plans to prosecute the former spy.[19]

The basis for these concerns was that Cairncross and his young partner, Gayle, planned to return to Britain, or at least another English-speaking country. If he were to make such a move, Cairncross had to be assured that he would not come back only to find himself serving the remainder of his life behind bars. After the renewal of MI5's interest in him following his brief stint in the United States in the 1960s, Cairncross' fears were understandable. Fortunately for the couple, the answer was an emphatic no: the Attorney General had no plans to prosecute.

In 1994 Allason again met with Cairncross, still living in the south of France and, on this occasion, the subject of 'An Agent for the Duration' came up. Allason showed some interest in the project. Since his early contact with Cairncross in the early 1980s, his reputation as an historian and record as an author had grown considerably, and he offered general advice on locating a literary agent and publisher. In the meantime, Cairncross had also been in contact with Anthony Cave Brown, who offered advice and assistance on the preparation of the manuscript.[20] Cave Brown, like Allason, was an author of spy-related literature and had a successful record when it came to prying secrets from former intelligence officers. Brown had been an early discoverer of the Ultra secret many years before in the early 1970s and had been threatened with 'a horse whipping' by the British government if he dared go to print with his material. In the end, the government asked the retired intelligence officer Group Captain Frederick Winterbotham to write his own carefully vetted memoirs, which were promptly rushed into print in 1974, in anticipation of Brown's unauthorised account, which came out the following year.[21]

Brown had been sent a draft copy of Cairncross' manuscript and was sufficiently impressed with the material to forward it to Frank Curtis, a New York literary agent. Gayle and Cairncross had also enlisted the aid of Basil MacTaggart, who helped the couple revise the manuscript. In early 1995, Allason once again resumed contact and indicated that he would be willing to involve himself in the production of the book. For Cairncross this was splendid news indeed, Allason had established the St Ermins Press as a vehicle for the production of his own literary work and could offer advice, experience and a production company all in one helpful package.[22] The relationship, however, proved to be a poisoned chalice for all concerned.

★

Cairncross was also increasingly aware of his mortality. In 1991, he had received news that Andrew was planning to publish another book, potentially quoting KGB documents about Cairncross. He concluded that he needed to get his own story published as soon as possible. First, this would address any new claims made about him. Second, as Graham Greene noted, if his and Andrew's book were to appear at around the same time 'the two books might well sell each other'. Third, he was aware that he might be running out of time, 'I'm in a hurry, because though not ill, I am rising 78, and I can't leave Gayle who has been a wonderful friend … without financial backing. Her singing career may come off, but I don't want to take chances.'[23]

At the time Greene was also very ill, suffering from leukaemia. Indeed, he was so unwell that his final letters to Cairncross, despite the secrecy of their correspondence in the wake of Andrew and Gordievsky's book, were dictated to his secretary, his niece Amanda Saunders.[24] Saunders wrote to Cairncross two months later to inform him that Greene's health was 'very bad'.[25] On 3 April 1991, Greene passed away. Cairncross learned of the news via a television bulletin and was 'shattered by this'. He wrote to Saunders some days later offering his condolences and said that he 'was relieved to learn that Graham's last days were peaceful and painless'.[26] Throughout his failing health, Greene had been a regular correspondent with Cairncross, offering advice and support regarding his ongoing troubles with the press, and the production of his autobiography.

In the final years of his life, he was, not unusually, in financial trouble with the French tax authorities and was borrowing money from Alec. However, in 1993, his sister, Margaret, died. Though he had lived outside of Britain for more than forty years by that point, he had been able to see Margaret and one of his other sisters, Anne, recently when they visited the south of France. Margaret had left him a 'fantastic bounty', likely £50,000, in her will, which solved his financial worries.[27] Meanwhile, Cairncross' health had remained strong throughout the opening years of the 1990s, even if his finances had not. In July 1993, he wrote to Alec and noted that, save from problematic blood pressure he had 'no health problems that I know of'. He wrote again in September stating that he had been for a health check and that 'the doctor was very satisfied'.[28] Later that year, however, he suffered a stroke. This slowed down the production of his book and led to the decision not to write a third section, covering his writing career. Nevertheless, despite troubles with his vision, he and Gayle continued to work on the autobiography.[29]

In May 1995, Cairncross and Gayle returned to Britain. However, in August he suffered a second stroke. Following the death of his first wife, Gabrielle, in September, the pair were married.[30] Days later, John Cairncross died on 8 October 1995 at the age of 82.

★

Though John Cairncross had passed away, his story was far from finished. Gayle continued to work on the autobiography. All was not well in the relationship between Gayle and Rupert Allason; she was becoming increasingly concerned regarding the direction his input was taking. Shortly before he died, Cairncross described a proposed introduction to the book, written by Allason, as 'fatal'. In particular, Cairncross had objected to the effort by Allason to paint him as the 'fifth man' – a notion that the book sought to demolish. Without having signed a contract, St Ermins Press had been in contact with the US publisher Little Brown for serial and US rights for the book. When a contract was eventually sent to Gayle, she considered elements of it to be irregular and sought professional advice. It transpired that the document did indeed include language deemed 'far from standard terms'.

Nevertheless, Gayle continued to hope that St Ermins Press would publish the autobiography and employed solicitors to negotiate a contract with the company. However, those efforts proved unsuccessful. Meanwhile, Gayle and one of the late Graham Greene's friends, Ronnie Challoner, set about editing the book. It came as a surprise, therefore, in December 1996 to receive an invoice for £15,000 (minus VAT) from Allason's company, Westintel (Research) Limited, for the work he had placed into the preparation of the book. By that time, Gayle had elected to publish the book through a different publisher, Random House. Westintel (Research) Limited initiated legal proceedings against Random House, the claim being that Allason had ghost-written the book and that the publisher was in breach of copyright.[31]

When the matter eventually came to court in 2001, Allason lost the case.

Afterword

John Cairncross' public exposure in 1990 produced a number of headlines and a minor media splash. Yet compared to the furore that met the missing diplomats scandal of 1951, the defection of Philby in 1963 and the exposure of Blunt in 1979, the Cairncross case was a muted affair. The historian Richard Davenport-Hines argues, in his iconoclastic book *Enemies Within* (2018), that the reason for this was that as the son of a shopkeeper, Cairncross did not fit the mould for public scandal.[1] He was a million miles away, in terms of his origins and social status, from the other four. Though not aristocrats, they were born into the privilege and relative affluence that came with a professional, upper middle-class family. The story just did not have the mileage of betrayal by members of the establishment.

Yet, for Davenport-Hines, the popular narrative regarding the Ring of Five has been ill judged by both journalists and historians. Far from being aristocrats who betrayed their class, the five came from less elevated families. Further, he challenges the assumption that the failure of the government to mount any prosecutions against the five was the result of an establishment cover-up. Finally, he also asserts that they did not gain their positions at the heart of Whitehall and the intelligence services as result of the old-school-tie network. The former argument is undoubtedly true, save Maclean the son of an MP, particularly in the case of Cairncross. As we have seen, he was the son of an ironmonger, from an impoverished region of south-central Scotland that was stricken by the economic calamities of the inter-war period. Being lower middle class, the Cairncross family did not have to suffer in the same fashion of the miners, but in terms of finances and social status he was not of the establishment. Indeed, in his own estimation, Cairncross was the subject of considerable snobbery once he entered Whitehall. On his second point, that prosecution was not a result of a cover-up, again Davenport-Hines is again clearly correct. The failure to prosecute Cairncross, and indeed the others, was not due to an intervention by friendly establishment benefactors, but because there was insufficient admissible evidence that would have been acceptable in a court of law. It was not as if hugely sensitive Venona decrypts could have been aired in open court.

Davenport-Hines' third argument, that the old-school-tie was not the basis for the Ring of Five's entry into Whitehall, is less clear cut. Cairncross had been to the prestigious Hamilton Academy, a fee-paying selective day school, which provided numerous generous bursaries – some of which Cairncross and his brothers won. Yet even so, his was not the kind of background that lent itself to easy entry into Whitehall; rather it was his intellectual achievements and university credentials that did so. His place at Trinity clearly served only to benefit his chances, as did his stellar performance in the entrance exam – yet had his briefly overt Communist activities at Cambridge been known, it seems doubtful he would have been offered a job. The other four spies all had far more obvious Communist connections from university, which either weren't explored or in Maclean's case they were deliberately overlooked. It is difficult to imagine that less privileged individuals, men who were not born 'gentlemen', would have been afforded such a charitable hearing from the Foreign Office.

Certainly, the Eton-educated Burgess saw a difference between himself and Cairncross: 'He … is of humbler origin than I. He speaks with a strong Scottish accent and one cannot call him a gentleman … He is a typical petit bourgeois who always thinks that he can achieve a great deal in bourgeois society.'[2] Davenport-Hines is correct that Blunt, Burgess, Maclean and Philby were not aristocrats, but they certainly were products of the establishment. Cairncross was not. So why did he betray his country to the Soviet Union?

It is clear that it was precisely Cairncross' failure to find establishment acceptance, or at least his perception that he had been rebuffed, which made him susceptible to Arnold Deutsch and the NKVD. Despite years of hard work, winning a place to Glasgow, then the Sorbonne, Cambridge and ultimately the Foreign Office, he was never embraced by those around him. Yet, the degree to which this was his perception, as opposed to reality, is debatable. Where he found snobbery, as Burgess' views amply confirm, others also saw carelessness and conceit. As Maclean described him to Deutsch, 'MOLIÈRE is very intelligent, but works badly and is mainly careless. This is because he considers himself more clever and better than all the others.'[3] His problems were compounded by his forgetfulness and quarrelsome temperament. But, as far as he was concerned, his problem was purely a glass ceiling erected by an establishment that didn't take kindly to an upstart from Lesmahagow.

Difficult to fully accept is Cairncross' own claim that his Lesmahagow upbringing had little to do with his eventual choice to become a spy. While he might not have directly endured the political and economic upheavals that befell the miners of Lesmahagow, he lived within that environment and saw the devastation of the period first hand. His casual dismissal of the poverty that surrounded him, which plainly loomed large in the memories of his brothers, is itself telling. More concretely important were the formative trips he took to Paris, Austria and Germany as a young man. It was on his travels that he was first introduced to Communists and Jewish refugees but, as importantly, the far-right in the form of Action Française and Nazis. His withering hatred of the latter in particular and their treatment of Jews was politically formative. While the candidness of his autobiography has rightly been called into question, his oft-stated belief that the best way to oppose fascism was to support the Soviet Union was undoubtedly genuine.

In short, Cairncross was inclined towards working for the NKVD at least in part because of the environment in which he was brought up. Key, however, were his early experiences of witnessing fascism and fascists first hand and the perceived slights he received at the hands of the English establishment.

★

This book has also been concerned with Cairncross' life as both a civil servant and spy. His career as an official was both mundane as well as extraordinary. It was exceptional in that he found himself at the heart of the British secret state, moving from one sensitive post to the next. Cairncross worked at the Foreign Office, the Treasury, the Ministry of Supply, but most crucially in Lord Hankey's Office, GC&CS, and MI6. During that time, the KGB files allege that he passed many thousands of important, secret documents from Whitehall to his handlers. These materials included: Foreign Office analysis of the pre-war situation in Europe; information on defence research and development; access to Britain's most secret source, Ultra intelligence; details on MI6's activities; and even early word that Britain was preparing to build atomic weapons.

Of course, Cairncross denied all of this, save that he had passed Ultra intelligence, particularly that of significance to the Battle of Kursk. However, the evidence levelled against his claims, from the testimony of former Soviet intelligence officers to materials published from the KGB archives, would suggest otherwise. The KGB claimed what he supplied was sensational. Yet it is clear that Cairncross was not a born spy. His forgetfulness, lack of technical facility and caustic temperament led him into farcical situations that undermined his security and nearly led to his exposure. The most obvious example was his and Modin's ill-fated car ride, where his all-thumbs approach to technology required their being rescued by a police officer – with top secret documents laid beside them for all the world to see. Meanwhile, his temperament saw him moved unceremoniously from the Foreign Office and his refusal to put up with night shifts led him to leave Bletchley Park.

His time as a civil servant, despite working for multiple ministries and secret departments, was mundane in that he was a low-level bureaucrat and disappointing in that he never reached the senior ranks of any department in which he worked. He would always serve as a junior and at most middling official, never running a sub-section of a department, let alone rising to the heights of a Civil Service mandarin. His jobs tended to be defined by the tedious grind of the lowly cog in a vast bureaucracy. Yet in a number of ways, this clearly helped his espionage career for the NKVD. He had risen just enough in the world to have access to secret materials, but never sufficiently elevated that such materials became out of reach – as Philby was in danger of doing in MI6.

Yet, despite the range of access he received to secret documents and the praise lavished upon him by the NKVD and latterly the KGB, it is difficult not to conclude that, a hugely important spy though he was, his significance requires qualification. For much of his time as a spy, until 1944, the NKVD was sufficiently wrapped in paranoia that it questioned the sincerity of its best British agents. Meanwhile, Cairncross also spent a significant period of time working for ministries and departments already infiltrated by other agents. Maclean worked with him in the Foreign Office and Philby in MI6. Certainly in the case of MI6, some materials Cairncross shared with the

NKVD were actually written by Philby. Without doubt, their access to sensitive materials was, at those stages at least, superior to Cairncross'.

Even Cairncross' own prized contribution, British intelligence on the disposition of German aircraft prior to the Battle of Kursk, was almost certainly available to Soviet commanders from other sources. Moreover, the raids to destroy those aircraft were subject to severe losses. Any suggestion that Cairncross turned the tide of the battle, let alone the war (as the subtitle of his autobiography suggests), lacks credibility. Finally, the suggestion that Cairncross was an early, if not the first, atomic spy, which he vehemently denied, amounts to surprisingly little. While the documents to which Cairncross had access signified Britain's intention to pursue such a project, such efforts were at an early stage, and before long the NKVD had access to much better-placed sources – not least Klaus Fuchs – at the heart of the Manhattan Project.

The other major question surrounding Cairncross' espionage career is whether or not he was the 'fifth man'. His own contention was that there was no 'Ring of Five', or 'Cambridge Five'. He was, he claimed, a lone operator. There is strong evidence to suggest that this was at least partially true – after all he leaked materials penned by Philby, so he certainly did not know Philby was a fellow spy. Clearly then, the five did not operate as a cohesive unit or cell as far as Cairncross was concerned. However, if taken more loosely to mean that the Ring of Five was comprised of five exceptionally productive agents, all of whom gained an education at Cambridge, then the situation changes. Indeed, had the Soviet defector Anatoliy Golitsyn not incorrectly stated that the five had attended university together, which was not true, then MI5's efforts to identify the final two chief suspects, Blunt and Cairncross, would certainly have proceeded more rapidly.

★

In addition to covering Cairncross' life as a spy, the other key objective of this book has been to narrate his post-espionage career. This aspect of his life had been almost entirely ignored by historians – save for brief narration of how MI5 eventually caught up with him. Yet it is clear that, though nearly entirely overshadowed by his spying, Cairncross' literary career was highly impressive. In addition to early work as a journalist, he published six volumes of translation of literature and poetry, which still remains significant; he also translated academic work and material for the UN's Food and

Agricultural Organisation. He was also an editor and worked on multiple reports into the question of the provision of food in developing nations.

What is surprising is that as an international civil servant, travelling the world, that the KGB did not attempt to reacquire him as an asset – certainly there is no evidence that they tried. This could have been because he didn't have the contacts with the KGB in Rome, Bangkok, Karachi or the other places he lived after 1952. Another possibility is that, as he claimed, he was glad to be out of the murky and dangerous world of Soviet espionage. Finally, he was, if not an entirely blown agent, under the suspicion of MI5 and dangerous for Soviet intelligence to maintain. Regardless of the reason, once Cairncross left spying behind him 1952, he never returned to it.

As it was, Cairncross was perfectly capable of landing himself in hot water entirely without the assistance of the KGB. This was typically financial in origin. It is no small irony that despite his years of illegal espionage on the behalf of the Soviet Union, the only (and very brief) time he spent in prison was for currency smuggling. This was the most serious of his financial misdeeds, but his post-espionage life was plagued by poor decisions when it came to money and assets. Had it not been for his brother Alec's repeated interventions, with loans and other assistance, it seems likely that Cairncross would have floundered in debt on many occasions. An excellent translator and linguist he undoubtedly was, but he would have made a terrible accountant.

Yet the greatest failure of Cairncross' life was that, save a year in the USA, he never acquired an academic post or the opportunity to fulfil his scholarly potential. Save during retirement, he was forced to share his time between his professional careers while also producing his translations, books and articles on seventeenth-century French literature. With the time and academic resources of a university behind him, it is very likely that his scholarly endeavours would have been still more impressive and numerous. Though increasingly out of fashion in the twenty-first century, his translations of Racine and Corneille, in particular, proved to be highly significant works of scholarship, remaining in print many years after they first appeared and were widely touted as among the finest efforts of their type.

Cairncross' choice to become a spy repeatedly came back to haunt him and ruined his ambition to forge a long-term career as a professional academic. His brief sojourn in academia was cut short in 1964 by MI5's renewed interest in his case. As noted, this interest did not arise, as alleged by the likes of Peter Wright, because Blunt had named Cairncross as a spy.

Instead, his move to the USA had brought him back on MI5's radar and there were those within the service, not least Arthur Martin, who had never been convinced by Cairncross' earlier confessions in 1952. Thereafter, the threat of prosecution hung over him. It was not until 1970 that he received some assurance that he would not be prosecuted, and even then it is clear that he never became entirely comfortable. Moreover, even if it was not MI5 he had to fear, after 1979 it was the press, keen to reveal details of his prior secret life.

Yet throughout all of his troubles, Cairncross was able to provoke considerable loyalty and could rely on both the support and belief of close friends and family. Even after 1990, when the details of his espionage activities began to be revealed more fully, Graham Greene, Gayle Cairncross and Sir Alec Cairncross never lost faith in John's innocence. Finally, the saga that was the publication of his memoirs itself was a source of fierce argument and litigation.

Fittingly, even in death, John Cairncross was a source of contention.

Appendices

Interviews with John Cairncross[*]
Appendix 1

PP.72493.
(Copy in: PP.604529 – BURGESS).
Interview with John CAIRNCROSS on 31. 3. 52

On the 31st March I saw the above-named in Mr. Jupe's office which was made available for me at the Treasury. He was called to the office by Mr. Griffiths who left us the moment the preliminary introduction had been effected. I told CAIRNCROSS my name and explained that he had already been seen by Mr. Martin and Mr. Whyte, colleagues of mine, but there were certain further matters which I wished to discuss with him. Before I did so I was anxious to clear up one or two matters arising from the earlier interrogations.

I reminded him that he had volunteered to Mr. Martin the information that he had known BURGESS casually 'since about 1937'. I told him that Mr. Martin had reported that CAIRNCROSS had said that the latter had not counted BURGESS among his friends but regarded him as a glib gossip who was unlikely to have any interests in common with his own. CAIRNCROSS thought this was quite an accurate report of what he had said, and I then asked him whether he would enlarge upon this so as to inform me fully of his relationship with BURGESS.

CAIRNCROSS said that he had not met BURGESS by the time that he came down from Cambridge and went to work at Foreign Office. He met him some time later and thought it must have been during 1937, and so far

---

[*]   All documents in these appendices are drawn from: TNA, KV 2/4108.

as he could recall the meeting came about through some Foreign Office link. Following their first meeting BURGESS invited CAIRNCROSS to more than one party but this was hospitality which CAIRNCROSS never thought it necessary or desirable to return. Some time in 1937, though he cannot remember precisely the circumstances in which it happened, CAIRNCROSS travelled with BURGESS from Cambridge to London by train. He recalled also that he visited BURGESS's Chester Square address and was somewhat flattered to find himself being asked to meet people of the calibre of Harold NICHOLSON and MOUNSEY of Foreign Office.

He also remembered a luncheon at a restaurant at which he felt singularly out of his element when the other people present were BURGESS, Tom WYLIE and Helmuth KATZ. The other four were clearly a homosexual gathering and the extravagant language was a considerable surprise to CAIRNCROSS.

Though he was mildly surprised at the interest shown in him by BURGESS, the friendship was not developed to any very considerable extent and their meetings were widely spaced over two or three years up to the outbreak of war. Even reviewing the situation to-day CAIRNCROSS was unable to recall any incident which with the latest information about BURGESS would indicate that he was engaged in any subversive activity. BURGESS was a voracious collector of political gossip and was violently interested in political affairs. His own political line was difficult to assess but it did not follow any positive course and nothing that he said or did at that time indicated to CAIRNCROSS that he was a member of the Communist Party or held similar views. Any impetus given to the relationship was generated by BURGESS, and CAIRNCROSS felt somewhat flattered as a provincial finding himself with a certain cachet through his Foreign Office employment in London.

CAIRNCROSS said that he had not indulged in any correspondence with BURGESS nor could he remember having any official relationship with him which would require him to make reports to BURGESS. I then showed him the 14 page document traced to BURGESS's possession and which was clearly in the hand-writing of CAIRNCROSS. I handed to him to peruse a photostatic copy but gave him a sight of the original which I retained in my possession. I asked him immediately if he recognised the writing and he thought it slightly familiar. I then said to him, 'I have some considerable experience in the examination of hand-writing and I have no doubt that the document was written by you. My opinion has been confirmed by independent experts and I want you to tell me the circumstances in which this paper was passed to BURGESS.' He asked to be allowed to examine it and as he did so it became apparent that he had suffered a major shock by the production of this document. He read the first page or two carefully and then passed quickly to the end, and he was practically speechless. I thought it was opportune at this moment to caution him, and I did so quite formally. He then said that he was at a loss to know what to say, since the legal position was not entirely clear to him and he would prefer to think before he made any precise statement about the document. I told him that I thought it quite possible that I could be helpful to him in this matter. I proposed, for the purpose of enabling us to continue the interview untrammeled [sic] by legal obligations, for a short time to discuss this matter with him off the record if he were prepared to trust me to that extent. He said that he felt no difficulty in following this course of action, and he then said that the document was clearly in his writing, and he had written it to the best of his recollection to assist his own reasoning, for it was prepared in a style which he adopted when considering any academic subject. This situation, immediately after the invasion of Czechoslovakia, was one which had ceased to interest him in so far as his official duties were concerned, for by this time he had left the Foreign Office and gone to the Treasury. At the same time he continued to take an active interest in political affairs and remained in touch with numerous contacts of similar rank who were still working at Foreign Office. He denied that he had particularly or purposely sought out the individuals named in the report but assured me that the report was of conversations which took place as a result of chance meetings. Everybody as the time was discussing the political situation, which was truly a matter of life or death.

The thing that shocked him the most was that this document should have been found amongst Burgess's belongings. If he had ever thought about it at all, he was sure that he had recovered it from him. Certainly he had a recollection of being vaguely uncomfortable for a short time that it had not been returned. This was the only paper that he had ever passed to BURGESS, and he made this statement in a confident way, even though I pointed out that there remained a vast amount of correspondence still to be processed.

CAIRNCROSS assured me that he had no idea that BURGESS was interested in obtaining this sort of information for the purpose of passing it on to any other power. He believed at the time that he talked to

BURGESS that he was merely discussing political matters with an individual who was vitally interested in them on their own account. He was at a loss to explain why such words as 'my informant' should appear in this document, and thought he would take a day or two to arrange his thoughts in a sufficiently orderly manner to give a cogent and reasoned explanation of the circumstances in which he passed the document to BURGESS. The relationship, casual though it was, ceased so far as he could recall with the outbreak of war. They may have met during the course of the war but he does not recall the occasion, and he only remembers one positive meeting with BURGESS since the end of the war, when he met him along with David FOOTMAN.

CAIRNCROSS assures me that he had done nothing which might be urged against him at any time since this document was passed to BURGESS, and I told him plainly that if this were so there would be no chance of his being prosecuted. I added that should further information come to hand to indicate other or similar activities of a later date, he would undoubtedly be prosecuted against. CAIRNCROSS was confident that no such circumstances would be discovered and was grateful that he would not suffer prosecution. I hastened to add, hoping that he would appreciate that I was anxious to be patently fair in the matter, that it was unlikely that his employers, who, at the highest level, were aware of this enquiry, would be agreeable to his continuing in their service in the light of his admissions. CAIRNCROSS understood this and said that he was not particularly alarmed at the prospect of losing his job. His career was of slight importance but he did fear that he would be unable to make a living in other fields, and so long as he could preserve his good name unsullied by convictions he was satisfied that he could face the future with equanimity. Having resolved the position I told CAIRNCROSS that it would be my duty to report to my colleagues the nature of his admissions, and I indicated that I should require him to provide me with the fullest possible information regarding his relationship with BURGESS and those of BURGESS's circle with whom he came in contact. CAIRNCROSS gave me an undertaking that he would tell me the whole truth about these matters, and expressing gratitude for the fair manner in which I had put the case against him, he promised to attend Room 055 at 3 p.m. on Wednesday, April 2nd, for the purpose of making a full statement.

We spoke about the immediate future and when I said that I thought that his presence was likely to be an embarrassment at the Treasury whilst these matters were being resolved, he indicated that he was quite prepared to go on holiday while they made up their minds in the matter.

CAIRNCROSS indicated that though it was difficult to believe, when one looked at the evidence again the most that could be urged against him was that he had been indiscreet. He said that he would not expect the authorities to regard this indiscretion either as such, or of such a character as would permit his continued employment in work of a confidential nature.

Before we parted I questioned CAIRNCROSS as to his political views and he described himself to me as a Churchillian. Admitting that whilst at Cambridge he had attended a couple of meetings of the Communist Party, he claimed that he had quickly seen the fallacy of believing that there was any room for Communism in the political structure of this country. He has never failed since leaving University to follow and agree with the beliefs and politics advanced and practised by the present Prime Minister.

At the conclusion of the interviews I suggested that CAIRNCROSS might like to note down my name and telephone number, whereupon he said that he had recognised my name upon being introduced to me, and believed that he had read of it in the context of cases in the public eye in recent years. The interview lasted from 11 a.m. till 12.10 p.m. and CAIRNCROSS was fairly well recovered by the time that he left my company.

———————

As 2.30 p.m., in accordance with arrangements made with Mr. John Winnifrith, Mr. Simkins and I saw him at the Treasury. I told him what had transpired at my meeting with CAIRNCROSS, and he expressed his appreciation of the fact that I had kept Treasury so firmly in mind in dealing with the subject. Mr. Winnifrith endeavoured whilst I was with him to find CAIRNCROSS so as to suspend him from duty in my presence, but unfortunately he could not be found. I heard at 4 p.m. that CAIRNCROSS had returned to the office shortly after 3 p.m. from lunch, that Mr. Winnifrith had seen him, suspended him, and that CAIRNCROSS had accepted his congé without comment. Mr. Winnifrith, wondering whether it was the right word, said that CAIRNCROSS was 'looking forward to his interview with Mr. Skardon at 3 p.m. on Wednesday, 2nd April'.

At 5 p.m. I saw Chief Supt. Evan Jones in Special Branch and arranged that CAIRNCROSS's description, passport particulars, etc. (without mentioning his occupation) should be circulated to Special Branch officers at all ports asking that, should he arrive at a port to embark for abroad at any time during the next ten days, a rigorous customs examination of his effects was to be sought and his presence at the port reported immediately by telephone to New Scotland Yard.

(signed) W. J. Skardon.
B.2.a.
1.4.52.

Appendix 2

STATEMENT of John CAIRNCROSS, Principal H. M. Treasury, who STATING:-

I am thirty-eight years of age. I went to Trinity College, Cambridge, in September 1934 after previous education at Hamilton Academy, Hamilton, Lanarkshire, Glasgow University and the Sorbonne, Paris. Prior to going to Cambridge I had no pronounced political views, but I had absorbed a fairly anti-German attitude and indeed a marked hostility to Nazism while in Paris. In Cambridge I came under Communist influence very gradually and ultimately attended two or three Party Member meetings, but thereafter I was repelled by the unrealistic and conspiratorial aspects of the doctrine. I should add that I was attracted to Communism in the first place by its clear desire to secure a line-up against Germany and also by its approach to the study of literature and philosophy whereby social developments were linked with the evolution of thought and art. While at Cambridge I was studying French and German and my studies brought me into contact with Anthony BLUNT (who occupied the room below mine) and James KLUGMAN [sic] – both at Trinity. Without any open breach with the Communist Party I dropped my association with it. I graduated in French and German in June 1936.

I entered the Foreign Office via the usual exam in October 1936 and was posted to the American Department. In March 1937 or thereabouts I was transferred to the Western Department where I made, for the first time, the acquaintance of Donald MaCLEAN to whom I worked. I never had any inkling that he was currently or since a Communist. On the contrary he seemed to me to be fairly markedly to the right, in particular he was very enthusiastic about the need to re-arm. I had however heard that he associated with the Communist Party while at Cambridge.

While in my first stages at the Foreign Office I used to take part in a club run by David LAYTON (Lord LAYTON's son) to discuss rather vague and idealistic plans about social developments and welfare. At a few of these meetings which took place at LAYTON's home I was asked by EWER 'whether I had anything to report'. Following my usual tactics of avoiding a showdown and argument I always replied that I had nothing to report or possibly on one occasion had resort to some publicly known piece of information. Thereafter the attempts ceased. EWER it should be explained knew me during my Party days at Trinity.

I cannot exactly pinpoint either as to time, place or occasion the start of my acquaintance with Guy BURGESS. However, I can remember meeting him, I think, in the Spring of 1937 in BLUNT's room in Trinity, where Louis MacNIECE was also present. This meeting was not however the main object of my trip to Cambridge, which, I think, was to see my very close friend and French tutor Dr. ASHTON. I made the trip back to London in Guy BURGESS's company. I remember he asked me whether I thought there was any glamour in being attached to the Foreign Office. I told him that, as far as I was concerned, it was solely a case of doing a job, on questions which interested me. We also discussed the role of Communism, particularly in this country – apparently because he knew of my previous association. I expressed the view that Communist agitation, particularly in this country, was perfectly futile and the only thing that counted was to get as many Powers together, whatever their political views, to resist Nazi aggression. He agreed with this. I also had lunch at about March 1937 with BURGESS. The others present were BLUNT, Tom WYLIE and Helmut KATZ, a dapper young man who had been in Finland and spoke both Finnish and Swedish fluently. He was a German refugee. The atmosphere of the party was markedly and unpleasantly homosexual. Politics were not discussed. As some point thereafter, BURGESS was in Paris at the same time as I and left a message at my hotel asking me to contact him at the Select (a homosexual cafe). I did not go, as I had neither the wish nor the time to do so.

Round about September 1937 he asked me to a party at his flat in Chester Square at which a number of celebrities including Harold NICHOLSON were present. NICHOLSON, who had been told I worked in the

F.O. Department dealing with Spain, asked me about KOESTLER who was then imprisoned by the France [sic] authorities. He asked if I could do anything to help, and when I said I doubted it, he asked for the name of the Head of the Department and the Under Secretary, which I gave him.

I saw BURGESS at intervals which varied from twice or thrice a fortnight to one in three months to the best of my recollection. We occasionally discussed politics and I was much impressed by his wide and apparently inside knowledge of what was going on and of the elevated and influential circles in which he moved. Round about the time of Munich we had one or two vigorous arguments about British foreign policy. By this time I had moved to the Central Department of the Foreign Office. BURGESS alleged that Chamberlain was deliberately trying to divert German expansion to Russia. I endeavoured to counter this view in the light of my knowledge of official policy, stressing Chamberlain's lack of understanding of the aggressive dynamism of Hitler and the military unpreparedness of France and ourselves and the lack of understanding on the part of the Dominions on the European crisis. I also revealed to him that I was keeping a diary (which I destroyed in 1941) summarising current events in Central Europe. He himself volunteered information to me about these happenings. There was therefore a two way flow. I was under the impression that he was in a secret department (an impression confirmed by some third party whose identity I cannot remember) and imagined that I was possibly ingratiating myself with someone in M.I.5 who might stand me in good stead if ever my Communist associations were brought against me. It was also possible, I thought, that his relations with senior Foreign Office officials might one day prove helpful to me. My description of Government policy was not in great detail and in giving it I was, among other things, yielding to the rather foolish impulse of showing myself as knowledgeable as BURGESS.

In October 1938 I moved to the Treasury but continued in the normal course of social relations to see something of my Foreign Office friends. I also carried on the habit of making occasional entries on European events in my diary on the basis of my discussions with these friends. Round about Easter 1939, after the invasion of Czechoslovakia by Hitler, BURGESS and I had lunch together and the previous argument about Chamberlain's intentions came up. He asked me to substantiate my views and I made notes, both of recent conversations and some held immediately after seeing BURGESS, and let him have access to them. I identify the originals which have now been shown to me. He promised to let me have them back but delayed doing so and when finally I insisted, he told me, if I remember correctly, that he had accidentally burnt them with some papers of his. I was somewhat alarmed about this and saw very much less of him thereafter. I did, however, run into him late in 1940 soon after I had been bombed at Dolphin Square when he commiserated with me. I saw him once or twice thereafter but was distinctly reserved and I saw nothing of him for the rest of the war. I did, however, see him socially on one or two social occasions after the war.

To the very best of my recollection BURGESS did not have any access to other secret information held by me either oral or written. In showing him the notes of April 1939 I felt I was committing at the most an indiscretion and not a serious one in view of what I took to be BURGESS's membership of a secret organisation. It was, so to speak, an interdepartmental exchange of information. I now naturally realise the enormity of my offence and it goes without saying that I am ready to make any amends for my action.

Since leaving the Foreign Office I saw Donald MACLEAN once or twice on his return to London for posting to the Foreign Office and then again, after a gap of years, in November 1950 and April 1951. In November I ran into him at the Traveller's Club and we had dinner together. In April I asked him to a large party I was giving to which I had invited an American research doctor and his wife in order that they could discuss America together. It was a profound surprise when I heard of his departure with BURGESS.

This statement has been read over by me and it is true. I am quite prepared to offer any further information which I may possess.

[signed] J. Cairncross

2.4.52

Statement taken down, read over and signature witnessed by me at Room 055, War Office, on 2nd April, 1952.

[signed] W. J. Skardon.

Appendix 3

Second Interview with John Cairncross on 2 April 1952

On the 2nd April I saw John CAIRNCROSS as arranged at War Office at 3 p.m. He said that he had spent the period between our meetings in making rough notes of his recollections of events in the years before the war, and would like to crystallise his thoughts by reciting the story to me orally before it was reduced to writing. I agreed to this course, and asked him certain questions arising out of the recital to clear up ambiguous statements. And he then dictated the statement which he read through and signed when it was complete.

There are certain discrepancies between this statement and my report concerning the interview with him on the 31st March which ought to be clarified. At our first interview he said that Mounsey of Foreign Office was present with Harold NICOLSON, whereas in fact that was a faulty recollection. Mounsey was at that time the Under Secretary whose name CAIRNCROSS gave to NICOLSON in connection with his enquiries on behalf of KOESTLER.

I ought to mention as well that in describing his anxiety after passing the report to BURGESS he said that his worries were to some extent engendered by the fear that BURGESS might, through the possession of such a paper, have a hold over CAIRNCROSS as would enable him to blackmail CAIRNCROSS into providing further secret information. This I feel almost certainly betokened a knowledge of the sinister possibilities of this association with BURGESS. At the very least it demonstrates that whatever he may have heard about BURGESS being employed in a secret department, he was not completely satisfied that BURGESS was entirely loyal.

The proceedings at Room 055 continued until 5.45 p.m. And at their conclusion CAIRNCROSS referred to his interview with Winnifrith on the 31st March, and indicated that whereas he was prepared to offer his resignation to the Treasury, he thought that his employers would want to sack him. He told me that he had expressed his view to Winnifrith, and he certainly made it clear to me, that he believed that to discharge him would lead to unnecessary and undesirable publicity. He thought that a formula for requiring his resignation could easily be found to satisfy, for example, his wife, in his associations with BURGESS and MACLEAN, whose behaviour is sufficiently notorious to provide sufficient reason for such a step.

I arranged with him that I should be communicating with him in due course to exploit his knowledge of people in whom we are interested, and we agreed that if I telephoned him at home I would do so in the name of SEDDON, for he has some fear that the mention of my proper name might create some alarm in his wife's mind.

[signed]

W. J. Skardon.

B.2.a.
4. 4. 52.

Appendix 4

Interview with Cairncross, 9 April 1952

On the 9th of April, 1952, with Mr. Anthony Simkins, I saw the above-named at Room 055, War Office. I told him straight away that his statement of the 2nd April had been passed to the Treasury for their consideration, and enquired whether he had heard anything from his employers. It appeared, as we well knew, that he had not, and it seemed that he believed we would be aware as soon as he was of any development.

I sought to convey the impression that our dealings with Treasury in this matter were at an end, and I told him that his statement had been examined quite critically by a number of my colleagues, and it was thought that there were certain matters in connection with it which were contradictory and required explanation. He expressed himself completely willing to assist in any way, and I immediately pointed out to him that there was an inconsistency shown in the paragraphs of his statement which detailed his unease at the non-recovery of the document from BURGESS after he had passed it, as he had said, to a person employed in secret work. I emphasised this point by reminding him that, although it did not appear in his statement, he had underlined his anxiety by saying he had thought that such a document might prove a useful instrument of blackmail in BURGESS's hands, the possession of which would enable him to enforce further disclosures from CAIRNCROSS. CAIRNCROSS thought that we were reading too much into his statement; in fact his attitude towards this matter at the time was much the same, so he said, as though it were an unpaid debt. He had lent the document to BURGESS, and it was an untidy situation that the latter should not have returned it to him. Those were his feelings then, but in the course of time, and certainly to-day, he was horrified to learn that it should have been found in BURGESS's possession, knowing now what BURGESS must have been.

It was quite impossible to shake him on this, and he seemed to be quite unaffected by the direct attack made upon him.

I then tried to clear up certain points in his statement which required, so it seemed, elucidation and gained from him as a result information concerning other people already mentioned in his statement. In addition I went through the list of BURGESS's contacts dated 5.7.51 to be found on the BURGESS F.F.604529. The results of these researches are summarised hereunder.

Membership of the Cambridge University Community Party

During his membership (1934-35) the following individuals were also actively associated with the Party:-

John CORNFORD	'Jake' EWER
James KLUGMANN	[illegible] BARLOWE

It was now a very big membership, and CAIRNCROSS thought that he might remember the names of other people, particularly one who was a student of medicine, given time. He has the strong impression that amongst the Party circles he heard BURGESS's name discussed, but he was referred to as a person who had 'ratted' from the Party, and it was generally believed that he had done so because of homosexual relationships with non-Party members.

Anthony BLUNT

As is said in his statement, CAIRNCROSS occupied rooms above those used by Anthony BLUNT. He knew him quite well and whilst he believed that he was thoroughly Communist in his outlook, it was a Communist Party slant on art and letters rather than upon matters of politics. BLUNT was always something of a patrician, very stand-offish and not very accessible to undergraduates outside his immediate circles. CAIRNCROSS, as reported elsewhere, met BLUNT again in the company of BURGESS, and also knew of his association with the Bentinck Street flat during the war. With this flat CAIRNCROSS associated with Lord ROTHSCHILD,

Kim PHILBY who was the link between Ryder Street when he was there and M.I.5, and David FOOTMAN. He also remembered the present Lady ROTHSCHILD as a member of this monage [sic].

[redacted section]

Countess BUDBERG (PFR. 3736).
Cairncross uncertain that BURGESS and Countess BUDBERG were intimates. He himself knows the Countess and has attended her salons, having found such people as Robin CHANCELLOR there, and having been first introduced to the circle by HALPERN.

Alexander HALPERN (PFR. 1620).
CAIRNCROSS met the HALPERNs through David FOOTMAN. This international lawyer is so very Bolshevist in his politics as to be unbelievable. He is an extremely pompous person who claims friendships on the Prime Ministerial level in all walks of life, perhaps with some justification and possibly due to the fact that he was once Minister in the Kerensky Government. He has found HALPERN to be extremely hospitable, especially in Russian emigre [sic] circles. He takes a wide interest in people of all shades of opinion, particularly in the worlds of art, literature and other cultural activities. He (CAIRNCROSS) has never seen any evidence that HALPERN has cultivated his society of friendship, or that of anybody else, for any subversive motive. It is true that he would not hesitate to seek information which might assist him in his professional interests as an international lawyer. It was through HALPERN that CAIRNCROSS was introduced to B.B.C. Officials and has since been provided with broadcasting work on the Third Programme and in certain foreign services.

Freddy KUH (PF. PP. 19500).
CAIRNCROSS once met the above-named at a party given by George MEIER, at Matlock Court during the war. He is able to date the occasion since he remembers that KUH was attacking the Government's policy in failing to open a second front.

James MacGIBBON (PF. 51559).
His only contact with MacGIBBON, gained through the HALPERNs with whom he is on terms because of his literary associations, has been to undertake a small piece of translation into the French as a sample for

MacGIBBON. At one time it was proposed to translate the whole of a work into French and to publish it in Paris. The project came to an end before reaching fruition. I asked CAIRNCROSS if he had realised that MacGIBBON was a member of the Communist Party, and he expressed great surprise to learn this to be the case. This surprise seemed to be quite genuine, and I think that he does not know MacGIBBON very well.

Wolfgang PUTLITZ. (PF. 48846).

CAIRNCROSS only recalls meeting him once and believes that he was the domineering foreigner at a party in BURGESS's house in Chester Square referred to elsewhere as the occasion upon which CAIRNCROSS met Harold NICOLSON.

Professor Alexander Kirkland CAIRNCROSS

CAIRNCROSS' brother and a Professor at Glasgow University. He was at Cambridge with PHILBY. CAIRNCROSS remembers this to be the case because PHILBY once mentioned to him, after making enquiries about Alexander, that his brother was so much better at economics than he (PHILBY) turned out to be. CAIRNCROSS said that his brother was very far removed from being a member of the Communist Party, and he indicated that he held quite contrary views.

Fred WARNER. PF. 604585).

CAIRNCROSS had some slight knowledge of WARNER, gained as a result of working with him in Foreign Office in his early days there.

Tom WYLIE.

His only association with Tom WYLIE was as described elsewhere, that he met him at a luncheon with BLUNT, Helmuth KATZ and BURGESS.

David LAYTON.

I explored with CAIRNCROSS his recollection of a club run by the above-named, and it is CAIRNCROSS's recollection that the meeting took place somewhere in North London at Lord LAYTON's home. He knew that it was near a Green Man public house somewhere, without being able positively to pinpoint the locality. This club had a very mixed membership and it was in no sense dominated by members of the Community Party.

I pressed CAIRNCROSS to discover whether he had given BURGESS a sight of the diary which he kept and which he told me had been destroyed in 1941. He swore that BURGESS had not seen it. In order to persuade him to be a little more forthcoming in his estimate of the character of BURGESS, I tried to assure CAIRNCROSS that no harm would accrue to him by being frank in discussing this matter with me. In spite of my inducements and blandishments, CAIRNCROSS averred that he had nothing to add. He assured us that at no time until the publicity of 1951 did he realise that he was in contact with the agent of a foreign power when he met BURGESS. Never by any word or action did BURGESS create this impression upon his mind, and he swore that, unlike the manner in which he had developed other sources (Goronwy REES), BURGESS had never hinted at his possible association with the Communist Party. All his talk was in direct contrast to the sort of conversation to be expected from a member of the Community Party.

Throughout the interview CAIRNCROSS behaved as though he had nothing to hide, and eventually satisfied me that he was 'coming clean' at every point. After an hour and a half I brought the interview to an end and it was arranged that CAIRNCROSS should telephone me at 2 p.m. On Wednesday, April 16th, for information and further instructions. I have the very pronounced feeling that he is completely under control. *(of whom!*)

I discussed with him at the suggestion of Mr. Simkins his plans for Easter, and discovered that he intended to go away of Thursday April 10th, returning to London on Easter Monday, and to stay in the meantime in the Cotswolds. I told CAIRNCROSS that I was only really interested in any project for foreign travel, and pointed out to him that his employers would undoubtedly regard with disfavour any foreign journey at the present time. He fully saw the point of this, and speculated as to whether he would be free to undertake a holiday in Italy in perhaps June. He had no plans for any earlier foreign travel than that. I did not ask him to surrender his passport, for in the circumstances I do not think it is justified or necessary.

W. J. Skardon
B.2.a.
15.4.52

★ The words 'of whom!' appear in pencil in the form of marginalia, presumably written by a sceptical official reading Skardon's report.

Notes

Introduction

1 'One of us', *Yes, Prime Minister*, BBC 2, 27 February 1986.

2 Yuri Modin, *My Five Cambridge Friends: Burgess, Maclean, Philby, Blunt and Cairncross by their KGB Controller*, trans. Anthony Roberts (New York: Headline Book Publishing, 1994), p. 43.

3 Andrew Boyle, *The Climate of Treason: Five Who Spied for Russia* (London: Hutchinson, 1979).

4 'Anthony Blunt', HC Deb 21 November 1979, vol. 974, cc. 402-520.

5 Roland Perry, *The Fifth Man* (London: Pan Books, 1994, 1995).

6 *The Imitation Game*, dir. Morten Tyldum, The Weinstein Company (2014).

7 Richard Langhorne, 'Francis Harry Hinsley, 1918–1998', *Proceedings of the British Academy*, 120 (2003), p. 265.

8 So ingrained was this internal agency belief in the absolute nature of Bletchley Park's secrecy, Peter Calvocoressi, the noted lawyer, publisher, historian and Bletchley Park veteran, made a point of rejecting the idea that Cairncross had been employed by Bletchley Park. However, he did concede that both Cairncross and Philby had probably visited the establishment. Peter Calvocoressi, *Top Secret Ultra* (Cleobury Mortimer: M & M Baldwin, 1980, 2011), p. 119.

9 David Leitch and Barrie Penrose, 'I was a spy for Soviets', *Sunday Times*, 23 December 1979.

10 Chapman Pincher, *Their Trade is Treachery* (London: Sidgwick & Jackson, 1981, 1982); Chapman Pincher, *Too Secret Too Long* (New York: St. Martin's Press, 1984).

11 Barrie Penrose and Simon Freeman, *Conspiracy of Silence: The Secret Life of Anthony Blunt* (London: Grafton, 1986); Peter Wright with Paul Greengrass,

Spycatcher (Victoria: William Heinemann Australia, 1987); Robert Cecil, *A Divided Life: A Biography of Donald Maclean* (London: The Bodley Head, 1988), p. 43.

12   Christopher Andrew and Oleg Gordievsky, *KGB: The Inside Story of its Foreign Operations from Lenin to Gorbachev* (London: Hodder and Sroughton, 1990).

13   John Costello and Oleg Tsarev, *Deadly Illusions* (New York: Crown Publishers Inc., 1993), p. 220.

14   Modin, *My Five Cambridge Friends*.

15   Three key books produced with rare, if limited, access to KGB records are Costello and Tsarev, *Deadly Illusions*; Genrikh Borovik, *The Philby Files: The Secret Life of the Master Spy*, Phillip Knightley ed. (London: Little, Brown, 1994); Nigel West and Oleg Tsarev, *The Crown Jewels: The British Secrets Exposed by the KGB Archives* (London: HarperCollins Publishers, 1999).

16   The National Archives [TNA], FCO 158/129; TNA, KV 2/4108; TNA; HO 532/4.

17   These include, but are not limited to: Christopher Andrew and Vasili Mitrokhin, *The Mitrokhin Archive: The KGB in Europe and the West* (London: Penguin, 1999, 2000); West and Tsarev, *The Crown Jewels*; Nigel West and Oleg Tsarev (eds.), *TRIPLEX: Secrets from the Cambridge Spies* (New Haven: Yale University Press, 2009); Keith Jeffrey, *MI6: The History of the Secret Intelligence Service, 1909–1949* (London: Bloomsbury, 2009); Christopher Andrew, *The Defence of the Realm: The Authorized History of MI5* (London: Penguin, 2009).

18   'The Squalid Truth.', *Sunday Pictorial*, 25 September 1955.

19   Boyle, *Climate of Treason*, p. 84.

20   Richard Davenport-Hines, *Enemies Within: Communists, The Cambridge Spies and the Making of Modern Britain* (London: William Collins, 2018), p. 245.

21   Andrew, *The Defence of the Realm*, p. 174.

22   TNA, KV 2/4108, Statement of John Cairncross, 2 April 1952. Appendix 2.

23   Bernard Levin, *The Times*, 13 October 1995, p. 20.

24   Rhodri Jeffreys-Jones, *In Spies We trust: The Story of Western Intelligence* (Oxford: Oxford University Press, 2013), p. 118; Andrew, *The Defence of the Realm*, pp. 173-174.

25   Cecil, *Maclean*, p. 162.

26   Wright, *Spycatcher*, p. 222.

27   Stewart Purvis and Jeff Hulbert, *Guy Burgess: The Spy Who Knew Everyone* (London: Biteback, 2016), p. 49.

28   For the evolution of the KGB see, Andrew and Oleg Gordievsky, *KGB*, passim. Andrew and Gordievsky also include a useful flowchart, p. xii.

Chapter 1

1   T.S. Cairncross, 'A Lost House: Cairncross of Colmslie', in *The Border Magazine*, vol. x, no. 115 (July, 1905), p. 139.

2   Robert Keith, John Spotiswood, Michael Russel and Walter Goodall, *An Historical Catalogue of the Scottish Bishops: Down to the Year 1688* (Edinburgh: Bell & Bradfute, 1824), pp. 190–91.

3   Cairncross, 'A Lost House', pp. 138–39.

4   Alec Cairncross, *Living With the Century* (Fife: iynx, 1998), p. 13.

5   John M'Ure, *The History of Glasgow: A New Ed.* (Glasgow: Hutchison & Brookman, 1830), pp. 41–42.

6   William Clelland, *Lesmahagow: The Parish and the People* (Greenock: Orr, Pollock and Co. Ltd, 1990), pp. 36, 42, 50.

7   J.B. Greenshields, *Annals of the Parish of Lesmahagow* (Edinburgh: The Caledonian Press, 1864), p. 270.

8   D.B. McCowan, 'Coalmining at Auchanbeg, Lesmahagow, 1700–1922: An Introduction', *The Scottish Genealogist*, vol. 37, no. 1 (1990), p. 20.

9   Clelland, *Lesmahagow*, p. 114.

10   Greenshields, *Lesmahagow*, p. 277; Clelland, *Lesmahagow*, p. 114.

11   Greenshields, *Lesmahagow*, p. 245; Clelland, *Lesmahagow*, p. 95.

12   Quoted in Alan Campbell, *The Scottish Miners, 1874–1939 – Volume One: Industry, Work and Community* (Aldershot: Ashgate, 2000), p. 1.

13   Campbell, *The Scottish Miners*, p. 20, 23.

14   Greenshields, *Lesmahagow*, p. 270.

15   Greenshields, *Lesmahagow*, p. 272.

16   Greenshields, *Lesmahagow*, p. 20.

17   Clelland, *Lesmahagow*, p. 116.

18   Cairncross, *The Enigma Spy*, p. 22.

19   University of Glasgow Archives [here after UGA], R8/5/51/2 – Matriculation Records, 1930–1931.

20   Glasgow City Archives [here after GCA], CO1/47/68 Valuation and Assessment Roll for the County of Lanark – Lesmahagow Parish, 1926–1927, pp. 5–6.

21   Ian MacDougall, *Voices From the Hunger Marches: Personal Recollections by Scottish Hunger Marchers of the 1920s and 1930s – vol. II* (Edinburgh: Polygon, 1991), p. 331.

22   University of Warwick, Modern Records Centre Website, 'Coal miners' average wages – 1914 to 1920', October 1920, www2.warwick.ac.uk/services/library/mrc/explorefurther/images/coal/.

23   Cairncross, *The Enigma Spy*, p. 23.

24   Cairncross, *The Enigma Spy*, p. 22.

25   Cairncross, *Living with the Century*, p. 11.

26   Cairncross, *Living with the Century*, p. 12.

27   Cairncross, *Living with the Century*, p. 17.

28 Derek H. Aldcroft, *The British Economy Between the Wars* (Oxford: Philip Allan, 1983), p. 13.

29 Sidney Pollard, *The Development of the British Economy, 1914–1980 – Third Edition* (London: Edward Arnold, 1962, 1983), p. 69.

30 Robert K. Middlemas, *The Clydesiders: A Left Wing Struggle for Parliamentary Power* (London: Hutchinson, 1965), p. 90.

31 Campbell, *The Scottish Miners*, p. 23.

32 Campbell, *The Scottish Miners*, pp. 113–22.

33 Campbell, *The Scottish Miners*, p. 124.

34 GCA, CO1/47/37 General register of Indexed Poor, 1921–1926; GCA, CO1/47/29, Record of application for poor relief, 1926–1930.

35 South Lanarkshire Archives and Records Centre, East Kilbride [here after SLARC], CO1/60/3/1 District Council Minute Book – Second District Council, 5 December 1935.

36 SLARC, CO1/47/161 – Clothing Stock Book For Poor Relief.

37 GCA, CO1/47/15, Minutes of the Clothing Committee, 1923–1930, 17 October 1923.

38 MacDougall, *Voices from the Hunger Marches*, p. 328.

39 GCA, 47/37 General register of Indexed Poor, 1921–1926; GCA, 47/29, Record of application for poor relief, 1926–1930.

40 MacDougall, *Voices from the Hunger Marches*, p. 328.

41 Middlemas, *The Clydesiders*, p. 26.

42 Cairncross, *The Enigma Spy*, p. 22.

43 MacDougall, *Voices from the Hunger Marches*, pp. 334–46.

44 MacDougall, *Voices from the Hunger Marches*, p. 335.

45 'Arts, Letters Society to Hear Guest Scholar', *El Paso Times*, 1 November 1964, p. 74.

46 Cairncross, *Living with the Century*, p. 31.

47 Cairncross, *Living with the Century*, p. 2.

48 MacDougall, *Voices from the Hunger Marches*, p. 328.

Chapter 2

1 Miranda Carter, *Anthony Blunt: His Lives* (London: Pan Books, 2001), pp. 43, 49; Tim Milne, *Kim Philby: A Story of Friendship and Betrayal* (London: Biteback Publishing, 2014), p. 13; Andrew Lownie, *Stalin's Englishman: The Lives of Guy Burgess* (London: Hodder & Stoughton, 2015), p. 27; Cecil, *A Divided Life*, p. 22.

2 Andrew and Mitrokhin, *The Mitrokhin Archive*, pp. 73–75.

3 Andrew, *Defence of the Realm*, pp. 164–68.

4 John Costello, *Mask of Treachery: The First Documented Dossier on Blunt, MI5, and Soviet Subversion* (London: Collins, 1988), pp. 117–18.

5   Carter, *Anthony Blunt*, p.106.

6   Quoted in Geoff Andrews, *The Shadow Man At the Heart of the Cambridge Spy
       Circle* (London: I.B.Tauris, 2015), p.31.

7   T.E.B. Howarth, *Cambridge Between Two Wars* (London: Collins, 1978), p.201.

8   James Denman and Paul McDonald, 'Unemployment statistics from 1881 to
       the present day', *Labour Market Trends*, vol. 104, no. 1 (1996), p.6.

9   Carter, *Anthony Blunt*, pp.106–07.

10   Michael Holzman, *Donald and Melinda Maclean: Idealism and Espionage* (New
       York, NY: Chelmsford Press, 2014), p.75.

11   Andrews, *The Shadow Man*, pp.36–38. Meyer would, after the Second
       World War, undergo an ideological conversion to staunch conservatism,
       and became a leading Conservative intellectual. See William C. Dennis,
       'Foreword', in Frank S. Meyer, *In Defense of Freedom and Related Essays*
       (Indianapolis, IN: Liberty Fund, 1966), pp.xi–xxiii.

12   George Orwell, *Orwell's England: The Road to Wigan Pier in the Context of
       Essays, Reviews, Letters and Poems* (London: Penguin, 2001), p.109.

13   Carter, *Anthony Blunt*, p.107.

14   Quoted in Andrews, *The Shadow Man*, p.36.

15   Cambridge University Library, Wladislaw Zlorin, 'King Kong', *Trinity
       Magazine*, May Term 1933, p.17.

16   Peter Stansky and William Abrahams, *Journey to the Frontier: Two Roads to the
       Spanish Civil War* (London: Constable, 1966), pp.107–08; Note that Richard
       Deacon also records this event. In his narrative, Bell was accompanied by
       David Haden-Guest and the 'reactionaries' were members of Jesus College
       club. Deacon records the year of this escapade as 1925; given that Bell would
       have been 17 years of age in 1925 and Haden-Guest a mere 14, this date
       is clearly erroneous on this point at least. Richard Deacon, *The Cambridge
       Apostles: A History of Cambridge University's Élite Intellectual Secret Society*
       (London: Robert Royce Limited, 1985), p.112.

17   Quoted in Stansky and Abrahams, *Journey to the Frontier*, p.109.

18   Howarth, *Cambridge between Two Wars*, p.201.

19   Andrews, *The Shadow Man*, p.44.

20   Cambridge University Library, D.G., 'Fascism—A Blind Alley', *Trinity
       Magazine*, May Term 1933, pp.19–21.

21   Denman and McDonald, 'Unemployment statistics from 1881 to the present
       day', p.6.

22   Quoted in: Deacon, *The Cambridge Apostles*, p. 108. Blunt made a similar
       statement to Moscow in a brief autobiographical sketch he provided for
       them in 1943. See: West and Tsarev, *The Crown Jewels*, p.129.

23   Eric Hobsbawm, *Interesting Times: A Twentieth Century Life* (London: Allen
       Lane, 2002), p.100.

24   Costello and Tsarev, *Deadly Illusions*, pp.115–16; Borovik, *The Philby Files*,
       p.202.

25 Kim Philby, *My Silent War: An Autobiography of a Spy* (New York, NY: The Modern Library, 2002), p.132.

26 Andrews, *The Shadow Man*, p.36.

27 Philby, *My Silent War*, p. xxx. [add?]

28 Ben Macintyre, *A Spy among Friends: Philby and the Great Betrayal* (London: Bloomsbury, 2015), pp. 37–38. For further details also see Borovik, *The Philby Files*, pp.14–22.

29 Sir Donald Maclean was also a disciple of H.H. Asquith and eventually, in 1918–1920, led the Liberal opposition to David Lloyd George's Conservative backed government.

30 Cecil, *A Divided Life*, p.14.

31 Holzman, *Donald and Melinda Maclean*, p.46.

32 Cecil, *A Divided Life*, p.19.

33 Holzman, *Donald and Melinda Maclean*, p.50.

34 Cecil, *A Divided Life*, pp.22–25.

35 Costello and Tsarev, *Deadly Illusions*, p.193.

36 Borovik, *The Philby Files*, p.42.

37 Lownie, *Stalin's Englishman*, pp.8–16.

38 Purvis and Hulbert, *Guy Burgess*, pp.8–13.

39 Named after the former Prime Minister, William Pitt the Younger.

40 Purvis and Hulbert, *Guy Burgess*, pp.15–24.

41 Lownie, *Stalin's Englishman*, pp.28–29.

42 Lownie, *Stalin's Englishman*, p.54.

43 Modin, *My Five Cambridge Friends*, p.53; Lownie, *Stalin's Englishman*, p.55. Further details are provided in Borovik, *The Philby Files*, pp.48–49.

44 Carter, *Anthony Blunt*, pp.18–32.

45 Carter, *Anthony Blunt*, pp.45–51, 70–71.

46 Andrews, *The Shadow Man*, pp.63–64.

47 Modin, *My Five Cambridge Friends*, pp.69–70.

48 Lownie, *Stalin's Englishman*, pp.34–35; Purvis and Hulbert, *Guy Burgess*, p.33; for a full list of members and their political affiliation, see Costello, *Mask of Treachery*, pp.189–90.

49 Carter, *Anthony Blunt*, pp.162, 131–32. Modin suggests that the trip was in 1934 and that Burgess also attended. Modin, *My Five Cambridge Friends*, p. 72.

50 Purvis and Hulbert, *Guy Burgess*, pp.51–52; Carter, *Anthony Blunt*, pp.162–63. Modin suggests that Blunt met Deutsch in 1934 while in the Soviet Union and remained in contact with him from that point forward. Modin, *My Five Cambridge Friends*, p.74.

51 Quoted in West and Tsarev, *The Crown Jewels*, p.130.

52 Andrews, *The Shadow Man*, p.85.

53 Deacon, *The Cambridge Apostles*, pp.113–14.

54 'Teacher Killed in Spain', *The New York Times*, 7 August 1938, p.26.

Chapter 3

1 Cecil, *A Divided Life*, p.24.

2 Cairncross, *The Enigma Spy*, pp.27–32.

3 Michael Pacione, *Glasgow: The Socio-spatial Development of the City* (Chichester: John Wiley & Sons, 1995), pp.130–38.

4 GB Historical GIS, University of Portsmouth, Glasgow ScoCofC through time | Work and Poverty Statistics | Claimant Count Unemployment, A Vision of Britain through Time, www.visionofbritain.org.uk/unit/10262811/cube/INSURED_UNEM (accessed: 2 July 2017).

5 Peter Reed, 'The Tenement City', in Peter Reed (ed), *Glasgow: The Forming of a City* (Edinburgh: Edinburgh University Press, 1999), p.104.

6 Charles McKean, 'Between the Wars', in Peter Reed (ed), *Glasgow: The Forming of a City* (Edinburgh: Edinburgh University Press, 1999), p.143.

7 Michael Moss, J. Forbes Munro and Richard H. Trainor, *University, City and State: The University of Glasgow since 1870* (Edinburgh: Edinburgh University Press, 2000), p.163.

8 A.L. Brown and Michael Moss, *The University of Glasgow: 1451–1996* (Edinburgh: Edinburgh University Press, 1996), p.118.

9 Moss, Forbes and Trainor, *University, City and State*, p.166.

10 Moss, Forbes and Trainor, *University, City and State*, p.167.

11 Moss, Forbes and Trainor, *University, City and State*, p.163.

12 University of Glasgow Archive [hereafter UGA], R8/5/51/2, Matriculation Records, 1930–1931; UGA, DC106 Additions, 10/26, Press cutting of Andrew S. Cairncross' obituary. No date or no publication title are provided. However, the obituary was certainly written between late December 1975 and early January 1976.

13 UGA, Sen10/72, The Glasgow University Calendar 1930–31, pp.807, 808, 811; UGA, Sen10/73, The Glasgow University Calendar 1931–32, p.831, 851.

14 UGA, R20/2, Results of Open Bursary Competition 1929–1940; UGA, R8/5/51/2 – Matriculation Records, 1930–1931.

15 UGA, Sen10/73, The Glasgow University Calendar 1931–32, pp.828, 831; UGA, Sen10/74, The Glasgow University Calendar 1932-33, p.834, 836.

16 UGA, DC106/6/1/5, Lecture notes of Alec Cairncross: Political Economy 1928–1929.

17 UGA, DC106/6/1/1, Lecture notes of Alec Cairncross: English A, 1928–1929; DC106/6/1/2, Lecture notes of Alec Cairncross: English B, 1928–1929.

18 Robert Campbell Garry, *Life in Physiology. Memoirs of Glasgow University's Institute of Physiology during the 1920s and 1930s* (Glasgow: Glasgow Wellcome Unit for the History of Medicine, 1992), p.174–76.

19 Cairncross, *Living with the Century*, p.42.

20 Cairncross, *The Enigma Spy*, p.28.

21 James F. McMillan, *Twentieth Century France: Politics and Society, 1898–1991* (London: Edward Arnold, 1991), p.106.

22 Cairncross, *The Enigma Spy*, p.30.

23 Cairncross, *The Enigma Spy*, pp.30–34.

24 Cairncross, *The Enigma Spy*, pp.36–37.

25 Cairncross, *Living with the Century*, p.41.

26 Cairncross, *The Enigma Spy*, pp.37–38.

27 CUL, *Trinity College Magazine*, 'Who's Who', Easter Term 1936.

28 Cairncross, *The Enigma Spy*, p.41–42

29 Cairncross, *The Enigma Spy*, pp.37–42

30 Appendix Four.

31 Cairncross, *The Enigma Spy*, p. 44.

32 Appendix Two.

33 Christopher Andrew, 'Cambridge Spies: the 'Magnificent Five', 1933–1945, in Sarah J. Ormrod (ed.) *Cambridge Contributions* (Cambridge, Cambridge University Press, 1998), p.216.

34 Cairncross, *The Enigma Spy*, p.46.

35 University of Glasgow Archives (UGA), DC106 additions 83/1-28, 8/23, Handwritten diary of Sir Alexander Cairncross, 1979, 22 December 1979.

36 TNA, FCO 158/129, John Cairncross [undated personal profile, likely produced in 1952/53].

37 West and Tsarev, *The Crown Jewels*, pp.204–05.

Chapter 4

1 Purvis and Hulbert, *Guy Burgess*.

2 Cairncross, *The Enigma Spy*, pp.47–49.

3 John Dickie, *Inside the Foreign Office* (London: Chapmans Publishers, 1992), p.13.

4 Dickie, *Inside the Foreign Office*, p.15.

5 Quoted in T.G. Otte, 'Old Diplomacy: Reflections on the Foreign Office before 1914', *Contemporary British History, vol. 18, no. 3* (2004), p.35.

6 Otte, 'Old Diplomacy: Reflections on the Foreign Office before 1914', pp.34–35.

7 William Strang, *The Foreign Office* (London: George Allen & Unwin, 1955), p.72.

8 Paul Bolton, Education: Historical statistics, House of Commons Briefing papers, SN04252 (2012) researchbriefings.parliament.uk/ResearchBriefing/Summary/SN04252.

9 A.H. Halsey, *Trends in British Society since 1900: A Guide to the Changing Social Structure of Britain* (London: Palgrave Macmillan, 1972), p.183.

10   Peter Hennessy, *Whitehall* (London: Fontana Press: 1990), pp.78–79.

11   Strang, *The Foreign Office*, p.69.

12   Zara Steiner, 'The Foreign and Commonwealth Office: Resistance and Adaptation to Changing Times', *Contemporary British History, vol. 18, no. 3* (2004), p.21.

13   Steiner, *The Foreign and Commonwealth Office: Resistance and Adaptation to Changing Times*, p.21.

14   Peter Hennessy, *Establishment and Meritocracy* (London: Haus Publishing, 2014), p.7.

15   Cairncross, *The Enigma Spy*, p.50.

16   Cairncross, *The Enigma Spy*, p.51.

17   Cairncross, *The Enigma Spy*, p.52.

18   Cairncross, *The Enigma Spy*, p.55, 62.

19   Gerald Howson, *Arms for Spain: The Untold Story of the Spanish Civil War* (London: John Murray, 1998), pp.34–36.

20   Quoted in: Howson, *Arms for Spain*, p.36.

21   Anthony Beevor, *The Battle for Spain: The Spanish Civil War, 1936–1939* (London: Phoenix, 1982, 2006), pp.147–49.

22   Macintyre, *A Spy Among Friends*, p.47.

23   Quoted in: *Phillip Knightley, Philby: The Life and Views of the K.G.B. Masterspy* (London: André Deutsch, 1988, 2003), p.59.

24   TNA, FO 371/21287, Damage to Madrid, W5173, 17 March 1937.

25   Cairncross, *The Enigma Spy*, p.56.

26   Beevor, *The Battle for Spain*, pp.272–73.

27   Arthur Koestler, *Spanish Testament* (London: Victor Gollancz, 1937), pp.219–26.

28   Beevor, *The Battle for Spain*, p.225.

29   Cairncross, *The Enigma Spy*, p.56.

30   Pincher, *Their Trade is Treachery*, pp.153–55.

31   Nigel West, *Molehunt: Searching for Soviet Spies in British Intelligence* (New York, NY: Berkley Books, 1987, 1991), p.35; Andrew and Gordievsky, *KGB*, p.172.

32   Modin, *My Five Cambridge Friends*, pp. 105–06.

33   Modin, *My Five Cambridge Friends*, p.105.

34   Modin, *My Five Cambridge Friends*, p.107.

35   Andrew and Mitrokhin, *The Mitrokhin Archive*, p.85, 767 (note 69); Andrew, *The Defence of the Realm*, p.173.

36   Andrew and Mitrokhin, *The Mitrokhin Archive*, p.85, 767 (note 69); Andrew, *The Defence of the Realm*, p.85. In the accompanying end note, Andrew and Mitrokhin attribute the incorrect date and minute number. See: TNA, FO 371/21287, 25 March 1937, W5214,

37   Cairncross, *The Enigma Spy*, p.57.

38   Penrose and Freeman, *Conspiracy of Silence*, p.369.

39   Cairncross, *Enigma Spy*, pp.58–59.

40   Appendix 2

41   Goronwy Rees latterly became the Principal of the University of Wales, Aberystwyth from 1953 to 1957. In the 1930s he was an ardent anti-fascist, Marxist and Soviet spy. He broke with the Soviet Union out of disgust with the Molotov-Ribbentrop Pact of 1939. See Cecil, *A Divided Life*, p.114.

42   Appendix 2. For Cairncross' later, very similar narrative in his autobiography, see: Cairncross, *Enigma Spy*, pp.58–63.

43   Cairncross, *Enigma Spy*, p.62; West and Tsarev, *The Crown Jewels*, p.210.

44   West and Tsarev, *The Crown Jewels*, pp.207–08.

Chapter 5

1   Cairncross, *The Enigma Spy*, p. 62.

2   'Executions in Moscow', *The Spectator*, 5 February 1937, p. 2; Walter Duranty, 'Soviet executes 13 as Trotskyists; Curtly Announces Sentences Have Been Carried Out, but Gives No Details', *The New York Times*, 2 February 1937, p.14.

3   Cairncross, *The Enigma Spy*, pp.71–72.

4   Cecil, *A Divided Life*, p.40.

5   Cairncross, *The Enigma Spy*, p.65.

6   Cairncross, *The Enigma Spy*, pp. 65–66. In the 1980s, Cairncross began rough drafts of a history of the appeasement era. In one such draft he described himself as being Churchillian in the 1930s. CUL, SC, MS Add. 10042 (Papers of John Cairncross), Large Box 2, Munich and After by David Jardine, p.6.

7   Cairncross, *The Enigma Spy*, pp. 181–82.

8   Pincher, *Their Trade is Treachery*, pp.153–54.

9   Andrew and Gordievsky, *KGB*, p.172; Cairncross, *Enigma Spy*, p.5.

10   Cairncross, *The Enigma Spy*, p.40.

11   Penrose and Freeman, *Conspiracy of Silence*, p.369.

12   Modin, *My Five Cambridge Friends*, p.107.

13   Cairncross, *The Enigma Spy*, p.52.

14   John Colville, *The Fringes of Power: Downing Street Diaries, 1939–1955* (London: Hodder and Stoughton, 1985), p.30. However, by 1945, Cairncross was noted as being 'less of a bore than he used to be'. Colville, Colville, *The Fringes of Power*, p.562.

15   Penrose and Freeman, *Conspiracy of Silence*, p.370.

16   West and Tsarev, *The Crown Jewels*, pp. 208–09.

17   Cairncross, *Living With the Century*, pp.300–01.

18   Cairncross, *The Enigma Spy*, p.51.

19   West and Tsarev, *The Crown Jewels*, p.211.

20   TNA, FCO 158/129, Edward Youde, Mr John Cairncross: Case History
      Derived From Head of Security Department File QPF 2/343 (H) [Draft],
      28 December 1979.

21   Andrew and Gordievsky, *KGB*, p.174. See note 162.

22   TNA, FCO 158/129, J.E.D. Street to Sir B[ernard] Burrows [The Deputy
      Under-Secretary for Foreign Affairs(Defence)], 19 February 1964.

23   TNA, FCO 158/129, Edward Youde, Mr John Cairncross: Case History
      Derived From Head of Security Department File QPF 2/343 (H) [Draft],
      28 December 1979.

24   Andrew and Gordievsky, *KGB*, p.172.

25   Andrew and Gordievsky, *KGB*, pp.143–44.

26   D. Cameron Watt, 'Francis Herbert King: A Soviet Source in the Foreign
      Office', *Intelligence and National Security, vol. 3, no. 4* (1988), p.62.

27   TNA, KV 2/815, Special Branch Report: Helen Wilkie, 17 October 1939;
      TNA, KV 2/815, Special Branch Report: J.H. King, 17 October 1939.

28   Andrew and Gordievsky, *KGB*, p.144.

29   TNA, KV 2/815, Statement of John Herbert King, 28 September 1939, p.3.

30   Andrew, *Secret Service*, p.182.

31   TNA, KV 2/815, Statement of John Herbert King, 28 September 1939, p.3.

32   Andrew and Gordievsky, *KGB*, p.174.

33   West and Tsarev, *The Crown Jewels*, p.209.

34   Cairncross, *The Enigma Spy*, p.75. *Rezidentura* meaning the base of operations
      or station of spies operating in a foreign country.

35   Modin, *My Five Cambridge Friends*, p.108.

36   West and Tsarev, *The Crown Jewels*, p.209.

37   Modin, *My Five Cambridge Friends*, p.108.

38   Cairncross, *The Enigma Spy*, pp.72–73.

39   Cairncross, *The Enigma Spy*, p.69.

40   West and Tsarev, *The Crown Jewels*, p.211.

41   Andrew and Mitrokhin, *The Mitrokhin Archive*, p.767 (note 72). SVR stand-
      ing for Sluzhba Vneshney Razvedki, the Foreign Intelligence Service of the
      Russian Federation.

42   Boris Volodarsky, *Stalin's Agent: The Life and Death of Alexander Orlov* (Oxford:
      Oxford University Press, 2015), pp.122–23.

43   Cairncross, *The Enigma Spy*, p.73; Andrew and Mitrokhin, *The Mitrokhin
      Archive*, p.104, 109.

44   Cairncross, *The Enigma Spy*, p.69.

45   West and Tsarev, *The Crown Jewels*, p.209.

46   Modin, *My Five Cambridge Friends*, p.108. The 'Lubyanka' being the head-
      quarters of the NKVD in Lubyanka Square, Moscow.

47   TNA, FCO 158/129, Edward Youde, Mr John Cairncross: Case History
      Derived From Head of Security Department File QPF 2/343 (H) [Draft],
      28 December 1979.

48   Hennessy, *Whitehall*, p.78.
49   Cairncross, *The Enigma Spy*, p.73.
50   Cairncross, *The Enigma Spy*, pp.81–83.
51   West and Tsarev, *The Crown Jewels*, p.212.
52   Andrew and Mitrokhin, *The Mitrokhin Archive*, pp.107–09.
53   Costello and Tsarev, *Deadly Illusions*, p.218.
54   Andrew and Mitrokhin, *The Mitrokhin Archive*, p.118.
55   Cecil, *A Divided Life*, p.66.
56   Cairncross, *The Enigma Spy*, p.73.
57   Modin, *My Five Cambridge Friends*, p.112.
58   Andrew, *Defence of the Realm*, p.280; Ben Wheatley, *British Intelligence and Hitler's Empire in the Soviet Union, 1941–1945* (London: Bloomsbury, 2017), p.41.

Chapter 6

1   Quoted in: Paul Kennedy, *The Rise and Fall of British Naval Mastery* (London: Penguin, 1976, 2001), p.290.
2   Alan Bullock, *Hitler and Stalin: Parallel Lives* (London: HarperCollins, 1991), p.544.
3   Henry Pelling, *Britain and the Second World War* (London: Collins, 1970), pp.22–23.
4   Penrose and Freeman, *Conspiracy of Silence*, p.207.
5   Quoted in: Lownie, *Stalin's Englishman*, p.95.
6   Donald Maclean, *British Foreign Policy Since Suez, 1956–1968* (London: Hodder and Stoughton, 1970), pp.39, 109, 286, 324.
7   CUL, SC, MS Add. 10042 (Papers of John Cairncross), Large Box 2, Munich and After by David Jardine.
8   Appendix 2.
9   Andrew and Mitrokhin, *The Mitrokhin Archive*, p.109.
10   Louis MacNeice, 'Primrose Hill', The Spectator, 25 August 1939, p.13.
11   John Harris, *Goronwy Rees* (Cardiff: University of Wales Press, 2001), p.58.
12   Quoted in Cecil, *A Divided Life*, p.114.
13   National Library of Wales, Goronwy Rees Papers, 2/2 – Cambridge Spy Ring Papers, David Footman, undated character description entitled 'Goronwy Rees'.
14   Harris, *Goronwy Rees*, p.59.
15   Quoted in: Robert McKay, *The Test of War: Inside Britain, 1939–1945* (London: Routledge, 1999), p.3. For some Conservatives, particularly in the wake of the Molotov–Ribbentrop Pact and Soviet expansionist policy in Eastern Europe, it was something of wonder that Britain was at war with Germany as opposed to the Soviet Union. 'I feel that it is rather pitiful,'

wrote the former MP Sir Cuthbert Headlam in his diaries, '[we] are shutting our eyes to Russia's aggression while we make such a to do about that of Germany ... the Bolshies are a greater menace to us than are the Nazis. I should sever [the] diplomatic relationship with Russia if I were in power ... This Russian method of grab is almost more intolerable than Hitler's.' Cuthbert Headlam, *Parliament and Politics in the Age of Churchill and Attlee: The Headlam Diaries 1935–1951*, ed. Stuart Ball (Cambridge: Cambridge University Press, 1999), p.72.

16   Wesley K. Wark, 'Appeasement Revisited', *The International History Review*, vol. 17, no. 3 (1995), p.560.

17   Michael Straight, *After Long Silence* (London: Collins, 1983), pp.144–45.

18   Cairncross, *The Enigma Spy*, pp.77–78.

19   Hansard, HC Debate, 3 September 1939, vol. 351 c. 292.

20   Max Hastings, *All Hell Let Loose: The World At War, 1939–1945* (London: Harper Press, 2012), pp.48–50.

21   Hansard, HC Deb, 7 May 1940, vol. 360, cc. 1164–65.

22   Philip Warner, *World War II: The Untold Story* (London: The Bodley Head, 1988), p.75.

23   Clive Ponting, *1940: Myth and Reality* (London: Hamish Hamilton, 1990), p.88.

24   'News of the Week', *Spectator*, no. 5840, 31 May 1940, p.1.

25   Juliet Gardiner, *Wartime: Britain, 1939–1945* (London: Headline, 2004), p.210.

26   Quoted in: Alan Bullock, *Hitler and Stalin: Parallel Lives* (London: Harper Collins, 1991), p.754.

27   J. Noakes and G. Pridham (eds.), *Nazism, 1939–1945 – Volume 3: Foreign Policy, War and Racial Extermination* (Exeter: University of Exeter Press, 1997), p.809.

28   Martin Marix Evans and Angus Mcgeoch, *Invasion!: Operation Sea Lion, 1940* (London: Routledge, 2004), p.68.

29   Quoted in: Phillips Payson O'Brien, *How The War Was Won: Air-Sea Power and Allied Victory in World War II* (Cambridge: Cambridge University Press, 2015), p.122. Note also that Operation Sea Lion plans were laden with insurmountable obstacles and the entire enterprise was rightly described by O'Brien as 'preposterous'.

30   TNA, FCO 158/129, J.E.D Street, John Cairncross, 19 February 1964.

31   Andrew and Mitrokhin, *The Mitrokhin Archive*, p.119.

32   West and Tsarev, *The Crown Jewels*, p.214.

33   Cairncross, *The Enigma Spy*, p.86.

34   Headlam, *Headlam Diaries*, 24 October 1939, p.172.

35   Cairncross, *The Enigma Spy*, pp.86–87.

36   Cairncross, *The Enigma Spy*, p.90.

37   Cairncross, *The Enigma Spy*, pp.90–91.

38   Commonwealth War Graves Commission, 'Cairncross, William Wishart',
      Service No: 5108015 www.cwgc.org/find-war-dead/casualty/2715805

39   Cairncross, *Living with the Century*, pp.75–76.

40   Cairncross, *The Enigma Spy*, pp.91–92.

41   Nigel West and Oleg Tsarev, eds., *TRIPLEX: Secrets From the Cambridge Spies*
      (New Haven, CT: Yale University Press, 2009), pp.190–233. See also the dia-
      ries of Guy Liddell, 2 March 1940. Guy Liddell, *The Guy Liddell Diaries, vol.
      1: 1939–1942 – MI5's Director of Counter-Espionage in World War II*, ed. Nigel
      West (London: Routledge, 2005), p.69.

42   West and Tsarev, *The Crown Jewels*, p.114.

43   Such is the seriousness of this charge, changing the nature and significantly
      elevating the importance of Cairncross' espionage work for the Soviet
      Union, it has been repeatedly discussed. For examples see: Richard Rhodes,
      Dark Sun: The Making Of The Hydrogen Bomb (New York, NY: Simon and
      Schuster, 1995, 2011), pp.52–53; Michael D. Gordin, *Red Cloud at Dawn:
      Truman, Stalin, and the End of the Atomic Monopoly* (New York, NY: Farrah,
      Straus and Giroux, 2009), pp.111–17; Michael S. Goodman, *Spying on the
      Nuclear Bear: Anglo–American Intelligence and the Soviet Bomb* (Stanford, CA:
      Stanford University Press, 2007), pp.82–83.

44   Andrew and Gordievsky, *KGB*, p.253.

45   *Newsnight*, BBC 2, 31 October 1990. See also: Cairncross, *Enigma Spy*,
      pp.8–10.

46   Costello and Tsarev, *Deadly Illusions*, p.218.

47   Pavel Sudoplatov and Anatoli Sudoplatov, *Special Tasks: The Memoirs of an
      Unwanted Witness – A Soviet Spymaster*, with Jerrold L. Schecter and Leona
      P. Schecter (London: Little, Brown and Company, 1994), pp.437–41, 463
      (note 2), 464 (note c).

48   Sheila Kerr, 'KGB sources on the Cambridge network of Soviet agents: True
      or false?', *Intelligence and National Security*, vol. 11, no. 3 (1996), pp.561–85;
      John Earl Haynes and Harvey Klehr, 'Special Tasks and Sacred Secrets on
      Soviet Atomic Espionage', *Intelligence and National Security*, vol. 26, no. 5
      (2011), pp.656–75; Nigel West, *Mortal Crimes: The Greatest Theft in History:
      The Soviet Penetration of the Manhattan Project* (New York, NY: Enigma, 2004),
      pp.15–17.

49   Nigel West, *The A to Z of British Intelligence* (Lanham, MD: Scarecrow Press,
      2009), p.310. It has also been suggested that these attributions to Maclean
      were deliberate attempts at obfuscation by the Russian intelligence services
      in an effort to protect Cairncross while he was still alive. See: Haynes and
      Klehr, 'Special Tasks and Sacred Secrets on Soviet Atomic Espionage',
      p.658–59 (note 7).

50   Modin, *My Five Cambridge Friends*, p. 109.

51   'Vassiliev Yellow Notebook #1', History and Public Policy Program Digital
      Archive, Alexander Vassiliev Papers, Manuscript Division, Library of Congress,

digitalarchive.wilsoncenter.org/document/112856, p.1. See also pages, 6, 29. On the subject of the veracity of this information, Philip Boobbyer, a specialist on modern Russian history, opined: 'Although there are still questions to ask about how and why Vassiliev had access to the particular documents that he saw, and how he found time to transcribe them all, there is no reason to doubt their reliability – even though scholars cannot check the actual originals'. Philip Boobbyer, 'Review: Spies: The Rise and Fall of the KGB in America by Haynes, John Earl; Klehr, Harvey; Vassiliev, Alexander', *The Slavonic and East European Review*, vol. 89, no.2 (2011), p.371.

52   West and Tsarev, *The Crown Jewels*, p.228; Michael Smith, 'The humble Scot who rose to the top – but then chose treachery', *The Daily Telegraph*, 12 January 1998. This evidence has not, however, been deemed sufficient by some scholars to rule out Maclean. See: Jerrold L. Schecter and Leona Schecter, *Sacred Secrets: How Soviet Intelligence Operations Changed American History* (Washington, DC: Brassey's 2002), pp.48, 348 (note 5).

53   Michael. S. Goodman, *The Official History of the Joint Intelligence Committee, Volume 1: From the Approach of the Second World War to the Suez Crisis* (London: Routledge, 2014), p.284.

54   Quoted in, Richard J. Aldrich (ed.), *Espionage, Security and Intelligence in Britain, 1945–1970* (Manchester: Manchester University Press, 1998), p.141.

Chapter 7

1   West and Tsarev, *The Crown Jewels*, p.217.

2   A.G. Denniston, 'The Government Code and Cypher School Between the Wars', in Christopher Andrew (ed.), *Codebreaking and Signals Intelligence* (London: Frank Cass, 1986), p.49.

3   Michael Smith, 'The Government Code and Cypher School and the First Cold War', in Michael Smith and Ralph Erskine (eds), *Action This Day: Bletchley Park from the Breaking of the Enigma Code to the Birth of the Modern Computer* (London: Transworld Publishers, 2001), pp.15–40.

4   Wesley K. Wark, *The Ultimate Enemy: British Intelligence and Nazi Germany, 1933–1939* (Oxford: Oxford University Press, 1986), p.17.

5   Pelling, *Britain and the Second World War*, pp.22–23; Kennedy, *The Rise and Fall of British Naval Mastery*, pp.289–92.

6   Frank Birch, *The Official History of Sigint: 1919–1945*, vol. 1 (part 1), John Jackson (ed.) (Milton Keynes, 2004), p.20.

7   For an excellent technical outline of how Enigma worked and the history of its development see, Simon Singh, *The Code Book: the Secret History of Codes and Codebreaking* (London: Fourth Estate, 1999, 2000), pp.127–42. See also, Ralph Erskine, 'Enigma's Security: What the Germans Knew', in Michael Smith and Ralph Erskine (eds), *Action This Day: Bletchley Park from*

the Breaking of the Enigma Code to the Birth of the Modern Computer (London: Transworld Publishers, 2001), pp.370–85.

8   Smith, *The Hidden History of Bletchley Park*, p. 7; Christopher Smith, 'How I Learned to Stop Worrying and Love the Bombe: Machine Research and Development and Bletchley Park', *History of Science*, vol. 52, no. 2 (2014), p.205–08.

9   R.A. Ratcliff, *Delusions of Intelligence: Enigma, Ultra, and the End of Secure Ciphers* (Cambridge, Cambridge University Press, 2006), p.75; Joel Greenberg, *Gordon Welchman: Bletchley Park's Architect of Ultra Intelligence* (London: Frontline Books, 2014), pp.24–25. The name Bomba, or Bomby, referred to the ticking noise made by the machine while in operation, Michael Smith, *Station X: The Codebreakers of Bletchley Park* (London: Pan Books, 1998, 2004), p.25–26.

10   Smith, *The Hidden History of Bletchley Park*, p.8.

11   Denniston, 'The Government Code and Cypher School Between the Wars', p.52.

12   For full length biographies of these individuals, see: Sara Turing, *Alan M. Turing* (London: W. Heffer and Sons, 1959); Andrew Hodges, *Alan Turing: The Enigma* (New York: Vintage, 1983, 2012); Dermot Turing, *Prof: Alan Turing Decoded* (Stroud: The History Press, 2015); Greenberg, *Welchman*.

13   Hodges, *Alan Turing*, p.549 (note 4.9).

14   TNA, HW 72/9, Alistair Denniston to C.E.D. Peters, 26 April, 1932.

15   TNA, HW 25/2, A.P. Mahon, *The History of Hut Eight 1939–1945*, p.28.

16   John Keen, Harold 'Doc' Keen and the Bletchley Park Bombe (Cleobury Mortimer: M & M Baldwin, 2003, 2012), p.30.

17   Kerry Johnson and John Gallehawk, eds, *Figuring it Out at Bletchley Park, 1939–1945* (Redditch: BookTower Publishing, 2007), p.167.

18   Smith, *The Hidden History of Bletchley Park*, pp.61–65.

19   Johnson and Gallehawk, *Figuring it Out*, p.3.

20   John Jackson (ed.) *Solving Enigma's Secrets: The Official History of Bletchley Park's Hut 6* (Redditch: BookTower Publishing, 2014), p.87.

21   John Jackson (ed.), *The Secret War of Hut 3: The First Full Story of How Intelligence from Enigma Signals Decoded at Bletchley Park was Used During World War Two* (Milton Keynes: Military Press, 2002), *The Secret War of Hut 3*, pp.11–12.

22   Jackson (ed.), *The Secret War of Hut 3*, pp.10–12.

23   Smith, *The Hidden History of Bletchley Park*, pp.71–96.

24   Ralph Bennett, *Behind the Battle: Intelligence in the War with Germany, 1939–1945* (London: Pimlico, 1994, 1999), pp.63–64.

25   Bennett, *Behind the Battle*, pp.57–59.

26   F.H. Hinsley, et al., *British Intelligence in the Second World War*, vol. 2, (London: HMSO, 1981), p.169.

27   For a fascinating account of the Ultra secret and its ultimate release in 1974, see: Christopher Moran, *Classified: Secrecy and the State in Modern Britain* (Cambridge: Cambridge University Press, 2013), pp.256–80.

28   Richard Trahair and Robert Miller, *Encyclopaedia of Cold War Espionage, Spies and Secret Operations* (Oxford: Enigma Books, 2012), pp.225–26.

29   West and Tsarev, *The Crown Jewels*, 217.

30   Tammy M. Proctor, 'Family Ties in the Making of Modern Intelligence', Journal of Social History, 39:2, *Kith and Kin: Interpersonal Relationships and Cultural Practices*, (Winter 2005), p.452. Also see, Rosemary F. Toy and Christopher Smith, 'Women in the shadow war: gender, class and MI5 in the Second World War', Women's History Review, early online access, DOI: 10.1080/09612025.2017.1345714, p.4.

31   Cited in Christopher Andrew, 'F.H. Hinsley and the Cambridge Moles', in Richard Langhorn (ed.) *Diplomacy and Intelligence During the Second World War: Essays in Honour of F.H. Hinsley* (Cambridge: Cambridge University Press, 2004), p.32.

Chapter 8

1   Cairncross, *The Enigma Spy*, p.96.

2   Hugh Denham, 'Bedford-Bletchley-Kilindini-Columbo', in F.H. Hinsley and Alan Stripp, *Codebreakers: The Inside Story of Bletchley Park* (Oxford: Oxford University Press, 1992, 2001), p.265.

3   Cairncross: *The Enigma Spy*, p.96.

4   R.A. Ratcliff, *Delusions of Intelligence: Enigma, Ultra, and the End of Secure Ciphers* (Cambridge: Cambridge University Press, 2006), pp.113–14.

5   John Colville, *The Fringes of Power: Downing Street Diaries, 1939–1955* (London: Hodder & Stoughton, 1985), 14 November 1940, p.250.

6   F.W. Winterbotham, *The Ultra Secret* (London: Weidenfeld and Nicolson, 1974).

7   Calvocoressi, *Top Secret Ultra*, pp.60–61.

8   TNA, HW 64/16, Guard at Bletchley Park, 15 December 1939.

9   TNA, HW 64/16, Challenge by Sentries, 6 April 1940.

10   TNA, HW 64/16, Careless Talk, 24 August 1940; HW 64/16, Security, 16 August 1941; HW 64/16, Indiscreet Talk, 9 September 1941

11   See: TNA, HW 62/8, passim; TNA, HW 64/71, passim.

12   TNA, HW 64/16, Security in G.C. & C.S., 11 May 1942.

13   It has also been suggested that the 'Lucy Ring', an anti-Nazi spy ring operating out of Switzerland, was also a clandestine British-controlled conduit for supplying the Soviet Union with Ultra. See, Anthony Read and David Fisher, Operation Lucy: Most Secret Spy Ring of the Second World War (New York, N.Y.: Coward, McCann & Geoghegan, Inc, 1981). This, however,

has proven to be a highly controversial thesis and roundly rejected by most historians. For a discussion of why that is the case, see: Phillip Knightley, *The Second Oldest Profession: Spies and Spying in the Twentieth Century* (New York, NY: W. W. Norton & Company, 1986, 1987) pp.202–04.

14   Cairncross, *The Enigma Spy*, pp.99–102.

15   West and Tsarev, *The Crown Jewels*, p.217; Smith, Station X, p. 163.

16   Simon Singh, *The Codebook: the Secret History of Codes and Code-Breaking* (London: Fourth Estate, 2000), p.142.

17   Wesley Wark, *The Ultimate Enemy: British Intelligence and Nazi Germany 1933–1939* (Oxford, Oxford University Press, 1986), p.18.

18   Frank Birch, *The Official History of Sigint: 1919–1945*, vol. 1 (part 1), John Jackson (ed.) (Milton Keynes: Military Press, 2004), p.20.

19   Smith, *The Hidden History of Bletchley Park*, pp. 48–50.

20   Smith, *The Hidden History of Bletchley Park*, pp.34–38.

21   Peter Calvocoressi, *Top Secret Ultra* (London: Cassell, 1980) p.55

22   These descriptions of the work of these sections is highly superficial and incomplete. For a fuller description of the blocks and sections at Bletchley Park, see: 'Bletchley Park Trust Report No. 18', *History of Bletchley Park Huts & Blocks 1939–1945*, revised by Arthur Bonsall (2009).

23   Calvocoressi, *Top Secret Ultra*, p. 56.

24   Cairncross, *The Enigma Spy*, p.97.

25   Cairncross, *The Enigma Spy*, p.98.

26   Calvocoressi, *Top Secret Ultra*, pp.54–58.

27   TNA, HW 64/56, Afternoon Tea, 20 May 1942.

28   GB Historical GIS, University of Portsmouth, Bletchley UD through time, Population Statistics, | Total Population, A Vision of Britain through Time, www.visionofbritain.org.uk/unit/10135849/cube/TOT_POP (access date: 27/6/2018).

29   Linda Monckton 'Bletchley Park, Buckinghamshire: the architecture of the Government Code and Cypher School', *Post-Medieval Archaeology*, 40(2), 2006, p.294.

30   Smith, *The Hidden History of Bletchley Park*, pp.100–05.

31   Quoted in Marion Hill, *Bletchley Park People: Churchill's Geese that Never Cackled* (Stroud: Sutton Publishing Limited, 2004), p.110.

32   Centre for Buckinghamshire Studies, DC 14/1/20, Bletchley Urban District Council, Minute book 1943–1944, 21 May 1943.

33   TNA, HW 64/70, [Anonymous author], Memorandum [no date given, but attached to Minutes dated 30 May 1942].

34   Bletchley Park Trust Archive, Dave Whitchuch (ed.), *Other People's Stories: Book 2 June Douglas*, in Dave Whitchuch, *Other People's Stories: Book 2*, 2001, p.48.

35   Cairncross, *The Enigma Spy*, pp.96–97.

36   Cairncross, *The Enigma Spy*, pp.96–97.

37   West and Tsarev, *The Crown Jewels*, p. 218.

38   West and Tsarev mistakenly contend that Tunny was an Enigma key. It was not, for full length discussions of this cipher system and the efforts to break it, see: B. Jack Copeland (ed.), *Colossus: The Secrets of Bletchley Park's Codebreaking Computers* (Oxford: Oxford University Press, 2006); Paul Gannon, *Colossus: Bletchley Park's Greatest Secret* (London: Atlantic Books, 2006).

39   West and Tsarev, *The Crown Jewels*, p.218.

40   Cairncross, *The Enigma Spy*, p.104.

41   Cairncross, *The Enigma Spy*, p.105.

42   Evan Mawdsley, *Thunder in the East: The Nazi-Soviet War, 1941–1945* (London: Bloomsbury Academic, 2005, 2011), p.266; Lloyd Clark, *Kursk: The Greatest Battle, Eastern Front 1943* (London: Headline Review, 2011), pp.220–21.

43   Mawdsley, *Thunder in the East*, pp.262–67.

44   Modin, *My Five Cambridge Friends*, pp.113–14.

45   Robin Cross, *The Battle of Kursk: Operation Citadel 1943* (London: Penguin, 1993, 2002), p.101–04; Mawdsley, *Thunder in the East*, p.265.

46   Modin, *My Five Cambridge Friends*, p.114.

47   Mawdsley, *Thunder in the East*, p.266.

Chapter 9

1   West and Tsarev, *The Crown Jewels*, p.219.

2   Cairncross, *The Enigma Spy*, p.109.

3   Robin Denniston, *Thirty Years Secret: A. G. Denniston's Work in Signals Intelligence, 1914–1944* (Trowbridge: Polperro Heritage Press, 2007), p.26.

4   Cairncross, *The Enigma Spy*, pp.109–10.

5   Cairncross, *The Enigma Spy*, p.110.

6   Cairncross, *The Enigma Spy*, p.110.

7   TNA, FCO 158/129, John Cairncross, 19 February 1964.

8   Lownie, *Stalin's Englishman*, pp.97–98.

9   Modin, *My Five Cambridge Friends*, p.58.

10   Modin, *My Five Cambridge Friends*, p.58.

11   Philby, *My Silent War*, pp.8–10.

12   F.W. Winterbotham, 'Recording of interview with Group Captain F.W. Winterbotham RAF On Sydney Radio in February 1977', ref BP250500, in Dave Whitchurch (ed.) *Other People's Stories*, vol. 1., The Bletchley Park Trust Archive (BPTA), p.11.

13   Andrew and Gordievsky, *KGB*, p.237.

14   Borovik, *The Philby Files*, p.184; John H. Waller, *The Unseen War in Europe: Espionage and Conspiracy in the Second World War* (London: I.B. Tauris, 1996), p.199.

15   Borovik, *The Philby Files*, p.186.

16   Borovik, *The Philby Files*, pp.xii–xv (Phillip Knightley, 'Introduction').

17   Philby, *My Silent War*, p.36.

18   Tim Milne, *Kim Philby: A Story of Friendship and Betrayal* (London: Biteback, 2014), p.94.

19   Philby, *My Silent War*, pp.92–100.

20   Richard Davenport-Hines, *Enemies Within: Communists, The Cambridge Spies and the Making of Modern Britain* (London: William Collins, 2018), p.314.

21   Stephen Dorril, *MI6: Inside the Covert World of Her Majesty's Secret Intelligence Service* (London: Touchstone, 2000, 2002), p.59.

22   Cairncross, *The Enigma Spy*, p.114.

23   John A. Taylor, *Bletchley Park's Secret Sisters: Psychological Warfare in World War II* (Dunstable: The Book Castle, 2005).

24   Cairncross, *The Enigma Spy*, p.113.

25   In his memoirs, Cairncross suggests, incorrectly, that the Sicherheitsdienst was the counter-intelligence unit of the Abwehr. Cairncross, *The Enigma Spy*, p.113.

26   Cairncross, *The Enigma Spy*, p.114.

27   Appendix Four.

28   Cairncross, *The Enigma Spy*, p.115, 13.

29   West and Tsarev, *TRIPLEX*, pp.233–48.

30   Andrew and Mitrokhin, *The Mitrokhin Archive*, p.165.

31   West and Tsarev, *The Crown Jewels*, pp.220–21.

32   Modin, *My Five Cambridge Friends*, p.114.

33   West and Tsarev, *The Crown Jewels*, p.220.

34   West and Tsarev, *The Crown Jewels*, p.220; Christopher Chant, 'Operation Ulm', *Code Names: Operations of the Section World War*, code names.info/operation/ulm/ [21 July 2018].

35   Norman Sherry, *The Life of Graham Greene*, vol. 2: 1939–1955 (London: Penguin, 1994, 2006), p.79; Milne, *Kim Philby*, p.123.

36   Cairncross, *The Enigma Spy*, p.118. Whether or not the theatre of this slightly theatrical narrative is wholly accurate remains unclear, what is certainly the case is that the two certainly met while in SIS and remained life-long correspondents.

37   Boris Volodarsky, 'Kim Philby: Living a Lie', *History Today*, vol. 60, no. 8 (August 2010).

38   Boston College, Burns Library (BCBL), Letters of Graham Greene, MS1995-03, Box 13, Folder 31, Graham Greene to Claymore [John Cairncross], 10 October 1967.

39   Graham Greene, *Our Man in Havana* (London: Vintage, 1958, 2004), p.195.

40   Graham Greene, 'Foreword' to Philby, *My Silent War*, p.xvii.

41   Cairncross, *The Enigma Spy*, pp.118–19.

42   Cairncross, *The Enigma Spy*, p.120.

Chapter 10

1   Victor Madeira, '"Because I Don't Trust Him, We are Friends": Signals Intelligence and the Reluctant Anglo-Soviet Embrace, 1917–24', *Intelligence and National Security*, vol. 19, no. 1 (2004), p.32.

2   Smith, 'The Government Code and Cypher School and the First Cold War', in Smith & Erskine (eds.), *Action This Day*, pp.25–27.

3   For more a detailed discussion of Soviet cipher systems see: John Earl Haynes and Harvey Klehr, *Venona: Decoding Soviet Espionage in America* (New Haven, CT: Yale University Press, 1999), pp.25–28.

4   Richard J. Aldrich, *GCHQ* (London: Harper Press, 2011), p.74.

5   National Security Agency, 'Venona: An Overview', *Cryptologic Almanac 50th Anniversary Series* (2002) www.nsa.gov/news-features/declassified-documents/crypto-almanac-50th/assets/files/VENONA_An_Overview.pdf [accessed: 30 May 2018]; see also: Haynes and Klehr, *Venona*, pp.28–29.

6   Roland Philipps, *A Spy Named Orphan: The Enigma of Donald Maclean* (London: The Bodley Head, 2018), p.179.

7   Paul Kennedy, *The Rise and Fall of the Great Powers: Economic Change and Military Conflict from 1500–2000* (London: Unwin Hyman, 1988), p.332.

8   Paul Kennedy, *The Rise and Fall of the Great Powers*, p.324.

9   Louis Kruh, 'Stimson, The Black Chamber, and the 'Gentlemen's Mail' quote', *Cryptologia*, vol. 12 no. 2 (1988), p.67.

10   Henry L. Stimson and McGeorge Bundy, *On Active Service in Peace and War* (New York: Harper & Brothers, 1947, 1948) p.188.

11   Kruh, 'Stimson, The Black Chamber, and the 'Gentlemen's Mail' quote', p.68.

12   William F. Friedman, 'From the Archives: A Brief History of the Signal Intelligence Service', 29 June 1942, *Cryptologia*, vol. 15 no. 3 (1991), p.269.

13   Friedman, 'From the Archives: A Brief History of the Signal Intelligence Service', p.270.

14   Bradley F. Smith, *The Ultra-Magic Deals: And the Most Secret, Special Relationship, 1940-1946* (Novato, CA: Presidio, 1992), p.6, 9.

15   Smith, *The Ultra-Magic Deals*, p.56.

16   Aldrich, *GCHQ*, p.75.

17   Jim Baggott, suggests he joined the project in 1946. Jim Baggott, *Atomic: The First War of Physics and the Secret History of the Atomic Bomb, 1939–49* (London: Icon Books, 2009, 2015)

18 National Security Agency | Central Security Service, Hall of Honour, 'Cecil Philips' www.nsa.gov/about/cryptologic-heritage/historical-figures-publications/hall-of-honor/2006/cphillips.shtml [accessed: 24 July 2018].

19 PBS, 'Red Files: Secrets Victories of the KGB', Interview with Cecil Philips, www.pbs.org/redfiles/kgb/deep/interv/k_int_cecil_philips.htm [Accessed: 24 July 2018].

20 *Daily Telegraph*, 'Obituary: Meredith Gardner', 20 August 2002; Harold Jackson, 'Obituary: Meredith Knox Gardner', *The Guardian*, 16 August 2002.

21 Richard Aldrich places the date of Gardner's initiation into Venona work in 1944. Aldrich, *GCHQ*, p.75. Others, such as Jim Baggott, suggest he joined the project in 1946. Baggott, *Atomic*, p.422.

22 National Security Agency | Central Security Service, Hall of Honour, 'Cecil Philips' www.nsa.gov/about/cryptologic-heritage/historical-figures-publications/hall-of-honor/2006/cphillips.shtml [accessed: 24 July 2018].

23 Robert J. Lamphere and Tom Shachtman, *FBI–KGB War: A Special Agent's Story* (Macon, GA: Mercer University Press, 1986, 1995), pp.82–83.

24 Nigel West, *Venona: The Greatest Secret of the Cold War* (London: HarperCollinsPublishers, 1999), pp.353–64.

25 West, *Venona*, pp.353–64.

26 West and Tsarev, *The Crown Jewels*, p.220.

27 Carter, *Anthony Blunt*, p.297.

28 Purvis and Hulbert, *Guy Burgess*, p.175.

29 Philipps, *A Spy Named Orphan*, p.139.

30 West and Tsarev, *The Crown Jewels*, p.220.

31 Cairncross, *The Enigma Spy*, p.92.

32 Milne, *Kim Philby*, pp.214–15.

33 Cairncross, *The Enigma Spy*, p.117.

Chapter 11

1 Cairncross, *The Enigma Spy*, p.117.

2 TNA, FCO 158/129, John Cairncross, 19 February 1964; West and Tsarev, *The Crown Jewels*, p.221.

3 Cairncross, *The Enigma Spy*, p.8.

4 West and Tsarev, *The Crown Jewels*, p.211.

5 Milovzorov's first name is sourced from: Roland Perry, *The Last of the Cold War Spies: The Life of Michael Straight, The Only American in Britain's Cambridge Spy Ring* (Cambridge, MA: Da Capo Press, 2005), p.136.

6 Modin, *My Five Cambridge Friends*, p.21, 145. For the date of Rodin's appointment, see Andrew and Mitrokhin, *The Mitrokhin Archive*, p.186.

7 Cairncross, *The Enigma Spy*, p.124.

8 West and Tsarev, *The Crown Jewels*, p.222.

9   Andrew and Mitrokhin, *The Mitrokhin Archive*, pp.181–83.

10   Modin, *My Five Cambridge Friends*, p.145.

11   Cairncross, *The Enigma Spy*, p.127; Modin, *My Five Cambridge Friends*, pp. 148–50. See also: West and Tsarev, *The Crown Jewels*, p.222.

12   West and Tsarev, *The Crown Jewels*, p.222

13   Modin, *My Five Cambridge Friends*, p.148.

14   West and Tsarev, *The Crown Jewels*, p.222; Modin, *My Five Cambridge Friends*, p.149.

15   West and Tsarev, *The Crown Jewels*, p.223.

16   Andrew and Mitrokhin, *The Mitrokhin Archive*, p.184.

17   Modin, *My Five Cambridge Friends*, p.150.

18   West and Tsarev, *The Crown Jewels*, p.223.

19   David Leitch, 'Introduction', in Modin, *My Five Cambridge Friends*, p.9.

20   Modin, *My Five Cambridge Friends*, p.144–47.

21   Modin, *My Five Cambridge Friends*, p.149.

22   Modin, *My Five Cambridge Friends*, p.169–71.

23   Cairncross, *The Enigma Spy*, p.17, 132.

24   TNA, FCO 158/177, Maclean and Burgess, II.B: Preliminary Investigations [No date].

25   Philipps, *A Spy Named Orphan*, pp.227–28.

26   TNA, KV 4/471, Diary of Guy Liddell, Deputy Director General of the Security Service, 1949, 28 January 1949, p. 18. William Hayter, later British Ambassador to the Soviet Union, was a British diplomat. He had, until 1944, been stationed at the British Embassy in Washington DC. He was replaced by Donald Maclean, the man he was now hunting.

27   TNA, FCO 158/177, Maclean and Burgess, II.B: Preliminary Investigations [No date]; For the records of the investigation, see TNA, FCO 158/2, passim.

28   TNA, FCO 158/177, Maclean and Burgess, II.B: Preliminary Investigations [No date]; TNA, KV 6/142, 337A, Telegram to S.L.O. Washington, 7 April 1951.

29   TNA, KV 4/473, Diary of Guy Liddell, Deputy Director General of the Security Service, 1951, 11 April 1951, p. 53.

30   Davenport-Hines, *Enemies Within*, p. 347.

31   TNA, FCO 158/177, Maclean and Burgess, I.A: Previous Histories of Maclean and Burgess [No date].

32   TNA, FCO 158/177, Maclean and Burgess, I.A: Previous Histories of Maclean and Burgess [No date]; TNA, PREM 8/1524, Mr G.F. De M. Burgess, 13 June 1951.

33   Purvis and Hulbert, *Guy Burgess*, pp.241–47.

34   Lamphere and Shachtman, *The FBI–KGB War*, p.230.

35   Modin, *My Five Cambridge Friends*, pp.197–200.

36   TNA, KV 6/143, 427a, Telegram, 31 May 1951.

37   TNA, FCO 158/27, The Peach Case, 7 December 1951.

38   Hansard, House of Commons, Debate, 7 November 1955, vol. 545 c. 1497.

39   Modin, *My Five Cambridge Friends*, pp.197–200.

40   Her death in 1995 was recorded with a touching obituary in the newsletter of the Association of Jewish Refugees in Great Britain, the *AJR Information*. C.N. Nathan, 'Gabrielle Cairncross', Obituaries, *AJR Information*, vol. 50, no. 11 (Nov 1995), p.15.

41   Cairncross, *The Enigma Spy*, p.128.

42   Margaret Jones, 'Ackroyd, Dame (Dorothy) Elizabeth [Betty] (1910–1987)', *Oxford Dictionary of National Biography*, ed., doi.org/10.1093/ref:odnb/63318 [accessed: 23 March 2017].

43   West and Tsarev, *The Crown Jewels*, pp.224–25.

44   Cairncross, *The Enigma Spy*, p.128.

45   Andrew and Mitrokhin, *The Mitrokhin Archive*, p.210.

46   Colville, *The Fringes of Power*, p.30; TNA, KV 2/4108, C.A.G. Simkins, Loose Minute, 4 March 1952.

47   Purvis and Hulbert, *Guy Burgess*, p.304. Purvis and Hulbert suggest that Cairncross' phone was tapped before the discovery of the note in Burgess' flat, noting that the tapping began in March. However, the note had been discovered by at least 4 March, suggesting that his phone was tapped as a response to the discovery.

48   TNA, KV 4/474, Diary of Guy Liddell, Deputy Director General of the Security Service, 1952, 4 March 1952, pp.234–38.

49   Cairncross, *The Enigma Spy*, pp.129–30.

50   TNA, KV 2/4108, Interview with John CAIRNCROSS on 31. 3. 52 [Transcribed in Appendix One of this volume]; TNA, KV 4/474, Diary of Guy Liddell, Deputy Director General of the Security Service, 1952, 3 April 1952, p.64.

51   Andrew, *In Defence of the Realm*, p.334.

52   Appendix One.

53   Cairncross, *The Enigma Spy*, p.130.

54   Appendix One.

55   TNA, KV 4/474, Diary of Guy Liddell, Deputy Director General of the Security Service, 1952, 3 April 1952, p.64.

56   Modin, *My Five Cambridge Friends*, p.215; Cairncross, *The Enigma Spy*, p.132.

57   Appendix Two.

58   Appendix Three.

59   Appendix Four. Of course, the marginalia was not necessarily added in 1952. It could have been added at any time, including by archivists in the aftermath of Cairncross' rather fuller 1964 confession.

60   TNA, FCO/129, John Cairncross, [no date].

Chapter 12

1   Cairncross, *The Enigma Spy*, p.132; Appendix Three.

2   Modin, *My Five Cambridge Friends*, p.164.

3   BCBL, Massachusetts, MS1995-03, box 13, folder 31, Graham Greene to Claymore, 5 June 1952.

4   Cairncross, *The Enigma Spy*, p.132.

5   Cairncross, *The Enigma Spy*, p.127.

6   Cairncross, *The Enigma Spy*, p.127.

7   'New AJR Secretary', *AJR Information*, vol. 29, no. 1. (January 1974), p.3.

8   Cairncross, *The Enigma Spy*, p.135.

9   Cairncross, *The Enigma Spy*, p.135.

10   John Cairncross, 'A Madonna Weeps in Italian Town', *The Boston Globe*, 6 June 1954, p.65

11   John Cairncross, 'Italian Population is Falling, Fewer Births', *Des Moines Tribune*, 22 March 1954, p.10; John Cairncross, 'Italians Find Treasures Old and New', *Des Moines Tribune*, 8 March 1954, p.10; John Cairncross, 'New Sicilian Wells Meet Nation's Needs', *The Boston Globe*, 3 June 1954, p.10; John Cairncross, 'Cannibalism Reported in Red Prison Camps', *Des Moines Tribune*, 10 March 1954, p.14.

12   Cairncross, *The Enigma Spy*, p.135.

13   Cairncross, *The Enigma Spy*, p.135.

14   For a particularly good example see: UGA, DC106 Additions, 87/8, John Cairncross to Mary Cairncross, 26 May 1956.

15   Cairncross, *The Enigma Spy*, p.126.

16   Cairncross, *The Enigma Spy*, p.126.

17   John Cairncross, *New Light on Molière: Tatuffe; Elomire Hypocondre* (Geneva: Librairie E. Droz, 1956).

18   Jaques Barzun, *From Dawn to Decadence: 500 Years of Western Cultural Life, 1500 to the Present* (New York, NY: HarperCollins Publishers, 2000), pp.344–47. It has been suggested by the historian Richard Davenport-Hines that Cairncross' love of Molière is a 'key' to understanding his character. Molière was, according to Davenport-Hines, 'the most protean of playwrights, a comic genius, a satirical moralist, a flatterer of bourgeois values, a toady to the nobility', shades of which were reflected in Cairncross' character. The difficulty with this proposition, however, is that Cairncross was interested in, admired and wrote about a wide variety of literary figures, most notably, La Fontaine, Corneille and Racine. In the case of the latter two, he undertook at least four major translation projects to produce English language volumes of their work that included scholarly analyses of the plays and biographies of their authors. Yet, where Molière wrote comedies and satires, Corneille and Racine were both tragedians and very different characters. Davenport-Hines, *Enemies Within*, p.258.

19   Cairncross, *New Light on Molière*, pp.1–4.

20   Cairncross, *The Enigma Spy*, p.38.

21   Cairncross, *New Light on Molière*, Raymond Picard, Preface, p.xi.

22   Raymond Picard, *Two Centuries of French Literature* (London: Weidenfeld & Nicolson, 1970).

23   Charlier Gustave, 'Cairncross (John). New Light on Molière, Tartuffe, Elomire hypocondre', Préface de Raymond Picard', In: *Revue belge de philologie et d'histoire*, vol. 35, no. 2 (1957), pp. 415–417; Marcel Gutwirth, 'Cairncross (John). New Light on Molière', *Modern Language Notes*, vol. 72, no. 5 (1957), pp.389–92.

24   John Cairncross, *By a Lonely Sea* (Hong Kong: Hong Kong University Press, 1959), p.93.

25   TNA, FCO 158/129, 'John Cairncross', D. Stephens to G. A. Carey-Foster, 9 February 1953.

26   TNA, FCO 158/129, D. Stephens to G.A. Carey-Foster, 9 February 1953.

27   TNA, FCO 158/129, 'John Cairncross', D. Stephens to G. A. Carey-Foster, 9 February 1953.

28   Andrew and Gordievsky, *KGB*, p.323.

29   Purvis and Hulbert, *Guy Burgess*, p.319.

30   Purvis and Hulbert, *Guy Burgess*, pp.318–20.

31   Hansard, HC Deb, 3 May 1954, vol. 527, cc. 6–8.

32   Purvis and Hulbert, *Guy Burgess*, pp.320–21.

33   Davenport-Hines, *Enemies Within*, p.473.

34   'College Principal Resigns', *Manchester Guardian*, 16 March 1957, p.1.

35   Cairncross, *The Enigma Spy*, pp.135–36.

36   TNA, FCO 158/129, J.E.D. Street, 'John Cairncross', 7 February 1964.

37   Cairncross, *The Enigma Spy*, pp.135–36.

38   Cairncross, *The Enigma Spy*, p.136.

39   Barzun, *From Dawn to Decadence*, p.342.

40   Patrick Swinden, 'Translating Racine', *Comparative Literature*, vol. 49, no. 3 (1997), p.209.

41   Jean Racine, *Phaedra*, trans. John Cairncross (Geneva: Librairie E. Droz, 1958), preface.

42   Jean Racine, *Andromanche and Other Plays* trans. John Cairncross (London: Penguin, 1967), Translators Foreword; For a similar argument, see: Jean Racine, *Iphigenia, Phaedra and Athaliah*, trans. John Cairncross (London: Penguin, 1970), Translators Foreword.

43   *Times Literary Supplement*, 'From the French', 2950, 12 September 1958, p.514.

44   UGA, DC106 Additions, 87/8, John Cairncross to Alec Cairncross, 4 November 1958.

45   BCBL, Letters of Graham Greene, MS1995-03 Box 13, folder 32, John Cairncross to Graham Greene, 4 August 1963. Op. Cit. is an

abbreviation of the Latin phrase *opere citato* or 'in the work cited'. Hippolyte Jean Giraudoux was an important French novelist and dramatist who achieved literary notoriety during the inter-war period. See: Laurent LeSage, *Jean Giraudoux: His Life and Works* (University Park, PA: Pennsylvania State Press, 1959).

46   Cairncross, *By a Lonely Sea*, p.vii.
47   UGA, DC106 Additions, 87/8, John Cairncross to Alec Cairncross, 1 December 1958.
48   UGA, DC106 Additions, 87/8, John Cairncross to Alec Cairncross, 4 November 1958.
49   UGA, DC106 Additions, 87/8, John Cairncross to Alec Cairncross, 15 February 1960.
50   Cairncross, *The Enigma Spy*, p.138.
51   UGA, DC106 Additions, 87/8, John Cairncross to Alec Cairncross, 1 March 1961.
52   *Journal of the Siam Society*, vol. 54, no. 2. (1964), p.269; *Journal of the Siam Society*, vol. 71 (1983), p.290.
53   Cairncross, *The Enigma Spy*, p.136.
54   BCBL, Letters of Graham Greene, MS1995-03 Box 13, folder 32, John Cairncross to Graham Greene, 4 August 1963.
55   Contrary to Cairncross' claim, Amina was not a member of the Royal family. Professionally known by her stage name, Princess Amina, Shirin Moynihan (nee Berry-Quereshi) was a Malaysian belly-dancer who married Anthony Moynihan, the third Baron Moynihan. While not royalty, she did briefly (she and Moynihan divorced in 1967) become a cause célèbre because of her marriage into British nobility. As *Ebony* magazine put it in 1966: she was '27, a slim, sloe-eyed, coffee-colored professional belly-dancer who, by the sudden death of her father-in-law, had become Lady Moynihan of Leeds, a peeress of the realm and the first non-white woman of child-bearing age to become a member of the English nobility'. See Charles Davis and Maria-Jesus Bellenger, 'Belly-dancer who became a lady', *Ebony*, vol. 21 no. 9 (July 1966), p.79.
56   BCBL, MS1995-03, box 13, folder 32, Graham Greene to Dr Crocker, 26 August 1963.

Chapter 13

1   Cairncross, *The Enigma Spy*, p.137.
2   UGA, DC106/10/3, Typed Manuscript of AK Cairncross' Diary – 1961–1969, 16 October 1963.

3   University of Bristol Special Collections [UBSC], Eunice Frost Papers, Penguin DM2843/70/Envelope A, John Cairncross to Eunice Frost, 2 October 1964.

4   TNA, FCO 158/129, Burke Trend to Prime Minister [Alec Douglas-Home], John Cairncross, 19 February 1964.

5   BCBL, Letters of Graham Green, MS1995-03 Box 13, folder 32, John Cairncross to Graham Greene, 27 April 1964.

6   TNA, FCO 158/129, [Redacted name] to J.E.D. Street, John Cairncross, 7 February 1964.

7   TNA, FCO 158/129, J.E.D. Street, John Cairncross, 7 February 1964.

8   TNA, FCO 158/129, B.A.B. Burrows. 12 February 1964.

9   Wright, *Spycatcher*, p.122.

10   Straight, *After Long Silence*, p.342.

11   Philby, *My Silent War*, p.185.

12   Cairncross, *The Enigma Spy*, p.128.

13   Cairncross, *The Enigma Spy*, pp.138–39

14   TNA, FCO 158/129, J.E.D. Street, Top Secret, 18 February 1964.

15   Cairncross, *The Enigma Spy*, p.139.

16   Andrew, *In Defence of the Realm*, p.435.

17   TNA, FCO 158/129, Director general of the Security Service [Sir Roger Hollis] to Bernard Burrows, 18 February 1964.

18   TNA, FCO 158/129, J.E.D. Street, John Cairncross, 19 February 1964.

19   Pincher, *Too Secret Too Long*, p.395.

20   Wright, *Spycatcher*, pp.218–19.

21   Stella Rimington, *Open Secret: the Autobiography of the Former Director General of MI5* (London: Arrow Books, 2001, 2002), p.119.

22   Cairncross, *The Enigma Spy*, p.39.

23   Cairncross, *The Enigma Spy*, p.45.

24   Cairncross, *The Enigma Spy*, p.139.

25   Cairncross, *The Enigma Spy*, pp.142–43.

26   In 1966, Blake escaped from Wormwood Scrubs and fled to the Soviet Union. For further details on Blake's near fantastical life, see: Roger Hermiston, *The Greatest Traitor: The Secret Lives of Agent George Blake* (London: Aurum Press, 2013).

27   TNA, FCO 158/129, Burke Trend, John Cairncross, 21 February 1964.

28   TNA, CAB 301/270, Burke Trend, John Cairncross, 28 February 1964.

29   TNA, FCO 158/129, Burke Trend to Timothy Bligh, 4 March 1964.

30   TNA, CAB 301/270, Burke Trend to Prime Minister [Alec Douglas-Home], 6 March 1964.

31   TNA, FCO 158/129, Timothy Bligh to Burke Trend, 9 March 1964.

32   Richard Aldrich and Rory Cormac, *The Black Door: Spies, Secret Intelligence and British Prime Ministers* (London: William Collins, 2016), p.219.

33   Stella Rimington, *Open Secret: The Autobiography of the Former Director-General of MI5* (London: Arrow, 2001, 2002), pp.119–20.

34   Wright, *Spycatcher*, pp.222–23.

35   Rimington, *Open Secret*, pp.119–20.

36   UBSC, Penguin Archive, DM1952, Box 331, 312, John Cairncross to James Cochrane, 19 September 1968.

37   UBSC, Penguin Archive, DM1952, Box 331, 312, John Cairncross to Will Sulkin, 19 October 1975.

38   Cairncross, *The Enigma Spy*, p.147; Alain Marcoux, *Population, Society and Agricultural Planning* (Rome: Food and Agriculture Organization of the United Nations, 1987), pp.157–58.

39   UBSC, Penguin Archive, DM1952, Box 331, 312, Contract Slip for Penguin Originals, 4 July 1968.

40   UBSC, Penguin Archive, DM1952, Box 331, 312, Will Sulkin to John Cairncross, 19 January 1974; Racine, Andromache, 1985 reprint, p.4.

41   Swinden, 'Translating Racine', p.214.

42   Rupert Christiansen, 'Alan Hollinghurst, interview: bringing Jean Racine's Berenice back to Britain', *Daily Telegraph*, 26 September 2012.

43   Jean Racine, *Andromache, Phaedra, Athaliah*, trans. Tim Chilcott (Ware: Wordsworth Editions Limited, 2000), p.xxxvi.

44   *Times Literary Supplement*, 'Cairncross and Molière', 5026, 30 July 1999, p.18.

45   UBSC, Penguin Archive, DM1952, Box 331, 312, John Cairncross to Will Sulkin, 27 August 1975.

46   UBSC, Penguin Archive, DM1952, Box 331, 312, John Cairncross to Will Sulkin, 19 October 1975; Will Sulkin to Lizzy Buchan, 9 October 1975.

47   UBSC, Penguin Archive, DM1952, Box 331, 312, Will Sulkin to John Cairncross, 16 June 1976.

48   Shih Shun Liu, *One Hundred And One Chinese Poems: With English Translation and Preface*, intro. Edmund Blunden, foreword by John Cairncross (Hong Kong: Hong Kong University Press, 1967).

49   John Cairncross, *After Polygamy Was Made a Sin: the Social History of Christian Polygamy* (London: Routledge & Keegan Paul, 1974).

50   T.B. Maston, 'Review: After Polygamy Was Made a Sin: The Social History of Christian Polygamy by John Cairncross', *Journal of Church and State*, vol. 20, no. 3 (1978), pp.553–54.

51   BCBL, Papers of Graham Greene, MS1995-03, box 13, folder 32, Graham Greene to Claymore [John Cairncross], 7 April 1975.

52   H. Gaston Hall, 'The Seventeenth Century', *The Year's Work in Modern Language Studies*, vol. 25 (1963), p.58.

53   J.-C., Tournand, 'Review: Molière bourgeois et libertin by John Cairncross', *Revue D'Histoire Littéraire De La France*, vol. 65, no. 2, (1965), pp.298–99.

54   *Times Literary Supplement*, 'N.B.', 5012, 25 June 1999, p.18.

55 John Cairncross, 'Tartuffe', ou Molière hypocrite', *Revue d'Histoire littéraire de la France*, 72e Année no. 5/6 (Sep–Dec 1972), pp.890–901; John Cairncross, *L' Humanite de Moliere* (Paris: Klincksieck, 1988).

Chapter 14

1   Boyle, *Climate of Treason*, p.431; Pincher, *Too Secret Too Long*, p.358; Andrew, *Defence of the Realm*, pp.653–55.

2   Richard Ingrams, 'Richard Ingrams's Week: Sir Anthony Blunt and my part in his downfall', *The Independent*, 24 July 2009, www.independent. co.uk/voices/columnists/richard-ingrams/richard-ingramsrsquos-week-sir-anthony-blunt-and-my-part-in-his-downfall-1760727.html (accessed: 21 February 2018).

3   Margaret Thatcher, Hansard, House of Commons Debate, 15 November 1979, vol. 973, cc.679-81W.

4   Barrie Penrose and Simon Freeman, *Conspiracy of Silence: The Secret Life of Anthony Blunt* (New York: Vintage, 1988), p.525.

5   David Leitch and Barrie Penrose, 'I was a spy for the Soviets', *Sunday Times*, 23 December 1979.

6   For examples see: 'Ex-Foreign Office Man Plays Down his Spying Career', *Aberdeen Press and Journal*, 24 December 1979; 'I gave away little, says Cairncross', *Birmingham Daily Post*, 24 December 1979; Gerald Bartlett, 'Cairncross case of commons', *Daily Telegraph*, 27 December 1979; David Leitch and Barrie Penrose, 'Calls for 'fifth man' enquiry', *Sunday Times*, 30 December 1979.

7   Michael Havers, Hansard, HC Deb, 17 January 1980, vol. 976, c. 817W.

8   Hansard, HC Deb, 18 January 1980, vol. 976, cc. 869–70W.

9   UGA, DC106 additions, 83/1-28, 8/23, Handwritten diary of Sir Alexander Cairncross, 22 December 1979.

10 UGA, DC106 Additions, 91/7, AK Cairncross Diary: corrected version 3, Jan 80/22 Sep 80; 7 February 1980.

11 BLBC, MS1995-03, box 13, folder 32, Graham Greene to John Cairncross, 22 February 1980.

12 *BBC Nine O'clock News*, BBC1, 20 November 1979.

13 UGA, DC106 Additions, 91/7, AK Cairncross Diary: corrected version 3, Jan 80/22 Sep 80, 7 February 1980.

14 UGA, DC106 Additions, 91/7, AK Cairncross Diary: corrected version 3, Jan 80/22 Sep 80, 14 February 1980.

15 UGA, DC106 Additions, 91/7, AK Cairncross Diary: corrected version 3, Jan 80/22 Sep 80, 5 May 1980.

16 UGA, DC106 Additions, 91/7, AK Cairncross Diary: corrected version 3, Jan 80/22 Sep 80, 4 March 1980.

17   UGA, DC106 Additions, 80/1, John Cairncross to Sir Alec Cairncross, 8 August 1977.

18   Boston College, Burns Library, MS1995-03, box 13, folder 34, John Cairncross to Graham Greene, 24 August 1980.

19   UGA, DC106 additions, 83/25, Handwritten Diary of Sir Alec Cairncross, 1982, pp.74–78.

20   Ronald Singleton, 'Ex-F.O. spy is arrested in border swoop', *Daily Mail*, 23 June 1982.

21   Leslie Childe, 'Burgess Contact Sentenced', *Daily Telegraph*, 26 June 1982. Both this and the *Daily Mail* appeared as cuttings in the Foreign Office file on John Cairncross: TNA, FCO 158/129.

22   BCBL, MS1995-03, box 13, folder 34, John Cairncross to Graham Greene, 3 July 1982.

23   BCBL, MS1995-03, box 13, folder 34, Graham Greene to John Cairncross, 16 July 1982.

24   BCBL, MS1995-03, box 13, folder 34, Graham Greene to John Cairncross, 6 July 1984.

25   BCBL, MS1995-03, box 13, folder 34, John Cairncross to Graham Greene, 12 May 1987.

26   Boston College, Burns Library, MS1995-03, box 13, folder 34, John Cairncross to Graham Greene, 20 December 1987.

27   UGA, DC106 additions, 83/25, Handwritten Diary of Sir Alec Cairncross, 1982, pp.74–78.

28   UGA, DC106 Additions 80/1, Elsie Cairncross to Sir Alec Cairncross, 27 April 1980.

29   UBSC, Penguin Archive: Eunice Frost Papers, Box 70, DM1843/70/ Envelope A, John Cairncross to Eunice Frost, 2 October 1964.

30   Cairncross, *The Enigma Spy*, p.xvi.

31   BCBU, MS1995-03, box 13, folder 34, John Cairncross to Graham Greene [no date, late 1985].

32   BCBU, MS1995-03, box 13, folder 34, passim.

Chapter 15

1   Cairncross, Enigma Spy, p. 2.

2   Sheila Kerr, 'Oleg Tsarev's Synthetic KGB Gems', International Journal of Intelligence and CounterIntelligence, vol. 14, no. 1 (2001), p. 100.

3   Cairncross, Enigma Spy, p. 1.

4   Kerr, 'Oleg Tsarev's Synthetic KGB Gems', p. 100.

5   Robert Porter, 'KGB confirms Cairncross as the Fifth Man', Sunday Telegraph, 21 October 1990, p. 1; Oleg Gordievsky, 'Letter: Spy-writers' views in conflict', The Times, 13 November 1990, p. 17.

6   Richard Deacon with Nigel West, *Spy!: Six Stories of Modern Espionage* (London: Crown Publications, 1980).

7   Nigel West, *MI5: British Security Service Operations, 1909–1945* (New York, NY: Stein and Day, 1981).

8   Cambridge University Library (CUL), Special Collections (SC), MS Add. 10042 (Papers of John Cairncross), Small Box 2, Rupert Allason Pt 1 Book & Lawyers (file 4), Nigel West to John Cairncross, 29 May 1981.

9   TNA, HO 532/4, [Author and recipients redacted], A04620, 3 April 1981.

10   Cutting contained in TNA, HO 532/4: Sue Reid, Harry Edgington and Fiona Barton, 'Traitor Cairncross admits he was a top Soviet agent', *Mail on Sunday*, 22 September 1991.

11   Cairncross, *The Enigma Spy*, p.14.

12   CUL, SC, MS Add. 10042, Large Box 2, John Cairncross to Sir Alec Cairncross, 2 December 1989.

13   Correlli Barnett, *The Collapse of British Power* (Stroud: Alan Sutton Publishing, 1982, 1984); Correlli Barnett, *The Audit of War: The Illusion and Reality of Britain as a Great Nation* (London: Macmillan, 1986); Correlli Barnett, *The Lost Victory: British Dreams, British Realities, 1945–50* (London: Faber and Faber, 1995, 2011); Correlli Barnett, *The Verdict of Peace: Britain Between her Yesterday and the Future* (London: Faber and Faber, 2001).

14   A.J.P. Taylor, *The Origins of the Second World War* (London: Penguin, 1961, 1963).

15   Paul Kennedy, *The Rise and Fall of the Great Powers: Economic Change and Military Conflict from 1500–2000* (London: Unwin Hyman, 1988), p.317.

16   CUL, SC, MS Add. 10042, Large Box 2, Munich and After by David Jardine, p.1.

17   CUL, SC, MS Add. 10042, Large Box 2, An Agent for the Duration (The Fifth Man that Never Was), Contents Page.

18   CUL, SC, MS Add. 10042, Small Box 2, Correspondence R Allason JC! (file 7), John Cairncross to Nigel West, 14 May 1991.

19   CUL, SC, MS Add. 10042, Small Box 2, Correspondence R Allason JC! (file 7) Patrick Mayhew to Rupert Allason, 6 February 1992.

20   CUL, SC, MS Add. 10042, Large Box 2, Gayle Brinkerhoff to Anthony Cave Brown, 2 November 1994.

21   Frederick Winterbotham, *The Ultra Secret* (London: Weidenfeld and Nicolson, 1974); Anthony Cave Brown, *Bodyguard of Lies* (New York: Harper and Row, 1975).

22   CUL, SC, MS Add. 10042, Small Box 2, Random Westintel Docs, Patrick Moloney, Instructions to Counsel to Settle the Defence.

23   CUL, SC, MS Add. 10042, Large Box 2, Correspondence with Graham Greene, Graham Greene to John Cairncross, 22 January 1991; John Cairncross to Graham Greene, 26 January 1991.

24   BCBL, MS1995-03, Box 13, folder 35, Graham Greene to John Cairncross, 22 January 1991.

25   BCBL, MS1995-03, Box 13, folder 35, Amanda Saunders to John Cairncross, 25 March 1991.

26   BCBL, MS1995-03, Box 13, folder 35, John Cairncross to Amanda Saunders, 14 April 1991.

27   CUL, SC, MS Add. 10042, Large Box 2, John Cairncross to Mary Cairncross, 24 April 1993; John Cairncross to Alec Cairncross, 6 May 1993; John Cairncross to Alec Cairncross, 20 June 1993; John Cairncross to Alec, 18 July 1993; John Cairncross to Alec and Mary Cairncross, 2 August 1993.

28   CUL, SC, MS Add. 10042, Large Box 2, John Cairncross to Alec, 18 July 1993; John Cairncross to Alec, 13 September 1993.

29   Cairncross, *The Enigma Spy*, p.xvii; CUL, SC, MS Add. 10042, Large Box 2, John Cairncross to Alec, 16 March 1994.

30   Cairncross, *The Enigma Spy*, p.xvii; C.N. Nathan, 'Gabrielle Cairncross', *AJR Information*, vol. 50, no. 11 (1995), p.15.

31   CUL, SC, MS Add. 10042, Small Box 2, Random Westintel Docs, Patrick Moloney, Instructions to Counsel to Settle the Defence, pp.8–12.

Afterword

1   Davenport-Hines, *Enemies Within*, pp.545–49.

2   West and Tsarev, *The Crown Jewels*, pp.204–05.

3   West and Tsarev, *The Crown Jewels*, p.209.

Bibliography

Archival Sources

Bletchley Park Trust Archive
Whitchurch, D., ed., *Other People's Stories*, vols. 1-2.

Burns Library, Boston College
MS1995-03, box 13, folder 31, Graham Greene Correspondence with John Cairncross

MS1995-03, box 13, folder 32, Graham Greene Correspondence with John Cairncross

MS1995-03, box 13, folder 33, Graham Greene Correspondence with John Cairncross

MS1995-03, box 13, folder 34, Graham Greene Correspondence with John Cairncross

MS1995-03, box 13, folder 35, Graham Greene Correspondence with John Cairncross

MS1995-03, box 64, folder 50, Graham Greene Correspondence with John Cairncross

Cambridge University Library, Special Collections
Guest, D., 'Fascism–A Blind Alley', *Trinity Magazine*, May Term 1933

MS Add. 10042, Large Box 2, Loose Correspondence and Papers

MS Add. 10042, Small Box 2, Rupert Allason Pt 1 Book & Lawyers (file 4)

MS Add. 10042, Small Box 2, Correspondence R. Allason JC! (file 7)

Trinity College Magazine, 'Who's Who', Easter Term 1936

Zlorin, W., 'King Kong', *Trinity Magazine*, May Term 1933

Centre for Buckinghamshire Studies

DC 14/1/20, Bletchley Urban District Council, Minute book 1943–1944

Glasgow City Archive

CO1/47/15, Minutes of the Clothing Committee, 1923–1930

CO1/47/29, Record of application for poor relief, 1926–1930

CO1/47/37, General register of Indexed Poor, 1921–1926

CO1/47/68 Valuation and Assessment Roll for the County of Lanark – Lesmahagow Parish, 1926–1927

National Archives

CAB 301/270, John Cairncross, former member of the Foreign Service: confession to spying

FCO 158/2, Investigation into the leak of Foreign Office telegrams from the British Embassy, Washington, DC, to the Russians, March 1945

FCO 158/27, Kim Philby (PEACH): file 1

FCO 158/129, John Cairncross: personal file

FCO 158/177, Investigation into the disappearance of Guy Burgess and Donald Maclean

FO 371/21287, Spain. Code 41 File 1 (papers 4954–5728)

HO 532/4, Espionage activities by individuals: John Cairncross

HW 25/2, A. P. Mahon, The History of Hut Eight 1939–1945

HW 62/8, GC&CS miscellaneous papers: Breaches of Security 1943–1945

HW 64/16, Security circulars

HW 64/56, Catering arrangements at Bletchley Park

HW 64/70, Staffing and conditions of work at Bletchley Park

HW 64/71, Security officers' reports

HW 72/9, Correspondence with universities on Junior Assistant recruitment for GC&CS

KV 2/815, John Herbert KING, alias 'MAG'

KV 2/4108, Guy Francis De Moncy BURGESS, aliases Roger STYLES, Jim Andreyevich ELIOT: British

KV 4/471, Diary of Guy Liddell, Deputy Director General of the Security Service, 1949

KV 4/473, Diary of Guy Liddell, Deputy Director General of the Security Service, 1951

KV 4/474, Diary of Guy Liddell, Deputy Director General of the Security Service, 1952

KV 6/142, Leakage of top secret Foreign Office telegrams in the USA

KV 6/143, Leakage of top secret Foreign Office telegrams in the USA

PREM 8/1524, Disappearance of Foreign Office officials, Donald Maclean and Guy Burgess

National Library of Wales, Aberystwyth
Goronwy Rees Papers, 2/2 – Cambridge Spy Ring Papers

South Lanarkshire Archives and Records Centre, East Kilbride
CO1/47/161, Clothing Stock Book For Poor Relief
CO1/60/3/1, District Council Minute Book – Second District Council

University of Bristol, Special Collections
Eunice Frost Papers, Penguin, DM2843/70/Envelope A, Frost Correspondence
    with John Cairncross
Penguin Papers, DM1952, Box 331, 312, Corneille. Translated by John Cairncross

University Of Glasgow Archive
DC106/6/1/1, Lecture notes of Alec Cairncross: English A, 1928–1929
DC106/6/1/2, Lecture notes of Alec Cairncross: English B, 1928–1929
DC106/6/1/5, Lecture notes of Alec Cairncross: Political Economy 1928–1929
DC106 Additions, 10/26, Press cutting of Andrew S. Cairncross' obituary
DC106 Additions, 80/1, Sir Alexander Cairncross Correspondence
DC106 Additions, 87/8, Miscellaneous Papers of Sir Alexander Cairncross
DC106 Additions, 83/1-28, 8/23, Handwritten diary of Sir Alexander Cairncross
DC106 Additions, 83/25, Handwritten Diary of Sir Alec Cairncross, 1982
DC106 Additions, 91/7, AK Cairncross Diary: corrected version 3
DC106/10/3, Typed Manuscript of AK Cairncross' Diary – 1961–1969
Sen10/72, The Glasgow University Calendar 1931–32
Sen10/73, The Glasgow University Calendar 1932–33
R8/5/51/2 – Matriculation Records, 1930–1931
R20/2, Results of Open Bursary Competition 1929–1940

Cairncross Articles, Books and Translations

Cairncross, J., *After Polygamy Was Made a Sin: The Social History of Christian Polygamy* (London: Routledge & Kegan Paul, 1974).
Cairncross, J., *An Approach to Food and Population Planning*, (Rome: Food and Agricultural Organization of the United Nations, 1978).
Cairncross, J., *By a Lonely Sea* (Hong Kong: Hong Kong University Press, 1959).
Cairncross, J. *La Fontaine Fables & Other Poems* (Gerrards Cross: Colin Smythe Limited, 1982).
Cairncross, J., *L' Humanité de Molière* (Paris: Klincksieck, 1988).
Cairncross, J., *Population and Agriculture in the Developing Countries* (Rome: Food and Agricultural Organization of the United Nations, 1980).

Cairncross, J., *New Light on Molière: Tatuffe; Elomire Hypocondre* (Geneva: Librairie E. Droz, 1956).

Cairncross, J., 'Tartuffe', ou Molière hypocrite', *Revue d'Histoire littéraire de la France*, 72e Année no. 5/6 (Sep–Dec 1972).

Cairncross, J., *The Enigma Spy, An Autobiography: The Story of the Man Who Changed the Course of World War Two* (London: Century, 1997).

Cairncross, J., *Things to Come: The World Food Crisis, The Way Out* (Rome: Food and Agricultural Organization of the United Nations, 1974).

Colombo-Sacco, D., López-Morales, G., *The Missing Half. Woman 1975*, Cairncross, J. collab. (Rome: Food and Agricultural Organization of the United Nations, 1975).

Corneille, P., *Polyeuctus/ The Liar/Nicomedes*, trans. Cairncross, J. (London: Penguin, 1980).

Corneille, P., *The Cid/Cinna/ The Theatrical Illusion*, trans. Cairncross, J. (London: Penguin, 1975).

Liu, S. S., *One Hundred And One Chinese Poems: With English Translation and Preface*, intro. Blunden, E., foreword Cairncross, J. (Hong Kong: Hong Kong University Press, 1967).

Picard, R., *Two Centuries of French Literature*, Cairncross, J. trans. (London: Weidenfeld & Nicolson, 1970).

Racine, J., *Andromache and Other Plays*, trans. Cairncross, J. (London: Penguin, 1967).

Racine, J., *Iphigenia/Phaedra/Athaliah*, trans. Cairncross, J. (London: Penguin, 1963).

Racine, J., *Iphigenia/Phaedra/Athaliah*, trans. Cairncross, J. with rev. foreword (London: Penguin, 1963, 1970).

Racine, J., *Phaedra*, trans. Cairncross, J. (Geneva: Librairie E. Droz, 1958).

Hansard

House of Commons, Debate, 3 September 1939, vol. 351

House of Commons, Debate, 7 May 1940, vol. 360

House of Commons, Debate, 3 May 1954, vol. 527

House of Commons, Debate, 7 November 1955, vol. 545

House of Commons Debate, 15 November 1979, vol. 973

House of Commons, Debate, 21 November 1979, vol. 974

House of Commons, Debate, 17 January 1980, vol. 976

House of Commons, Debate, 18 January 1980, vol. 976

Historic Newspaper Articles

'Arts, Letters Society to Hear Guest Scholar', *El Paso Times*, 1 November 1964.

Bartlett, G., 'Cairncross case of commons', *Daily Telegraph*, 27 December 1979.

Cairncross, J, 'A Madonna Weeps in Italian Town', *The Boston Globe*, 6 Jun 1954.

Cairncross, J., 'Cannibalism Reported in Red Prison Camps', *Des Moines Tribune*, 10 March 1954.

Cairncross, 'Italian Population is Falling, Fewer Births', *Des Moines Tribune*, 22 March 1954.

Cairncross, J., 'Italians Find Treasures Old and New', *Des Moines Tribune*, 8 March 1954.

'Cairncross and Molière', *Times Literary Supplement*, 5026, 30 July 1999.

Cairncross, J., 'New Sicilian Wells Meet Nation's Needs', *The Boston Globe*, 3 June 1954.

Cairncross, T.S., 'A Lost House: Cairncross of Colmslie', in *The Border Magazine*, vol. x, no. 115 (July, 1905).

Childe, L., 'Burgess Contact Sentenced', *Daily Telegraph*, 26 June 1982.

'College Principal Resigns', *Manchester Guardian*, 16 March 1957.

Duranty, W., 'Soviet executes 13 as Trotskyists; Curtly Announces Sentences Have Been Carried Out, but Gives No Details', *The New York Times*, 2 February 1937.

'Executions in Moscow', *The Spectator*, 5 February 1937.

'Ex-Foreign Office Man Plays Down his Spying Career', *Aberdeen Press and Journal*, 24 December 1979.

'From the French', *Times Literary Supplement*, 2950, 12 September 1958.

Gordievsky, O., 'Letter: Spy-writers' views in conflict', *The Times*, 13 November 1990.

'I gave away little, says Cairncross', *Birmingham Daily Post*, 24 December 1979.

Ingrams, R., 'Richard Ingrams's Week: Sir Anthony Blunt and my part in his downfall', *The Independent*, 24 July 2009, www.independent.co.uk/voices/columnists/richard-ingrams/richard-ingramsrsquos-week-sir-anthony-blunt-and-my-part-in-his-downfall-1760727.html

Levin, B., *The Times*, 13 October 1995.

Leitch, D., Penrose, B., 'Calls for "fifth man" enquiry', *Sunday Times*, 30 December 1979.

Leitch, D., Penrose, B., 'I was a spy for the Soviets', *Sunday Times*, 23 December 1979.

'N.B.', *Times Literary Supplement*, 5012, 25 June 1999.

Norton-Taylor, R., '"Lying" former Tory MP faces criminal charge', *The Guardian*, 17 October 2001, www.theguardian.com/uk/2001/oct/17/politics.books.

Singleton. R., 'Ex-F.O. spy is arrested in border swoop' *Daily Mail*, 23 June 1982.

'News of the Week', *Spectator*, 31 May 1940.

Porter, R., 'KGB confirms Cairncross as the Fifth Man', *Sunday Telegraph*, 21 October 1990.

Reid, S., Edgington, H., Barton, F., 'Traitor Cairncross admits he was a top Soviet agent', *Mail on Sunday*, 22 September 1991.

'Teacher Killed in Spain', *The New York Times*, 7 August 1938.

'The Squalid Truth.', *Sunday Pictorial*, 25 September 1955.

Published Primary Sources, Autobiographies and Memoirs

Aldrich, R.J. (ed.), *Espionage, Security and Intelligence in Britain, 1945–1970* (Manchester: Manchester University Press, 1998).

Birch, F., *The Official History of Sigint: 1919–1945*, vol. 1 (part 1), Jackson, J., ed. (Milton Keynes, 2004).

Bletchley Park Trust Report No. 18, *History of Bletchley Park Huts & Blocks 1939–1945*, revised by Arthur Bonsall (2009).

Cairncross, A., *Living With the Century* (Fife: iynx, 1998).

Robert Campbell Garry, *Life in Physiology. Memoirs of Glasgow University's Institute of Physiology during the 1920s and 1930s* (Glasgow: Glasgow Wellcome Unit for the History of Medicine, 1992).

Calvocoressi, P., *Top Secret Ultra* (Cleobury Mortimer: M & M Baldwin, 1980, 2011).

Charlier, G., 'Cairncross (John). *New Light on Molière, Tartuffe, Elomire hypocondre*', Préface de Raymond Picard', In: *Revue belge de philologie et d'histoire*, vol. 35, no. 2 (1957).

Colville, J., *The Fringes of Power: Downing Street Diaries, 1939–1955* (London: Hodder and Stoughton, 1985).

Davis, C., Bellenger, M., 'Belly-dancer who became a lady', *Ebony*, vol. 21 no. 9 (July, 1966).

Denham, H., 'Bedford-Bletchley-Kilindini-Columbo', in Hinsley, F.H. and Stripp, A., eds., *Codebreakers: The Inside Story of Bletchley Park* (Oxford: Oxford University Press, 1992, 2001).

Denniston, A.G., 'The Government Code and Cypher School Between the Wars', in Andrew, C., ed., *Codebreaking and Signals Intelligence* (London: Frank Cass, 1986).

Friedman, W., 'From the Archives: A Brief History Of The Signal Intelligence Service', 29 June 1942, *Cryptologia*, vol. 15, no. 3 (1991).

Hall, H.G., 'The Seventeenth Century', *The Year's Work in Modern Language Studies*, vol. 25 (1963).

Greene, G., *Our Man in Havana* (London: Vintage, 1958, 2004).

Gutwirth, M., 'Cairncross (John). *New Light on Molière*', *Modern Language Notes*, vol. 72, no. 5 (1957).

Headlam, C., *Parliament and Politics in the Age of Churchill and Attlee: The Headlam Diaries 1935–1951*, Stuart Ball, ed. (Cambridge: Cambridge University Press, 1999).

Hobsbawm, E., *Interesting Times: A Twentieth Century Life* (London: Allen Lane, 2002).

Jackson, J., ed., *Solving Enigma's Secrets: The Official History of Bletchley Park's Hut 6* (Redditch: BookTower Publishing, 2014).

Jackson, J. ed., *The Secret War of Hut 3: The First Full Story of How Intelligence from Enigma Signals Decoded at Bletchley Park was Used During World War Two* (Milton Keynes: Military Press, 2002).

Johnson, K., Gallehawk, J., eds., *Figuring it Out At Bletchley Park, 1939–1945* (Redditch: BookTower Publishing, 2007).

Journal of the Siam Society, vol. 54, no. 2. (1964).

Journal of the Siam Society, vol. 71 (1983).

Koestler, A., *Spanish Testament* (London: Victor Gollancz, 1937).

Liddell, G., *The Guy Liddell Diaries, vol. 1: 1939–1942 – MI5's Director of Counter-Espionage in World War II*, West, N., ed. (London: Routledge, 2005).

MacDougall, I., *Voices From the Hunger Marches: Personal Recollections by Scottish Hunger Marchers of the 1920s and 1930s – vol. II* (Edinburgh: Polygon, 1991).

Maclean, D., *British Foreign Policy Since Suez, 1956–1968* (London: Hodder and Stoughton, 1970).

MacNeice, L., 'Primrose Hill', *The Spectator*, 24 August 1939.

Maston, T.B., 'Review: After Polygamy Was Made a Sin: The Social History of Christian Polygamy by John Cairncross', *Journal of Church and State*, vol. 20, no. 3 (1978).

Milne, T., *Kim Philby: A Story of Friendship and Betrayal* (London: Biteback Publishing, 2014).

Modin, Y., *My Five Cambridge Friends: Burgess, Maclean, Philby, Blunt and Cairncross by their KGB Controller*, trans. Anthony Roberts (New York: Headline Book Publishing, 1994).

Nathan, C.N., 'Gabrielle Cairncross', Obituaries, *AJR Information*, vol. 50, no. 11 (1995).

'New AJR Secretary', *AJR Information*, vol. 29, no. 1. (1974).

Noakes, J. Pridham, G. eds., *Nazism, 1939–1945 – Volume 3: Foreign Policy, War and Racial Extermination* (Exeter: University of Exeter Press, 1997).

Orwell, G., *Orwell's England: The Road to Wigan Pier in the Context of Essays, Reviews, Letters and Poems* (London: Penguin, 2001).

Philby, K., *My Silent War: An Autobiography of a Spy* (New York, NY: The Modern Library, 2002).

Rimington, S., *Open Secret: The Autobiography of the Former Director-General of MI5* (London: Arrow, 2001, 2002).

Stephenson, W.S., *British Security Coordination: The Secret History of British Intelligence in the Americas 1940–45*, West, N., ed. (New York: Fomm International Publishing, 1998).

Stimson, H.L., Bundy, M., *On Active Service in Peace and War* (New York: Harper & Brothers, 1947, 1948).

Straight, M., *After Long Silence* (London: Collins, 1983).

Strang, W., *The Foreign Office* (London: George Allen & Unwin, 1955).

Sudoplatov, P., Sudoplatov, A., *Special Tasks: The Memoirs of an Unwanted Witness – A Soviet Spymaster*, with Jerrold L. Schecter and Leona P. Schecter (London: Little, Brown and Company, 1994).

Tournand, J.-C, 'Review: Molière bourgeois et libertin by John Cairncross', *Revue D'Histoire Littéraire De La France*, vol. 65, no. 2 (1965), pp. 298–299.

West, N., Tsarev, O., eds., *TRIPLEX: Secrets From the Cambridge Spies* (New Haven, CT: Yale University Press, 2009).

Winterbotham, F.W., *The Ultra Secret* (London: Weidenfeld and Nicolson, 1974).

Wright, P., with Greengrass P., *Spycatcher* (Victoria: William Heinemann Australia, 1987).

Online Sources

GB Historical GIS, University of Portsmouth, A Vision of Britain through Time, www.visionofbritain.org.uk.

University of Warwick, Modern Records Centre Website, 'Coal miners' average wages – 1914 to 1920', October 1920, www2.warwick.ac.uk/services/library/mrc/explorefurther/images/coal/.

'Vassiliev Yellow Notebook #1', History and Public Policy Program Digital Archive, Alexander Vassiliev Papers, Manuscript Division, Library of Congress, digitalarchive.wilsoncenter.org/document/112856.

Articles and Chapters

Andrew, C., 'Cambridge Spies: the "Magnificent Five", 1933–1945', in Sarah J. Ormrod (ed.) *Cambridge Contributions* (Cambridge, Cambridge University Press, 1998).

Andrew, C., 'F.H. Hinsley and the Cambridge Moles', in Langhorn, R., ed., *Diplomacy and Intelligence During the Second World War: Essays in Honour of F.H. Hinsley* (Cambridge: Cambridge University Press, 2004).

Boobbyer, P., 'Review: Spies: The Rise and Fall of the KGB in America by Haynes, John Earl; Klehr, Harvey; Vassiliev, Alexander', *The Slavonic and East European Review*, vol. 89, no.2 (2011).

Christiansen, R., 'Alan Hollinghurst, interview: Bringing Jean Racine's Berenice back to Britain', *Daily Telegraph*, 26 September 2012.

Daily Telegraph, 'Obituary: Meredith Gardner', 20 August 2002.

Denman, J., McDonald, P., 'Unemployment statistics from 1881 to the present day', *Labour Market Trends*, vol. 104 no. 1 (1996).

Dennis, W.C., 'Foreword', in Meyer, F.S., *In Defense of Freedom and Related Essays* (Indianapolis, IN: Liberty Fund, 1966).

Erskine, R., 'Enigma's Security: What the Germans Knew', in Smith, M. and Erskine, R. eds., *Action This Day: Bletchley Park from the Breaking of the Enigma Code to the Birth of the Modern Computer* (London: Transworld Publishers, 2001).

Haynes, J.H., Klehr, H., 'Special Tasks and Sacred Secrets on Soviet Atomic Espionage', *Intelligence and National Security,* vol. 26, no. 5 (2011).

Jackson, H., 'Obituary: Meredith Knox Gardner', *The Guardian*, 16 August 2002.

Kerr, S., 'KGB sources on the Cambridge network of Soviet agents: True or false?', *Intelligence and National Security*, vol. 11, no. 3 (1996).

Kerr, S., 'Oleg Tsarev's Synthetic KGB Gems', *International Journal of Intelligence and Counter Intelligence*, vol. 14, no. 1 (2001).

Kruh, L., 'Stimson, The Black Chamber, and the "Gentlemen's Mail" quote', *Cryptologia*, vol. 12 no. 2 (1988).

Langhorne, R., 'Francis Harry Hinsley, 1918–1998', *Proceedings of the British Academy*, 120 (2003).

Leitch, D., Penrose, B., 'I was a spy for Soviets', *Sunday Times*, 23 December 1979.

Madeira, V., '"Because I Don't Trust Him, We are Friends": Signals Intelligence and the Reluctant Anglo-Soviet Embrace, 1917–24', *Intelligence and National Security*, vol. 19, no. 1 (2004).

McCowan, D.B., 'Coalmining at Auchanbeg, Lesmahagow, 1700-1922: An Introduction', *The Scottish Genealogist,* vol. 37, no. 1 (1990).

McKean, C., 'Between the Wars', in Reed, P. ed., *Glasgow: The Forming of a City* (Edinburgh, Edinburgh University Press, 1999).

Monckton, L. 'Bletchley Park, Buckinghamshire: The architecture of the Government Code and Cypher School', *Post-Medieval Archaeology*, vol. 40, no. 2 (2006).

Otte, T.G., 'Old Diplomacy: Reflections on the Foreign Office before 1914', *Cotemporary British History*, vol. 18, no. 3 (2004).

Proctor, T., 'Family Ties in the Making of Modern Intelligence', *Journal of Social History*, 39:2, Kith and Kin: Interpersonal Relationships and Cultural Practices, (Winter 2005).

Reed, P., 'The Tenement City', in Reed, P. ed., *Glasgow: The Forming of a City* (Edinburgh, Edinburgh University Press, 1999).

Smith, B., *The Ultra-Magic Deals: And the Most Secret, Special Relationship, 1940–1946* (Novato, CA: Presidio, 1992).

Smith, C., 'How I Learned to Stop Worrying and Love the Bombe: Machine Research and Development and Bletchley Park', *History of Science*, vol. 52, no. 2 (2014).

Smith, M., 'The Government Code and Cypher School and the First Cold War', in Smith, M. and Erskine, R. eds., *Action This Day: Bletchley Park from the*

Breaking of the Enigma Code to the Birth of the Modern Computer (London: Transworld Publishers, 2001).

Smith, M., '*The humble Scot who rose to the top* – but then chose treachery', *The Daily Telegraph*, 12 January 1998.

Steiner, Z., 'The Foreign and Commonwealth Office: Resistance and Adaptation to Changing Times', *Cotemporary British History*, vol. 18, no. 3 (2004).

Swinden, P., 'Translating Racine', *Comparative Literature*, vol. 49, no. 3 (1997).

Toy, R.F., Smith, C., 'Women in the shadow war: Gender, class and MI5 in the Second World War', *Women's History Review*, early online access, DOI: 10.1080/09612025.2017.1345714.

Volodarsky, B., 'Kim Philby: Living a Lie', *History Today*, vol. 60, no. 8 (August 2010).

Wark, W.K., 'Appeasement Revisited.', *The International History Review*, vol. 17, no. 3 (1995).

Watt, D.C., 'Francis Herbert King: A Soviet Source in the Foreign Office', *Intelligence and National Security*, vol. 3, no. 4 (1988).

Books

Aldcroft, D.H., *The British Economy Between the Wars* (Oxford: Philip Allan, 1983).

Aldrich, R.J., *GCHQ* (London: Harper Press, 2011).

Aldrich, R.J., Cormac, R., *The Black Door: Spies, Secret Intelligence and British Prime Ministers* (London: William Collins, 2016).

Andrew, C., *The Defence of the Realm: The Authorized History of MI5* (London: Penguin, 2009).

Andrew, C., Gordievsky O., *KGB: The Inside Story of its Foreign Operations From Lenin to Gorbachev* (London: Hodder and Stoughton, 1990).

Andrew, C., Mitrokhin, V., *The Mitrokhin Archive: The KGB in Europe and the West* (London: Penguin, 1999, 2000).

Andrews, G., *The Shadow Man At the Heart of the Cambridge Spy Circle* (London: I.B. Tauris, 2015).

Baggott, J. *Atomic: The First War of Physics and the Secret History of the Atomic Bomb, 1939–49* (London: Icon Books, 2009, 2015).

Barnett, C., *The Audit of War: The Illusion and Reality of Britain as a Great Nation* (London: Macmillan, 1986).

Barnett, C., *The Collapse of British Power* (Stroud: Alan Sutton Publishing, 1982, 1984).

Barnett, C., *The Lost Victory: British Dreams, British Realities, 1945–50* (London: Faber and Faber, 1995, 2011).

Barnett, C., *The Verdict of Peace: Britain Between her Yesterday and the Future* (London: Faber and Faber, 2001).

Bibliography

Barzun, J., *From Dawn to Decadence: 500 Years of Western Cultural Life, 1500 to the Present* (New York, NY: HarperCollins Publishers, 2000).

Beevor, A., *The Battle for Spain: The Spanish Civil War, 1936–1939* (London: Phoenix, 1982, 2006).

Bennett, R., *Behind the Battle: Intelligence in the War with Germany, 1939–1945* (London: Pimlico, 1994, 1999).

Borovik, G., *The Philby Files: The Secret Life of the Master Spy*, Knightley, P., ed. (London: Little, Brown, 1994).

Boyle, A., *The Climate of Treason: Five Who Spied for Russia* (London: Hutchinson, 1979).

Brown, A.L., Moss, M., *The University of Glasgow: 1451–1996* (Edinburgh: Edinburgh University Press, 1996).

Bullock, A., *Hitler and Stalin: Parallel Lives* (London: HarperCollins, 1991).

Campbell, A., *The Scottish Miners, 1874–1939 – Volume One: Industry, Work and Community* (Aldershot: Ashgate, 2000).

Carter, M., *Anthony Blunt: His Lives* (London: Pan Books, 2001).

Cave Brown, A., *Bodyguard of Lies* (New York, Harper and Row, 1975).

Cecil, R., *A Divided Life: A Biography of Donald Maclean* (London: The Bodley Head, 1988).

Clark, L., *Kursk: The Greatest Battle, Eastern Front 1943* (London: Headline Review, 2011).

Clelland, W., *Lesmahagow: The Parish and the People* (Greenock: Orr, Pollock and Co. Ltd., 1990).

Copeland, B. J. (ed.), *Colossus: The Secrets of Bletchley Park's Codebreaking Computers* (Oxford: Oxford University Press, 2006).

Costello, J., *Mask of Treachery: The First Documented Dossier on Blunt, MI5, and Soviet Subversion* (London: Collins, 1988).

Costello, J., Tsarev, O., *Deadly Illusions* (New York: Crown Publishers Inc., 1993).

Cross, R., *The Battle of Kursk: Operation Citadel 1943* (London: Penguin, 1993, 2002).

Davenport-Hines, R., *Enemies Within: Communists, The Cambridge Spies and the Making of Modern Britain* (London: William Collins, 2018).

Deacon, R., *The Cambridge Apostles: A History of Cambridge University's Élite Intellectual Secret Society* (London: Robert Royce Limited, 1985).

Deacon, R., with West, N., *Spy!: Six Stories of Modern Espionage* (London: Crown Publications, 1980).

Denniston, R., *Thirty Years Secret: A. G. Denniston's Work in Signals Intelligence, 1914–1944* (Trowbridge: Polperro Heritage Press, 2007).

Dickie, J., *Inside the Foreign Office* (London: Chapmans Publishers, 1992).

Dorril, S., *MI6: Inside the Covert World of Her Majesty's Secret Intelligence Service* (London: Touchstone, 2000, 2002).

Evans, M.M., Mcgeoch, A., *Invasion!: Operation Sea Lion, 1940* (London: Routledge, 2004).

Gannon, P., *Colossus: Bletchley Park's Greatest Secret* (London: Atlantic Books, 2006).

Gardiner, J., *Wartime: Britain, 1939–1945* (London: Headline, 2004).

Goodman, M.S., *Spying on the Nuclear Bear: Anglo-American Intelligence and the Soviet Bomb* (Stanford, CA: Stanford University Press, 2007).

Goodman, M.S., *The Official History of the Joint Intelligence Committee, Volume 1: From the Approach of the Second World War to the Suez Crisis* (London: Routledge, 2014).

Gordin, M.D., *Red Cloud at Dawn: Truman, Stalin, and the End of the Atomic Monopoly* (New York, NY: Farrar, Straus and Giroux, 2009).

Greenberg, J., *Gordon Welchman: Bletchley Park's Architect of Ultra Intelligence* (London: Frontline Books, 2014).

Greenshields, J.B., *Annals of the Parish of Lesmahagow* (Edinburgh: The Caledonian Press, 1864).

Halsey, A.H., *Trends in British Society since 1900: A Guide to the Changing Social Structure of Britain* (London: Palgrave Macmillan, 1972).

Harris, J., *Goronwy Rees* (Cardiff: University of Wales Press, 2001).

Hastings, M., *All Hell Let Loose: The World At War, 1939–1945* (London: Harper Press, 2012).

Haynes, J.E., Klehr, H., *Venona: Decoding Soviet Espionage in America* (New Haven, CT: Yale University Press, 1999).

Hennessy, P., *Establishment and Meritocracy* (London: Haus Publishing, 2014).

Hennessy, P., *Whitehall* (London: Fontana Press: 1990).

Hermiston, R., *The Greatest Traitor: The Secret Lives of Agent George Blake* (London: Aurum Press, 2013).

Hill, M., *Bletchley Park People: Churchill's Geese that Never Cackled* (Stroud: Sutton Publishing Limited, 2004).

Hinsley, F.H., Thomas, E.E., Ransom, C.F.G., Knight, R.C., *British Intelligence in the Second World War*, v. 2., (London: HMSO, 1981).

Hodges, A., *Alan Turing: The Enigma* (New York: Vintage, 1983, 2012).

Holzman, M., *Donald and Melinda Maclean: Idealism and Espionage* (New York, NY: Chelmsford Press, 2014).

Howarth, T.E.B., *Cambridge Between Two Wars* (London: Collins, 1978).

Howson, G., *Arms for Spain: The Untold Story of the Spanish Civil War* (London: John Murray, 1998).

Jeffrey, K., *MI6: The History of the Secret Intelligence Service, 1909–1949* (London: Bloomsbury, 2009).

Jeffreys-Jones, R., *In Spies We trust: The Story of Western Intelligence* (Oxford: Oxford University Press, 2013).

Keen, J., *Harold 'Doc' Keen and the Bletchley Park Bombe* (Cleobury Mortimer: M & M Baldwin, 2003, 2012).

Keith, R., Spotiswood, J., Russel, M., Goodall, W., *An Historical Catalogue of the Scottish Bishops: Down to the Year 1688* (Edinburgh, Bell & Bradfute, 1824).

Kennedy, P., *The Rise and Fall of British Naval Mastery* (London: Penguin, 1976, 2001).

Kennedy, P., *The Rise and Fall of the Great Powers: Economic Change and Military Conflict from 1500–2000* (London: Unwin Hyman, 1988).

Knightley, P., *Philby: The Life and Views of the K.G.B. Masterspy* (London: André Deustch, 1988, 2003).

Knightley, P., *The Second Oldest Profession: Spies and Spying in the Twentieth Century* (New York, NY: W. W. Norton & Company, 1986, 1987).

Lamphere, R.J., Shachtman, T., *FBI–KGB War: A Special Agent's Story* (Macon, GA: Mercer University Press, 1986, 1995).

LeSage, L., *Jean Giraudoux: His Life and Works* (University Park, PA: Pennsylvania State Press, 1959).

Lownie, L., *Stalin's Englishman: The Lives of Guy Burgess* (London: Hodder & Stoughton, 2015).

Macintyre, B., *A Spy Among Friends: Philby and the Great Betrayal* (London: Bloomsbury, 2015).

Marcoux, A., *Population, Society and Agricultural Planning* (Rome: Food and Agriculture Organization of the United Nations, 1987).

Masterman, J.C., *The Double-Cross System In the War of 1939 to 1945* (London: Yale University Press, 1972).

Mawdsley, E., *Thunder in the East: The Nazi–Soviet War, 1941–1945* (London: Bloomsbury Academic, 2005, 2011).

McKay, R., *The Test of War: Inside Britain, 1939–1945* (London: Routledge, 1999).

Middlemas, R.K., *The Clydesiders: A Left Wing Struggle for Parliamentary Power* (London: Hutchinson, 1965).

Moran, C., *Classified: Secrecy and the State in Modern Britain* (Cambridge: Cambridge University Press, 2013).

Moss, M., Forbes Munro, J., Trainor, R.H., *University, City and State: The University of Glasgow since 1870* (Edinburgh: Edinburgh University Press, 2000).

M'Ure, J., *The History of Glasgow: A New Ed.* (Glasgow: Hutchison & Brookman, 1830).

O'Brien, P.P., *How The War Was Won: Air-Sea Power and Allied Victory in World War II* (Cambridge: Cambridge University Press, 2015).

Pacione, M., *Glasgow: The Socio-spatial Development of the City* (Chichester: John Wiley & Sons, 1995).

Pelling, H., *Britain and the Second World War* (London: Collins, 1970).

Penrose, B., Freeman, S., *Conspiracy of Silence: The Secret Life of Anthony Blunt* (London: Grafton, 1986).

Perry, R., *The Fifth Man* (London: Pan Books, 1994, 1995).

Perry, R., *The Last of the Cold War Spies: The Life of Michael Straight, The Only American in Britain's Cambridge Spy Ring* (Cambridge, MA: Da Capo Press, 2005).

Philipps, R., *A Spy Named Orphan: The Enigma of Donald Maclean* (London: The Bodley Head, 2018).

Pincher, C., *Their Trade is Treachery* (London: Sidgwick & Jackson, 1981, 1982).

Pincher, C., *Too Secret Too Long* (New York, NY: St. Martin's Press, 1984).

Pollard, S., *The Development of the British Economy, 1914–1980 – Third Edition* (London: Edward Arnold, 1962, 1983).

Ponting, C., *1940: Myth and Reality* (London: Hamish Hamilton, 1990).

Purvis, S., Hulbert, J., *Guy Burgess: The Spy Who Knew Everyone* (London: Biteback, 2016).

Racine, J., *Andromache, Phaedra, Athaliah*, trans. Tim Chilcott (Ware: Wordsworth Editions Limited, 2000).

Ratcliff, R.A., *Delusions of Intelligence: Enigma, Ultra, and the End of Secure Ciphers* (Cambridge, Cambridge University Press, 2006).

Read, A., Fisher, D., *Operation Lucy: Most Secret Spy Ring of the Second World War* (New York, NY: Coward, McCann & Geoghegan, Inc, 1981).

Rhodes, R., *Dark Sun: The Making Of The Hydrogen Bomb* (New York, NY: Simon and Schuster, 1995, 2011).

Schecter, Jerrold L., Schecter, L., *Sacred Secrets: How Soviet Intelligence Operations Changed American History* (Washington, DC: Brassey's 2002).

Singh, S., *The Codebook: The Secret History of Codes and Code-Breaking* (London: Fourth Estate, 2000).

Sherry, N., *The Life of Graham Greene, Volume 2: 1939–1955* (London: Penguin, 1994, 2006).

Smith, C., *The Hidden History of Bletchley Park: A Social and Organisational History* (Basingstoke: Palgrave Macmillan, 2015).

Smith, M., *Station X: The Codebreakers of Bletchley Park* (London: Pan Books, 1998, 2004).

Stansky, P., Abrahams, W., *Journey to the Frontier: Two Roads to the Spanish Civil War* (London: Constable, 1966).

Taylor, A.J.P., *The Origins of the Second World War* (London: Penguin, 1961, 1963).

Taylor, J.A., *Bletchley Park's Secret Sisters: Psychological Warfare in World War II* (Dunstable: The Book Castle, 2005).

Trahair, R., Miller, R., *Encyclopaedia of Cold War Espionage, Spies and Secret Operations* (Oxford: Enigma Books, 2012).

Turing, D., *Prof: Alan Turing Decoded* (Stroud: The History Press, 2015).

Turing, S., *Alan M. Turing* (London: W. Heffer and Sons, 1959).

Volodarsky, B., *Stalin's Agent: The Life and Death of Alexander Orlov* (Oxford: Oxford University Press, 2015).

Waller, J.H., *The Unseen War in Europe: Espionage and Conspiracy in the Second World War* (London: I.B. Tauris, 1996).

Wark, W.K., *The Ultimate Enemy: British Intelligence and Nazi Germany, 1933–1939* (Oxford: Oxford University Press, 1986).

Warner, D., *World War II: The Untold Story* (London: The Bodley Head, 1988).

West, N., *MI5: British Security Service Operations, 1909–1945* (New York, NY: Stein and Day, 1981).

West, N., *Molehunt: Searching for Soviet Spies in British Intelligence* (New York, NY: Berkley Books, 1987, 1991).

West, N., *The A to Z of British Intelligence* (Lanham, MD: Scarecrow Press, 2009).

West, N., *Venona: The Greatest Secret of the Cold War* (London: HarperCollins Publishers, 1999).

West, N., Tsarev, O., *The Crown Jewels: The British Secrets Exposed by the KGB Archives* (London: Harper Collins Publishers, 1999).

Other

Bolton, P., Education: Historical statistics, House of Commons Briefing papers, SN04252 (2012), researchbriefings.parliament.uk/ResearchBriefing/Summary/SN04252.

Commonwealth War Graves Commission, 'Cairncross, William Wishart', Service No: 5108015, www.cwgc.org/find-war-dead/casualty/2715805

Chant, C., Code names: Operations of the Section World War, code names.info/operation/ulm/.

Jones, M., 'Ackroyd, Dame (Dorothy) Elizabeth [Betty] (1910–1987)', *Oxford Dictionary of National Biography* ed. (2004), www.oxforddnb.com.

Newsnight, BBC 2, 31 October 1990.

National Security Agency, 'Venona: An Overview', *Cryptologic Almanac 50th Anniversary Series* (2002), www.nsa.gov/news-features/declassified-documents/crypto-almanac-50th/assets/files/VENONA_An_Overview.pdf.

National Security Agency | Central Security Service, Hall of Honour, 'Cecil Philips', www.nsa.gov/about/cryptologic-heritage/historical-figures-publications/hall-of-honor/2006/cphillips.shtml.

Parsons, S.R. *Communism in the professions: the organisation of the British Communist Party among professional workers, 1933–1956* (PhD thesis: University of Warwick, 1990).

PBS, 'Red Files: Secrets Victories of the KGB', Interview with Cecil Philips, www.pbs.org/redfiles/kgb/deep/interv/k_int_cecil_philips.htm.

The Imitation Game, dir. Morten Tyldum, The Weinstein Company (2014).

Yes, Prime Minister, 'One of us', BBC 2, 27 February 1986.

Index

Akhmerov, Iskhak 74

Allason, Rupert *see* West, Nigel

Andrew, Christopher 17, 49, 55–6, 57, 59, 62, 66–7, 69, 80–1, 105–6, 171–2, 173, 176, 178

Andrews, Geoff 33, 39

Apostles 38, 39, 89

appeasement 71–2, 74, 84, 174–6

Arlington Hall *see* Signals Intelligence Service (Arlington Hall)

atomic secrets 14, 15, 80–2, 122, 126, 127, 130, 153, 171–2, 182–3, 184

Baldwin, Stanley 42, 70

Barclay, Cecil 111

Barnett, Correlli 174

Bell, Julian 33, 34, 38, 39, 40

Birch, Francis 'Frank' 86, 105–6

Blake, George 155

Bletchley Park 13, 14, 77, 83–90, 92–102, 105–6, 108, 112, 115, 119, 158
  Cairncross at 13, 92–102, 103, 104, 153, 158, 183

Blunt, Anthony 12, 14, 17, 30, 34, 36, 38–40, 48, 57, 58, 59, 67, 69, 73, 89, 123, 126, 162–3, 164, 181
  and Cairncross 48, 49, 56, 154, 155, 185, 193, 194, 200–1, 202
  exposure of 12, 13, 17, 64, 154, 162–3, 165, 172, 180, 184

Bolton, Guy 23, 27, 28, 29

Bondy, François 46

Boyle, Andrew 12, 17, 162–3

Brinkerhoff, Gayle (John's second wife) 14, 170, 174, 177–8, 186

British Scientific Advisory Committee (BSAC) 80, 81, 171

Brown, Anthony Cave 177

Budberg, Countess 201

Bukharin, Nikolai 60

Burgess, Guy 12, 17, 30, 33, 34, 37–8, 39, 50, 57, 71, 73–4, 89, 130, 154, 163
  and Cairncross 14, 17, 49, 55–6, 57–8, 59, 65, 67, 72, 133, 134–5, 136, 153, 166, 181–2, 187–90, 194–6, 197–8, 199–200, 202, 203
  exposure and defection of 12, 15, 16, 132, 133, 143–4, 153, 154, 163, 196
  at Foreign Office 82, 123, 131, 133, 187–8
  in MI6 90, 105, 106

Cairncross, Sir Alec (John's brother) 23, 24, 27, 29, 43, 44–5, 47, 48, 79, 138, 140, 146, 147, 156, 169, 178, 185
  on John 49, 63, 149, 164, 165–6, 167–8, 186

Cairncross, Alexander (John's father) 21, 23, 26

Cairncross, Andrew (John's brother) 23, 28, 43, 140–1

Cairncross, Bill (John's brother) 79

Cairncross, David (John's nephew) 164–5

Cairncross, John
  academic life 50, 139, 140–3, 145–7,
    148, 150–1, 155, 159–61, 167, 184–5
  character 62–3, 150, 182
  communist sympathies 17–18, 48–9,
    55, 58, 61–2, 69, 135–6, 157, 164, 181,
    191, 193, 194
  early life 18, 21, 23–4, 25, 28, 29, 41,
    62–3, 180–1, 182
  The Enigma Spy (autobiography) 14–15,
    114, 155, 173, 174, 176–7
  financial problems 149–50, 167–8, 178,
    185, 190
  intelligence passed to Soviet Union 13,
    14, 61, 66–7, 68, 69, 80, 101–2, 110,
    111, 123–4, 132, 182–3
  marriages 132, 138, 147, 149–50, 170
  motivation 14, 61, 62–3, 82, 125, 176,
    181–2
  poetry of 143, 146–7, 160, 167, 184
  and technology 124, 128, 183
  tradecraft of 66, 68, 126, 183
Cairncross, Margaret (John's sister) 178
Calvocoressi, Peter 93, 100
Cambridge University 11
  Apostles 38, 39, 89
  Cairncross at 34, 40, 41, 47–9, 55–6, 61,
    62, 155, 200
  communism at 30–40, 41, 45, 48, 49,
    61, 106, 136, 158, 164, 181, 191,
    193–4, 200
  Ring of Five 12, 13, 14, 16–17, 18,
    30, 83, 90, 91, 122, 123, 129, 131–2,
    153–4, 162, 172, 173, 180, 181, 184
  Trinity College 14, 30, 31, 32, 33–4, 35,
    37–8, 39, 41, 47–8, 49, 165, 181, 193
  Trinity Hall 30, 36
Cecil, Robert 14, 17, 36, 37, 69
Chamberlain, Neville 70, 71, 72, 75, 77, 84,
    174, 175, 176, 195
Channon, Henry 'Chips' 74
China 70, 116
Churchill, Winston 14, 61, 71, 75, 76, 77,
    78, 93, 116, 122, 130, 176
Clarke, Carter W. 119–20
class system 11, 16, 17, 18, 23, 24, 29, 33,
    37, 44, 45, 49, 51–2, 62, 85, 91, 113,
    180, 181

Colville, John 'Jock' 13–14, 63, 93, 133, 163
communism 17, 18, 53, 58, 73, 107, 109,
    134
  and Cairncross 17–18, 48–9, 55, 58,
    61–2, 69, 135–6, 157, 164, 181, 191,
    193, 194
  at Cambridge University 30–40, 41,
    45, 48, 49, 61, 106, 136, 158, 164, 181,
    191, 193–4, 200
Communist Party of Great Britain (CPGB)
    28, 30–1, 32, 37, 40, 48, 49, 56, 62,
    140, 188, 191, 193, 194, 200, 202, 203
Compton, E.G. 128
Corneille 46, 141, 159, 160, 167, 185
Cornford, John 34, 40, 200
Cornforth, Maurice 31, 32, 33, 34
Costello, John 15, 81
Cowgill, Felix 107, 123
Czechoslovakia 65, 71, 72, 143, 189, 195

Daladier, Édouard 71
Davenport-Hines, Richard 180–1
Denniston, Alastair 83, 85, 96, 103
Deutsch, Arnold ('Otto') 30, 32, 35, 37,
    38, 55, 57, 58–9, 60, 61, 63, 66, 67,
    69, 182
Dickie, John 51
Dobb, Maurice 31, 35
Douglas-Home, Alec 20, 156, 157
Dukes, Paul 90–1
Dunkirk 76, 79, 88, 175–6

Enigma 84–5, 86, 87–8, 89, 96, 115, 119
The Enigma Spy (Cairncross) 14–15, 114,
    155, 173, 174, 176–7
establishment, the 35, 39, 51–2, 53, 54, 56,
    71, 90–1, 106, 107–8, 109, 111,
    180–2
Eton College 37, 38, 51, 52

FAO (Food and Agriculture Organisation)
    139, 143, 157, 158–9, 160, 161, 184–5
Fetterlein, Ernst 115–16
First World War 25, 41, 46, 52, 84, 85, 96
Footman, David 74, 107, 109, 190, 200–1
Foreign Office 12, 72, 77, 82, 105, 108,
    109, 143, 151, 153–4, 189, 195
  Burgess at 82, 123, 131, 133, 187–8

Cairncross at 13, 14, 15, 50–9, 60–3,
  64, 65, 66–8, 163, 174, 182–3, 187–8,
  193–5, 202
  elitism of 51–2, 61, 62–3, 64, 66, 68,
    113–14, 181
  Maclean at 14, 61, 63, 64, 65–6, 123,
    130–1, 183, 193–4, 196
France 30, 36, 57, 74, 76, 87, 119, 175–6,
  195
  Cairncross in 41, 45–6, 58, 62, 169, 171,
    176–7, 178, 182, 193, 194
Freeman, Simon 14, 62, 63
Frost, Eunice 150–1, 170
Fuchs, Klaus 122, 130, 134, 152, 184

Gardner, Meredith Knox 121–2
GC&CS (Government Code and Cypher
  School) *see* Bletchley Park
General Strike 18, 27, 28, 29, 36, 44, 53
Germany 18, 32, 36, 49, 53, 55, 57, 61, 62,
  66, 70, 71, 83–4, 96, 107, 134, 175, 193
  Cairncross in 46, 50–1, 182
  Second World War 67, 72–7, 86, 87–9,
    97, 101–2, 105, 106–7, 108, 110, 111,
    115, 117, 118, 119, 123, 124, 175–6
Glasgow 21, 22, 24, 25, 27–8, 41–2
  Glasgow University 25, 41, 42–6, 140–1
Golitsyn, Anatoliy ('Kago') 12, 153–4, 184
Gordievsky, Oleg 14, 55–6, 62, 63, 65,
  80–1, 105–6, 171, 173, 176
Gorsky, Anatoli Veniaminovich ('Henry')
  67, 68, 69, 72, 77, 80, 81, 90, 95, 100,
  101, 103
Gouzenko, Igor 126
Grafpen, Grigori 68
Great Depression 18, 24, 25, 26, 28, 29,
  31–2, 41–2, 44–5, 62, 71
Green, Frederick 104
Greene, Graham 16, 111–14, 139, 146,
  147–8, 150–1, 160–1, 165, 167, 168,
  170, 178, 186
Greenshields, J.B. 22

Haden-Guest, David 32, 33, 40
Hallock, Lieutenant Richard 120, 121
Halpern, Alexander 201
Hankey, Lord Maurice 13, 53, 77–8, 79–81,
  95, 124, 139, 182

Hardie, Keir 28
Havers, Sir Michael 164
Hennessy, Lord Peter 68
Hitler, Adolf 32, 34, 35, 46, 53, 71, 73, 76,
  84, 88, 96, 100–1, 175, 195
Hobsbawm, Eric 34
Hollis, Sir Roger 153–4, 157
homosexuality 16–17, 37–8, 39, 58, 131,
  144, 157, 162–3, 188, 194, 200

Italy 53, 54, 55, 70, 84, 107, 140
  Cairncross in 140, 152, 155, 157, 158–9,
    163–4, 166–9

Japan 55, 62, 70, 84, 92, 106, 107, 119, 121
Jeffreys-Jones, Rhodri 17

Kapitsa, Pyotr 31
Katz, Helmut 194, 202
Kennedy, Paul 174, 175
Kerr, Shelia 171–2
KGB (book) 80, 171, 172, 174, 176
KGB (Komitet Gosudarstvennoy
  Bezopasnosti) 12, 19, 60, 90, 120, 153,
  157
  and Cairncross 13, 14, 15, 59, 63, 65,
    66–7, 69, 95, 129, 140, 154, 155,
    171–2, 178, 182–3, 185
  see also NKVD (Narodnyy Komissariat
    Vnutrennikh Del)
King, John Herbert 64–5
Kislitsyn, Filip Vasilyevich 143
Klugmann, James 32–3, 34, 36, 39, 49,
  56–9, 67, 193, 200
Knox, Dillwyn 84
Koestler, Arthur 55, 194–5, 197
Krötenschield, Boris Mikhailovich
  ('Kretchin') 110, 123
Kuh, Freddy 201
Kukin, Konstantin Mikhailovick ('Igor')
  110
Kursk, Battle of 101–2, 110, 183, 184

Labour Party 27–8, 35, 37
Layton, David 194, 202
Lees, Jim 38
Leitch, David 13–14, 128
Lesmahagow 20–9, 46, 182

Levin, Bernard 17
Liddell, Guy 129, 130, 133, 134, 135–6
Lloyd, Selwyn 144
Long, Leo 89, 95
Lownie, Andrew 37
Luftwaffe 76–7, 79, 84, 87, 88, 101, 175–6

MacGibbon, James 201–2
Maclean, Donald 12, 14, 15, 17, 30, 32, 34,
    36–7, 38, 61, 71–2, 73, 81, 138, 171,
    180, 181, 194
    and Cairncross 14, 63, 64, 65–6, 133,
    134, 182, 193–4, 196
    exposure and defection of 12, 16,
    129–32, 133, 143–4, 152, 153, 154,
    163, 196
    at Foreign Office 14, 61, 63–6, 123,
    130–1, 183, 193–4, 196
Macmillan, Harold 78, 156–7
MacNeice, Louis 73, 194
Maly, Theodore 54, 57, 59, 65, 67
Manhattan Project 80, 122, 184
Margesson, David 53–4
Martin, Arthur 134, 151, 152–3, 154, 176,
    187
Mawdsley, Evan 102
Maxse, Marjorie 106
Mayhew, Sir Patrick 176–7
McMillan, James F. 45
MI5 13, 15, 18, 30–1, 57, 79–80, 90, 104,
    132, 133, 143, 153–4, 172, 184, 195–6
    Cairncross interrogations 15, 48–9, 58,
    72, 134–7, 151–4, 155, 157–8, 162,
    164, 173, 176, 186, 187–203
MI6 (SIS) 74, 79–80, 85, 90, 93, 99, 104–5,
    108, 112, 131, 143, 155
    Burgess in 90, 105, 106
    Cairncross in 13, 14, 104, 107–11,
    123–4, 125, 126, 153, 165, 182, 183
    Philby in 14, 82, 90, 105–6, 107,
    109–10, 111, 123, 124, 130, 131–2,
    183–4
    see also Bletchley Park
MI8 95, 118
Milne, Tim 107, 124
Milovzorov, Ivan 126
mining 21–9, 182
Ministry of Supply 13, 128, 132, 153

Mitrokhin, Vasili 57, 59, 66–7, 69
Modin, Yuri 12, 14, 56, 62, 65, 67–8, 69, 81,
    101–2, 105, 110, 126–7, 128–9, 132,
    136, 138, 183
Modrzhinskaya, Elena 69
Molière 46, 47, 57, 59, 98, 140, 141–3, 161
Molotov–Ribbentrop Pact 72–5
Muggeridge, Malcolm 112
Munich agreement 71, 72, 174–6, 195

Nicholls, F.W. 95
Nicholson, Harold 188, 194–5, 197, 202
NKVD (Narodnyy Komissariat
    Vnutrennikh Del) 19, 30, 38, 39, 40,
    56, 67, 69, 71, 72, 83, 89, 111, 183
    and Cairncross 57, 61, 62, 63, 65, 67,
    77, 79, 81, 123, 126, 182, 183–4
    see also KGB (Komitet
    Gosudarstvennoy Bezopasnosti)
Norway 75, 87

Oppenheim, Gabrielle (John's first wife)
    132, 138, 139, 140, 143, 144, 147, 149,
    154, 165–6, 169, 179
Oram, George 127
Orwell, George 32
Oxford University 11, 32, 73, 85, 139, 158

Pakistan 147–8
Pascal, Roy 31, 48
Penrose, Barrie 13–14, 57, 62, 163
Petrov, Vladimir 143
Philby, Kim 12, 14, 17, 18, 30, 34–6, 37,
    38, 40, 54, 72, 112, 113, 126, 131, 152,
    153–4, 181, 201, 202
    and Cairncross 14, 56, 109–10, 200–1
    exposure and defection of 12, 35, 112,
    132, 154
    in MI6 (SIS) 14, 82, 90, 105–6, 107,
    109–10, 111, 123, 124, 130, 131–2,
    183–4
    and the Spanish Civil War 40, 54
Philips, Cecil J. 120, 121
Pincher, Chapman 14, 55, 61–2, 154, 155,
    172
Poland 46, 72–5, 85
Putlitz, Wolfgang 202

Racine 46, 142, 145–6, 159–60, 185
Rees, Goronwy 58, 73–4, 144, 203
Rejewski, Marian 85
Rimington, Dame Stella 154, 158
Ring of Five from Cambridge 12–14,
    16–18, 30, 83, 90, 91, 122–3, 129,
    131–2, 153–4, 162, 172–3, 180–1, 184
Rome 139–40, 143, 147, 150, 165–6, 170,
    185
Rosenberg, Julius and Ethel 122
Rothschild, Victor 12, 200–1

Second World War 13, 14, 35, 67, 70–82,
    83, 86–9, 92–102, 104–8, 115–16, 174,
    175–6, 195–6
Signals Intelligence Service (Arlington
    Hall) 117, 118, 119, 121–2, 129
Simkins, Anthony 191, 199, 203
SIS (Secret Intelligence Service) *see* MI6 (SIS)
Skardon, Jim 134–5, 136–7, 138, 151, 163,
    176, 187–92, 193–6, 197–8, 199–203
Sorbonne 41, 45–7, 62
Soviet Union 11–12, 18, 31, 55, 58–9, 69,
    74, 83, 89–90, 94–5, 96, 106–7, 116,
    122, 125–6, 157
    archives 13, 15–16, 57, 59, 65–8, 81–2,
    125, 183
    cipher systems 115–17, 119–22
    defectors from 12, 14, 16, 57, 115, 126,
    143
    and Philby 18, 35, 106, 109–10, 124
    and Second World War 14, 61, 71, 72–3,
    74–5, 76, 82, 95, 101–2, 106, 110, 111,
    117, 119, 123, 140, 184
    Spanish Civil War 40, 53, 57
    terror 60–1, 65, 67–8, 71
    see also KGB; NKVD
Spanish Civil War 40, 53–5, 57, 65, 84
Stalin 13, 60, 65, 67, 74, 75, 132
Straight, Michael 14, 74, 152
Strang, Lord 51, 52

Street, J.E.D. 64, 151, 153
Sudoplatov, Pavel 81

Taylor, A.J.P. 174, 175
Thailand 145, 147, 154
Thatcher, Margaret 12, 163, 172
Tiltman, John 92
Travis, Edward 94, 96, 104
Treasury, Cairncross at 13, 63–5, 68–9, 72,
    77, 124–9, 153, 189, 190–1, 195, 198–9
Trinity College, Cambridge 14, 30, 31, 32,
    33–4, 35, 37–8, 39, 41, 47–8, 49, 165,
    181, 193
Trinity Hall, Cambridge 30, 36
Tsarev, Oleg 14, 59, 66–7, 81, 90, 125, 126,
    132
Turing, Alan 13, 85–6

US (United States) 71, 74, 80, 81, 82, 88–9,
    115–23, 129–32, 153, 174
    Cairncross in 144–5, 148, 150–6, 170,
    186

Vassall, John 157
Vassiliev, Alexander 81
Venlo incident 104–5
Venona project 115–24, 129–32, 181
Vienna 18, 30, 35, 37, 38, 45

Warner, Fred 202
Welchman, Gordon 85–6
West, Nigel (Rupert Allason) 15, 55–6, 59,
    65–7, 90, 125–6, 132, 172, 176–7, 179
Winnifrith, John 191, 198
Winterbotham, F.W. 93, 106, 177
Wittgenstein, Ludwig 31
Wright, Peter 14, 18, 1545, 157–8, 162,
    185
Wylie, Tom 58, 188, 194

Yes, Prime Minister 11, 16